India's Evolving National Security Agenda

Modi and Beyond

India's Evolving National Security Agenda

Modi and Beyond

Edited by

Harsh V. Pant

Konark Publishers Pvt Ltd
New Delhi • Seattle

Konark Publishers Pvt Ltd
206, First Floor,
Peacock Lane, Shahpur Jat,
New Delhi - 110 049
Phone: +91-11-41055065
Mob: +91 93552 93900, +91 93552 94900
e-mail: india@konarkpublishers.com
website: www.konarkpublishers.com

Konark Publishers International
8615, 13th Ave SW,
Seattle, WA 98106
Phone: (415) 409-9988
e-mail: us@konarkpublishers.com

Cataloging in Publication Data—DK
Courtesy: D.K. Agencies (P) Ltd. <docinfo@dkagencies.com>

India's evolving national security agenda : Modi and beyond / edited by Harsh V. Pant.
pages cm
Contributed articles.
Includes bibliographical references and index.
ISBN 9788193555439

1. National security—India. 2. India—Military policy. 3. India—Politics and government—2014- I. Pant, Harsh V., editor.

LCC UA840.I53 2019 | DDC 355.033054 23

Edited by Deepak Goel
Cover Jacket by Dushyant Parasher
Typeset by The Laser Printers, New Delhi
Printed and bound in India by Thomson Press India Ltd.

Contents

Preface *vii*

Introduction – Harsh V. Pant *ix*

1 Narendra Modi's Defence Policy: Ideation, Management, and Capabilities 1
Abhijnan Rej

2 Defence Modernisation and Production: Enduring Challenges 26
Kapil Patil

3 Maritime Security and India: India as a Regional Security Provider 45
Tuneer Mukherjee

4 India's Evolving Space Programme and Policy: A Story of Rising Ambitions 72
Rajeswari Pillai Rajagopalan and Vidya Sagar Reddy

5 Countering Terrorism in India: The Challenges of Ad-hoc Policies 89
Kabir Taneja

6 India's Counter-insurgency Strategy and Maoist Challenge: A Success Story? 106
Niranjan Sahoo

7 India's Cyber Defence Future: Issues and Challenges 126
Bedavyasa Mohanty

8 Environmental Security Challenges and India 141
Aparna Roy

9 Towards a Gender Responsive National Security Policy 156
Vidisha Mishra

List of Contributors 174

Index 178

Preface

NATIONAL Security challenges facing India are multidimensional and complex. As the global order changes and India redefines its global role as a 'leading' power, these challenges are only going to become more pressing for Indian policymakers. The Indian state is faced with a varied set of threats in the conventional, sub-conventional and nuclear domains. Unlike most states, the division between internal and external security domains is also hard to ascertain. Yet even as the security environment in and around India continues to remain highly challenging, the institutional apparatus that is required to address it is inadequate to respond to the challenges.

For years, Indian security response has been characterised as reactive, one that has attempted to address security threats sporadically as and when they arose. This has led to ad hoc responses by the Indian policymakers even as there has been no national security doctrine which has been articulated by New Delhi. This is as much a result of a lack of political consensus on the nature of security threats and the ways of addressing them as of an institutional infrastructure that is just not up to the mark.

This book examines the five years of the Narendra Modi government as it has grappled with a range of national security challenges and draws broader deductions for the future Indian policymakers. It leads off from the principal challenges to India—long, disputed, and militarised borders with Pakistan and China and visible capability gaps vis-à-vis the ever-widening threat spectrum. It addresses India's ambitions as a maritime power and as the net security provider in the Indian Ocean. Budgetary constraints also mean that the armed forces will not be able to invest in technological solutions wholly to catapult India's war fighting capabilities. The government and the armed forces need to prepare themselves for these challenges.

The volume also seeks to go beyond the traditional security framework and develop ideas around 'new' security challenges that confront India including countering violent extremism online, environment, cyber and gender inclusivity.

I would like to thank Konark Publishers for pushing me to pursue this project. It would not have been possible without an excellent team of researchers at the Observer Research Foundation (ORF), New Delhi. Thanks to all the contributors from ORF and beyond who decided to make time for this volume. If this volume is able to generate an informed discussion on the national security priorities of India, it would have served its purpose.

Harsh V. Pant

Introduction

Harsh V. Pant

AS a concept, national security remains a highly contested term. According to Arnold Wolfers, it is 'an ambiguous symbol meaning different things to different people.' Security is not an objective term that leads to an agreed set of issues and remedies. As a consequence, what is considered a security threat varies across time and cultures. There has been a vigorous debate in the academic literature on the concept and its implications for policymaking.

Indian security policy has largely been characterised as reactive—one that has attempted to address security threats sporadically as and when they arose. One of the major impediments in articulating an agreed national security strategy has been a lack of political consensus in not only understanding the nature of security threats but also in ways of addressing them. This lack of consensus has occasioned ad hoc responses to security challenges which are driven prominently by the nature and instincts of the top political leadership.

The Narendra Modi government came to office calling for a robust response to national security issues. This volume aims to take stock of the Modi government's performance in the realm of national security across various domains and assesses the policy issues which the new government will face after the 2019 parliamentary polls. It leads off from the principal challenges to India—long, disputed, and militarised borders with Pakistan and China and visible capability gaps vis-à-vis the ever-widening threat spectrum. It addresses India's ambitions as a maritime power and as the net security provider in the Indian Ocean. Budgetary constraints also mean that the armed forces will not be able to invest in technological solutions wholly to catapult India's war fighting capabilities. The government and the armed forces need to prepare themselves for these challenges.

The volume also seeks to go beyond the traditional security

framework and develop ideas around 'new' security challenges that confront India, including countering violent extremism online, environment, cyber and gender inclusivity.

An Evolving Security Landscape

The rapidly evolving security environment facing India continues to pose significant challenges to the nation's policymakers. A combination of internal and external as well as state and non-state-based threats have emerged that have made the Indian security scenario complicated. Internally, Indian security is challenged by a plethora of insurgencies which are a product of a range of factors, including a desire for greater autonomy to left-wing radicalism to prevailing socio-economic inequities. Externally, India's immediate neighbourhood continues to pose challenges to India's statecraft. Traditionally, India's national security discourse has been dominated by external state-based threats, especially China and Pakistan.

Even today, one of the most serious challenges to Indian security is deemed to come from the rise of China in the region and beyond. India and China are two major powers in Asia with global aspirations and some significant conflicting interests. As a result, some amount of friction in their bilateral relationship is inevitable. China's defence modernisation and the ambiguity surrounding China's arms build-up is generating apprehensions in New Delhi and has forced India to pursue its own defence modernisation programme. The Doklam crisis of 2017 has alerted India to the consequences of a rapidly expanding capability gap between the two Asian giants.

Another significant challenge has come from the growing turmoil around India's periphery. The instability in Pakistan, Afghanistan, Bangladesh, Nepal, Sri Lanka and Myanmar is a major inhibiting factor for India to realise its dream of becoming a major global player. India is surrounded by several weak states that view New Delhi's hegemonic status in the region with suspicion. A policy of 'splendid isolation' is not an option and Indian strategic elites recognise that India's desire to emerge as a major global player will remain just that — a desire, unless it engages its immediate neighbourhood more meaningfully and becomes a net provider of regional security.

Internally, from left-wing extremism to right-wing religious fundamentalism, the Indian State has faced multiple challenges that have threatened to derail the story of a rising India. The Maoist insurgency, too, has spread from the margins to the centre stage with former Prime Minister Manmohan Singh identifying the Naxalites as the 'greatest internal security threat' facing the nation. The Maoists have taken the fight to the geographic heart of India, to the vast swathe of territory comprising impoverished villages in central India.

India is also a vulnerable target for Islamist extremism. Technology has radically altered the dimensions of this challenge. India had long prided itself on the fact that not one person in a country that has the second largest Muslim population in the world is linked to al-Qaeda or to any international terror plot. This has turned out to be a myth with the exposure that every major Islamist urban terror cell in the country since 1993 has seen a preponderance of Indian nationals. India is fast emerging, both as a target and a recruitment base for organisations like al-Qaeda and attacks are being carried out with impunity by home-grown jihadist groups, trained and aided by organisations in neighbouring Pakistan and Bangladesh. The emergence of the Islamic State in Iraq and Syria (ISIS), also known as *Daesh* and ISIL (Islamic State of Iraq and Levant), has added another dimension to this debate. As ISIS competed with groups like al-Qaeda for influence over Islamist extremist groups around the world, the world witnessed another round of vicious extremism and the ability of the international community to effectively counter this threat seemed seriously limited. The impact of ISIS on South Asia and India has also been a matter of concern for the policymakers in India and the neighbourhood. While India has had relatively negligible exposure to ISIS so far, the threat remains potent.

India's rising global economic profile has made the world take India more seriously as a major power and has made Indian elites more ambitious in defining their global role and aspirations. There is clearly an appreciation in the Indian policymaking circles of India's rising capabilities. It is reflected in a gradual expansion of Indian foreign policy activity in recent years, in India's attempt to reshape its defence forces, in India's desire to seek greater global influence. India, the world's fourth-largest military power, had embarked on an ambitious plan to modernise its largely Soviet-era arms since late 1990s, as it started asserting its political and military profile in South Asia and the Indian Ocean region. India's armed forces had become increasingly ambitious, talking of their own revolution in military affairs. In line with India's broadening strategic horizons, its military acquisition is seeing a marked shift from conventional land-based systems to means of power projection such as airborne refuelling systems and long-range missiles. India is setting up bases abroad, patrolling the Indian Ocean to counter piracy and protecting the crucial sea-lanes of communication, and demonstrating a military assertiveness hitherto not associated with it. Yet lack of any credible military option against Pakistan has brought into sharp relief the fundamental weaknesses of Indian defence policy over the last several years. The terrorist strikes in Mumbai in November 2008 exposed vast gaps in India's security system. The three-day siege of India's financial capital became a pivotal point in the country's drive to beef up and modernise its armed forces and its arsenal. With extremist violence growing in Afghanistan and Pakistan, India's ability to prevent attacks through intelligence gathering and defensive measures has become more urgent than ever. Successive Indian governments have struggled to cope with this challenge. The Modi government's 'surgical strikes' of 2016 and airstrikes in February 2019 after the Pulwama attack are attempts at altering the tactical and operational status quo vis-à-vis Pakistan. But its consequences remain far from clear at this stage.

India's military power remains constrained by several factors, including the fact that not a single major platform is produced in India. Indian defence policy has suffered from an archaic bureaucracy and ineffective procurement procedures. Decision-making remains slow as politicians and bureaucrats are wary of approving purchases due to a series of arms procurement scandals since the late 1980s. The political opposition to the Rafale fighter deal underlines the challenge for Indian policymakers in concluding defence deals. Most large procurement programmes get delayed resulting in cost escalation and technological or strategic obsolescence of the budgeted items. India's military modernisation strategy, as a result, lacks focus and effectiveness.

In this day and age, India's national security perimeter is not limited to traditional security issues alone. Non-traditional security issues pertaining to cyber, environment and gender are equally critical. In fact, the line between traditional and non-traditional security issues is getting blurred rapidly. Though this has been neglected in the past, Indian decision-makers today can no longer afford to ignore them.

India needs a national security policy that can actually take on all these challenges simultaneously. It is a difficult task to accomplish given the fact that the multiplicity and variety of challenges that India faces often require varied responses. Yet compared to any other time in its history, India faces an international environment that has so far allowed it to pursue a 'multi-vector' defence policy as its relations with all major global powers are on a stable footing. The problems in charting out a credible defence policy remain largely internal.

The Modi Approach

In August 2018, India's defence planning architecture underwent a significant change with the Narendra Modi government deciding to establish an overarching Defence Planning Committee (DPC) under National Security Adviser (NSA). The aim is to leverage this cross-governmental body—comprising the Chairman of the Chiefs of Staff Committee, three service chiefs, and the defence, expenditure and foreign secretaries—to enhance India's ability to do some long-term strategising.

The DPC has been tasked with drafting reports on 'national security strategy, international defence engagement strategy, roadmap to build a defence manufacturing ecosystem, strategy to boost defence exports, and priority capability development plans'. Four subcommittees have been created under the DPC to focus on policy and strategy, plans and capability development, defence diplomacy, and the defence manufacturing ecosystem. Appointment of two more deputy National Security Advisers, as opposed to just one NSA in the earlier structure, is part of a major restructuring.

It has also been reported that a National Security Strategy document has been finalised though it is unlikely that it will be made public. Given the growing focus of Indian security policy on China, the Ministry of External Affairs (MEA) is now running the Centre for Contemporary China Studies, an in-house think-tank which is exclusively devoted to studying China. It has personnel from across various branches of the government and will aim to provide inputs to policymakers on managing China, both on a day-to-day and long-term basis.

With Pakistan, the Modi government has shifted the goal posts in significant ways—first with 'surgical strikes' of 2016 and then with airstrikes post Pulwama attack in 2019. These are important markers in India's approach to counter-terror, which has been hobbled by the Pakistani nuclear bluff. India has all but called that bluff, and Pakistan's decision to downplay these strikes underlines Islamabad's reluctance to retaliate. With these strikes, India has managed to convey to Pakistan and to other external stakeholders that Pakistan's nuclear blackmail has no legs to stand on and that India has military room to operate below the threshold that would trigger major conventional, or even nuclear, escalation. India is also trying to shape a counter narrative about the ability of India to inflict pain on Pakistan. By constantly deciding not to react militarily to Pakistani provocations, New Delhi was losing its deterrence credibility, further fuelling Pakistan's adventurism. The Modi government is trying to change that calculus.

While addressing the Combined Commanders Conference in December 2015, Prime Minister Narendra Modi had underlined: 'At a time when major powers are reducing their forces and rely more on technology, we are still constantly seeking to expand the size of our forces. Modernisation and expansion of forces at the same time is a difficult and unnecessary goal. We need forces that are agile, mobile and driven by technology, not just human valour.' In line with this, certain steps have been taken.

In the first such exercise of its kind since Independence to be completed by the end of 2019, the Modi government is also moving ahead with major restructuring of the Indian Army with a view to enhancing its combat capabilities as well as streamlining budgetary allocation. The Defence Ministry had constituted a committee under Lt Gen (retd.) D.B. Shekatkar to recommend measures for enhancing combat capability and rebalancing defence expenditure of the armed forces which had submitted its report in December 2016. Most of its recommendations (65 out of 99) have been accepted and are now in various stages of implementation.

The very nature of warfare is evolving rapidly and India's neighbours are undertaking their own restructuring. The Indian armed forces cannot remain beholden to their past practices without an assessment of the rapid evolution in technological and socio-political forces. The 1.3-million-strong Indian Army hardly has any funds for modernisation, burdened as it is by revenue expenditure and pensions. A planned Army restructuring, aimed at reducing its strength by 1.5 lakh men, is expected to save up to Rs 7,000 crore a year in revenue expenditure.

These decisions come at a time when Indian defence planning stands at the crossroads. The silo-driven approach to defence planning has resulted in the lack of an integrated view. The three services as well as the civilian and defence agencies are often seen to be working at cross-purposes. Such an ad hoc approach has meant that, more often than not, issues like threat perception and force structure are not managed via a centralised and authoritative overview. Instead, individual services tend to be driving the agenda at their own levels.

This lack of synchronisation is manifested in various ways. On the one hand, the Indian Army Chief has been talking of a two-front war. On the other, the Vice Chief of Army Staff testified before the Parliamentary Standing Committee on Defence in 2018 that the Budget allocated to the defence forces was hardly enough to complete the committed payments for the emergency procurements already made, let alone for pursuing an ambitious defence modernisation plan.

The headlines on Indian defence policy often tend to be completely divorced from the ground reality. India's US$250-billion military modernisation programme is often talked about. But even as New Delhi remains keen on acquiring significant weapons platforms, there have been persistent doubts about its ability to harness these resources in service of a long-term strategy. Indeed, the absence of an Indian 'grand strategy' that sets out political objectives for Indian power projection—and then ensures military, economic, intelligence and educational development—coordinated toward these objectives, has been a perennial topic of discussion within Indian strategic circles.

India's defence reform campaign has existed nearly as long as the current system itself. This drive focuses on extending resource integration and coordination throughout defence policymaking. Moreover, it recommends a state infrastructure, able to adequately implement political judgements and to combine state resources to meet these judgements. This is currently missing in India.

Since the very beginning, the defence reform drive has implicitly targeted the need for a sufficiently integrative and coordinative state structure—required for an operationally effective defence policy. But not much success has been achieved. Reforming this system remains a core requirement for India to adequately manage its scarce resources and align these with political objectives.

Effective defence planning and force structuring is a function of an institutional framework that allows for a clear delineation of political goals, efficient mobilisation of resources and effective use of these resources for developing instrumentalities of state power. The Modi government seems to have finally acknowledged the need for new structures and processes but time is not on India's side.

At a time when advances in technology are revolutionising warfare, India is still debating the need to move towards leaner force structures.

India needs to cut the flab on an urgent basis as over half of the annual defence Budget going to meet salary and pension requirements is clearly not sustainable. The priorities of India's 'Make in India' initiative and cumbersome defence procurement process will also have to be brought in sync with each other. India's status as the world's largest arms importer hardly does justice to its ambitions to emerge as a defence manufacturing hub. The debate on integration, both among the services headquarters, and between the services and the Ministry of Defence, also continues unabated and should be concluded.

Effective national security planning tends to put a premium on assuring future strategic and operational adaptiveness. In the Indian context, a transformative shift in mindset, structures and processes is needed. Rapidly evolving security environment as well as a near permanent pressure on scarce resources underscores the need for strategic national security planning.

Volume Overview

Contributors to this volume examine a range of issues and assess the performance of the Modi government in their own domains. Abhijnan Rej takes a broader look at the Modi government's defence policy through the three dimensions of ideation, management and capabilities. He argues that 'the most pronounced imprint of the Modi government on Indian defence policy has been in the realm of ideation, namely in developing and emphasising security doctrines and strategy'. He also credits the Modi government for pushing through some managerial and bureaucratic reforms though the results have not been stellar. For Rej, it is in the realm of new capability acquisitions, that the Modi government's performance has been lacklustre. Going forward, he is suggesting a focus on developing India's conventional military strength, reform of the military bureaucracy and mainstreaming of asymmetric capabilities.

Kapil Patil examines the issue of defence modernisation and procurement in detail. He argues that 'defence reforms and modernisation under the Modi government have gained significant pace compared to the previous UPA government. The Modi government has not only addressed a number of long-standing issues including those relating to the morale and welfare of the military personnel but also introduced major institutional changes which are expected to bring a structural shift in India's strategic planning and outlook". Patil also agrees, however, that 'in view of the complex challenges facing the country, it is imperative to move swiftly and complete many of the pending reforms in the areas of military modernisation. Given the inherently dynamic nature of military change, a more forceful enactment of reforms would go a long way in eliminating structural flaws in India's national security framework and secure its core strategic interests in the turbulent world order.'

This is followed by a chapter on maritime security by Tuneer Mukherjee wherein he argues that the Modi government 'has attempted to accentuate India's status as a stakeholder in regional maritime security and outlined plans to build a modern navy to fulfil that role' as Modi 'understands that as India realises its strategic niche, maritime security will be key to securing India's economic and political future'. Mukherjee suggests that 'Modi's enthusiasm for across the seas diplomacy, stretching from the South Pacific to the Western Indian Ocean, has made cooperation in the maritime arena a cornerstone of India's outreach to the world.'

Rajeswari Pillai Rajagopalan and Vidya Sagar Reddy outline major developments relating to India's space programme and policy during the five years of the Modi government. They underline two key decisions of the Modi government in linking space more clearly with Indian foreign and security policy priorities: inducting India's Foreign Secretary into the Space Commission and gifting a South Asia satellite to the neighbourhood. Rajagopalan and Reddy conclude that 'India cannot remain oblivious to the emerging challenges in the security and strategic domains in the Indo-Pacific region. In fact, the changing security dynamics in the broader region will compel India to re-orient its space programme to developing certain military characteristics to its space programme.'

Kabir Taneja surveys the counter-terrorism policy of the Modi government which, he argues, has retained the 'ad hocism' of the past.

Suggesting that the expectations of the BJP government have fallen tremendously short, Taneja underlines that 'while Kashmir remains the harbinger of almost every counter-terror policy India has, the rise of global jihadist groups such as the Islamic State of Iraq and the Levant (ISIS/ISIL), known as *Daesh* in Arabic, single-handedly made much of the global counter-terror practices obsolete.' He concludes that despite its historic mandate, the Modi government 'has only managed to continue with the snail-paced bureaucratic procedures to develop a modern, adaptive and robust counter-terror understanding and infrastructure akin to the needs of the twenty-first century threat.'

Niranjan Sahoo shifts the gaze to internal security as his chapter attempts to evaluate the successes (and failures) of counter-insurgency (COIN) strategy and tactics with regard to Maoist insurgency from a comparative perspective. Sahoo examines the policies and strategies of the successive governments that have invested on COIN and pioneered many of the tactics against Maoist insurgency and concludes that 'while there is no denying the critical role of previous government in mounting a comprehensive COIN which began hitting rebels hard as early as 2012, the real acceleration of such trend began in 2015 and continues to corner the rebels. The Modi government's early recognition of kind of threats posed by Maoists seems to have helped it put a coherent and aggressive COIN against rebels.' Though challenges remain, the Modi government's success in countering the Maoist cannot be underestimated.

Bedavyasa Mohanty examines India's cyber defence landscape and argues that 'the Modi government's performance on cyber security has been adequate in certain domains while remaining vastly wanting in others.' Cyber diplomacy is one area where India has achieved significant maturity in the last five years even as the absence of an overarching cyber security policy and adequate civilian and military institutional infrastructure continues to remain a serious problem.

Aparna Roy focuses on the environmental security challenges India faces and argues that while 'the Modi government have tried to address environmental security concerns by framing more stringent laws on conservation of natural resources, limiting the environmental impacts of industrialisation, and offering compensation to sufferers of industrial impacts,' India continues to rank 'highest in the world on the rate of environmental conflicts'. She blames the top-down approach to environmental security as the one responsible for the lack of implementation of policies which, more often than not, are sound. Roy also expresses her dissatisfaction with the Modi government's inability to shape a larger regional approach to environmental security.

In the final chapter, Vidisha Mishra examines the integration of gender-related issues into India's national security discourse and policy. She argues that, 'it is certain that under Prime Minister Modi's administration, gender has been more central in core national security and foreign policy discussions than before' with the induction of two female leaders in powerful positions in the Cabinet Committee on Security. But she suggests that 'women's political gains do not automatically translate to substantive differences in national security outcomes which, in practice, intersect with gender in a complex manner and, therefore, require broader measures in addition to representational parity.'

Overall, the Modi government seems to have taken a plethora of new initiatives and streamlined some of the old ones. But, as most contributors point out, the expectations from the government were so high that disappointment at some level was only natural. The aim of this volume is also to look beyond the Modi government and underline the challenges for the future policymakers. And these challenges continue to be structural and institutional as well as of implementation. Perhaps no other question continues to agitate the Indian strategic community as the need for a publicly articulated National Security Strategy (NSS) that bears the imprimatur of the Prime Minister and the Cabinet Committee on Security. Such an NSS will signal India's strategic intent to friends and adversaries alike. It will also shape defence procurement and modernisation plans, and direct India's sub-conventional, conventional, as well as nuclear force posture. Defence procurement processes right now are broken, with endemic cost overruns as well as confusion about the lack of strategic direction to it hobbling the entire process. The 'L1 system', critics argue, leads to acquisition of inferior weapons systems.

Meanwhile, indigenisation of arms production seems to be stalled due to lack of political will in seeing it through, as well as due to the lack of a proper ecosystem to make advanced weapons in India. These have considerable national-security consequences. A quite global revolution is underway right now where countries are leveraging new dual-use technologies to obtain cutting-edge asymmetric advantages over their adversaries. Such technologies include artificial intelligence and swarms, drones, quantum technology, as well as nano-biology. Should India fall behind in these critical areas, its military edge stands to be significantly eroded. At the same time, Indian policymakers will have to also ponder the strategic value of these gen-next weapons, and how they could significantly weaken our adversaries' extant capabilities. Intelligence reforms continue to be extremely high in the list of national-security priorities. They include the need for more effective information collection from trouble spots in India's immediate neighbourhood, the desirability of a much stronger analytical wing (consisting of multidisciplinary specialists) as well as a robust special-operations division for covert kinetic operations. Finally, Indian national security policy will have to start viewing non-traditional domains of environment and gender more integral to the nation's priorities.

1

Narendra Modi's Defence Policy: Ideation, Management, and Capabilities

Abhijnan Rej

NARENDRA Modi's election in 2014 as the 14th Prime Minister of India on the back of an electoral landslide marked a sharp turn away from India's coalition politics that had been the hallmark of the past three decades. Promising effective governance and a break from the policy paralysis that characterised the second term of the Congress-led United Progressive Alliance (UPA), Modi was widely seen by many—in India as well as abroad—as someone who would usher in sweeping reforms. Inside the security community in Delhi and beyond, there was palpable excitement that he would usher in fundamental changes in India's defence policy and security posture. This expectation stemmed—in equal parts—from Modi's ideological roots in the Hindu Right which has, historically, put a premium on power as a determining variable in international politics, as well as from his self-promoted strong-man image. Noting that the previous Bharatiya Janata Party (BJP)-led National Democratic Alliance (NDA) had demonstrated India as a nuclear-weapons state, bested Pakistan in a limited war over Kargil, as well as initiated key reforms of the national-security bureaucracy, optimists expected him to consolidate and further the country's hard-power capabilities.

To be sure, five years ago Modi inherited an extremely challenging strategic environment which has continued to deteriorate. The comprehensive power gap between India and China, steadily widening since 1979, put the latter squarely as a strategic competitor, superior to India irrespective of the metric used. Chinese actions—such as continuing to support Pakistan economically and militarily as well as explicitly thwarting India's global ambitions—and Beijing's goal to establish itself as a peer of the United States pose a direct challenge to India's own quest to become a power of consequence in Asia and beyond. These structural imperatives demand a fundamental reimagination of Indian defence policy. Long obsessed with a manifestly-weaker albeit persistently-irritating adversary, India's strategic orientation under Modi would become qualitatively different, many hoped—one that would be able to square up to China, end Pakistan's intransigence, and consolidate its position as the regional hegemon.

The desiderata for examination of a given government's defence policy are the following three interrelated dimensions: First, it must investigate new *ideational* elements that that government may have introduced. These would manifest themselves in terms of new strategies and doctrines, both explicit and implicit. Second, it must unearth *management* reforms (if any) of the bureaucratic architecture that must support the ideational component and allocate scant resources in the most efficient way to that effect. Third and finally, it must also examine new *capabilities* that the government in question has sought to further the new doctrines and strategies it has introduced—again, if it has indeed done so. Examining Modi's record five years later using these three dimensions, a middling picture emerges. While the Modi government has enthusiastically engaged in ideation—albeit to uncertain effect—as well as instituted modest—and in some views, questionable—management reforms, its record when it comes to acquiring new capabilities is disappointing. The summa of Modi's defence policy is that of what he failed to achieve despite early signals that he would indeed deliver. While India's strategic environment promises perils, in the final assessment, Modi's legacy would be that of the perils of promise.

Ideation

The most pronounced imprint of the Modi government on Indian defence policy has been in the realm of ideation, namely in developing and emphasising security doctrines and strategy. It has included commencement of work on a national security strategy, publication of two new conventional military doctrines, as well as reaffirmation of India's existing declaratory nuclear doctrine. Furthermore, Modi's maritime diplomacy and push to acquire specific capabilities also reveal important strategic and doctrinal preferences. Put together, these ideational elements demonstrate remarkable continuity with that of previous governments—a function of 'stickiness' of Indian defence policy—albeit with certain key innovations.

In order to discern the continuity and the changes as well as to examine whether they match Modi's strategic intent, it is useful to examine public expressions and demonstration of the latter. Within a year of Modi's election, his top national security officials pledged to make India a 'leading power', in contrast to a merely balancing one; they also noted that 'India [...] punches below its weight', promising that the country has to 'increase [its] weight and punch proportionately.'[1] India under Modi has rhetorically endorsed the normative construct of the Indo-Pacific in three different ways. First, it has adopted this nomenclature in official documents. Second, it has participated in the reinvented quadrilateral dialogue (the 'Quad') with the US, Japan and Australia, embarked on vigorous defence diplomacy with Indian Ocean littorals, as well as engaged in other bilateral and trilateral arrangements with a maritime focus. Third, it has entered into naval-logistics agreements with the US and France and has sought to acquire a naval base in Seychelles. Taken together, they signal the Modi government's interest in promoting India as a significant maritime player in the region.[2]

On land, New Delhi under Modi has continued to search for ways to enforce deterrence in face of Pakistan's intransigence. Responding to a serious terrorist attack on a military base in September 2016, Indian Special Forces carried out a limited cross-Line of Control (LoC) operation. Notably, these 'surgical strikes'—as the Modi government termed them—were *avowed* indicating New Delhi's interest in escalation dominance.[3] More significantly, on 26 February 2019, the Indian Air Force carried out an air attack in mainland Pakistan as a response to a terrorist attack on a CRPF convoy in Pulwama, Jammu and Kashmir, 12 days before—the first use of air power against that country in almost 50 years. But Modi's muscular intent has not been communicated to Pakistan alone. His decision to engage in a tense months-long military standoff with China over the disputed Bhutanese region of Doklam in the summer of 2017 was read by many as India's new-found assertiveness in dealing with Chinese 'salami-slicing' tactics.

Welcome as these developments are, India's responses to external security challenges continue to be sporadic, ad-hoc, and lacking grand-strategic direction. While India responded to the Pakistan-sponsored attack on the military base in Uri in September 2016 with cross-LoC special operations, its reaction to another similar attack two months later—on a military base in Nagrota, Jammu and Kashmir—was muted.[4] The terror attack in Pulwama also showed that the 'surgical strikes' of September 2016 failed in terms of deterring Pakistan-backed proxies; whether the Balakot strikes act as a deterrent for these groups remain to be seen. While the Indian Army prevented Chinese road construction in Doklam in the summer of 2017, New Delhi remains impervious to Chinese activity in that region despite admitting itself that the People's Liberation Army (PLA) continues to consolidate its presence there.[5] Finally, while India endorses the Quad, it continues to exclude Australia in the US-India-Japan Malabar naval exercise.[6]

The blame for much of this inexplicable behaviour must lie with New Delhi's inability to formulate and publicly present a National Security Strategy (NSS). Such a document should, ideally, (1) delineate India's strategic outlook, interests, and threats, (2) signal posture to both allies and adversaries, (3) provide direction to the national-security bureaucracy (the foreign office, the Defence Ministry, the armed forces, and the intelligence services) and, most importantly, (4) supply a politically-sanctioned intellectual framework that guides allocation of scarce national resources. An NSS would then lead to a national defence strategy which would go on to inform military doctrines and budgeting.[7] The need for formulation of a comprehensive Indian NSS was advanced by the Naresh Chandra Committee—tasked with an across-the-board examination of India's national security—in 2011 though there is an indication that the push for such a document, with a narrower scope, had started much earlier.[8] The Indian Integrated Defence Staff Headquarters had suggested a national security and defence strategy as early as 2008.[9] Going further back, the 2001 Group-of-Ministers (GoM) on National Security had already indicated the need for a document that will translate national security objectives into defence objectives.[10] However, despite at least three attempts since to create such a document,[11] New Delhi has yet to come up with it.

The Modi government has accepted the need for an NSS, and informed observers have noted that a formal document is indeed in the works. If India adopts an NSS by the end of Modi's term in 2019, this would be a significant innovation in Indian defence policy. However, from the scant publicly available information, it seems that instead of a national *security* strategy, the document under finalisation is a narrower national *defence* strategy—akin to the erstwhile US Quadrennial Defence Review or its new (mostly classified) avatar of a National Defence Strategy. The Indian NSS in the works apparently focuses on national-security bureaucracy reforms (discussed later in this chapter), seeks to guide military doctrines, and focusses on capabilities generation and resource allocation.[12] It remains unclear what relationship this document will have with the *Raksha Mantri's* Operational Directive which has been the principal tool through which the civilian leadership has provided strategic guidance to the Indian armed forces so far. Similarly, its relationship with the Long-Term Integrated Perspective Planning mechanism (LTIPP) —a classified 15-year plan that focuses on prospective defence budget, planning, and intra- and inter-services allocations—is yet to be elucidated.[13]

But more significantly, if the Modi NSS was to be a *classified* document obsessed with minutiae of management, it would fail to communicate India's strategic posture to its citizenry, allies and adversaries. If the NSS is kept inside locked safes, democratic India's citizenry would remain unconvinced about the direction of the country's defence policy; its international partners are concerned about India's shared commitments, and its adversaries unsure about New Delhi's resolve. In such an event, there will also be lingering suspicion that the NSS is a bureaucratic fiat to consolidate the powers of the Prime Minister's Office (PMO) and *inter alia* that of the National Security Advisor's (NSA), especially under a government that has focused on both.

Nowhere did the need for an NSS to guide military doctrines become clearer than in the instance of the 2017 Joint Doctrine of the Indian Armed Forces (JDIAF)—the first of its kind that was publicly released. Widely pilloried for its amateurish style, consequential gaffes, logical inconsistencies, and even instances of plagiarised content,[14] the JDIAF succeeded in inadvertently communicating India's default strategic posture—a continental view of threats that obsesses over Pakistan, values restraint, overemphasises the role of the army, downplays force projection (especially naval), and focuses on jointness insofar as the other two services (the air force in particular) support the army's operational objectives.[15] Significantly for a document of its kind, the JDIAF did not mention India's sole conventional tri-service Andaman and Nicobar Command (A&NC) once. Far from being a truly joint doctrine, it came across as an expression of what the Indian Army—the overwhelmingly predominant service—thinks about jointness, with questionable effect.[16]

However, the JDIAF did indicate two unique elements in Modi's military policy towards Pakistan. First, it formally situated cross-LoC strikes (such as the one carried out in September 2016) inside India's escalation calculus.[17] Second, the JDIAF gave a few—albeit incomplete—signals that India indeed has a proactive limited-aims strategy directed at Pakistan (colloquially known as 'Cold Start'), consolidating a doctrinal position that emerged with the classified (and subsequently leaked) Part-II of the 2004 Indian Army Doctrine.[18] In the recent past, the second element has become clear. In January 2019, Indian Army Chief General Bipin Rawat reiterated what he first explicitly announced in January 2017: That not only does the Indian Army have a proactive limited-aims strategy to enforce deterrence-by-punishment, but that it is actively reconfiguring its forces to implement the same.[19] This was a public reiteration of precepts laid down in the new 2018 Land Warfare Doctrine of the Indian Army which revises and supersedes the public 2004 document.[20]

In order to deter any such proactive campaign by India, Pakistan continues to develop and test the *Nasr* tactical nuclear missiles, advertising them as 'pouring cold water over Cold Start'. The proposition that such a move on Rawalpindi's part puts considerable pressure over the credibility of India's extant declaratory nuclear doctrine has been well examined.[21] Modi's 2014 election manifesto reflected the growing need to examine India's nuclear posture in face of such challenges. It had promised to 'study in detail India's nuclear doctrine, and revise and update it, to make it relevant to challenges of current times'.[22] Modi's first Defence Minister also inadvertently cast significant doubt over India's nuclear doctrine, especially its posture of 'no first use'.[23] However, what is remarkable is that the Modi government has not revised the declaratory nuclear doctrine—or even indicated that it is 'studying' it to that effect despite vocal calls from influential quarters.[24] This is a pronounced continuity with previous governments. Indeed, there is no indication that India's nuclear arsenal has grown significantly larger (which would be a requirement for a first-strike and/or nuclear war-fighting posture).

'If India opts to develop limited nuclear options, policymakers should refrain from announcing a capability before it exists,' two American analysts noted in 2016.[25] Indeed, it is quite possible that the Modi government has sought to acquire capabilities that would expand India's nuclear options. Such revealed doctrinal preferences can be seen in two distinct ways. First, despite considerable American pressure to the opposite, the Modi's government has gone ahead with the purchase of the S-400 *Triumf* anti-aircraft weapon system. India's acquisition of the S-400 system could potentially further a damage-limitation strategy along with the implicit ballistic missile defence (BMD) capability demonstrated through the anti-satellite (ASAT) missile test of 27 March 2019. Through this strategy India could enhance the survivability of its nuclear command-and-control apparatus (especially if, as speculated, some fraction of the acquired S-400 batteries as well as indigenous BMD systems are deployed to protect Delhi[26]) should Pakistan respond following an *Indian* counterforce strike against its nuclear assets. In this context, it is important to note that India has never, publicly at least, ascribed to mutual nuclear vulnerability that characterised the Cold-War mutually-assured destruction (MAD) posture with Pakistan (or China, for that matter) so New Delhi's interest in damage limitation would be unsurprising.

Second, one explanation that has been proffered for the enhanced unit cost of the Rafale Medium Multi-Role Combat Aircraft (MMRCA) is that they incorporate 'Indian-specific enhancements' that could allow the aircrafts' induction as part of the nuclear air vector.[27] At the very least—coupled with the symbolic attention the Modi government has paid to the sea-leg of the nuclear triad[28]—this indicates a renewed commitment to a robust Indian nuclear deterrent. More speculatively, the Rafale MMRCA could also be deployed by India to retaliate against Pakistani tactical nuclear-weapon (TNW) use without acquiring TNWs itself.[29]

Management

Like new strategies and doctrines, bureaucratic and managerial reforms also reveal specific signatures of a government's defence policy. Here, the impact—or lack thereof—of the Modi government has been visible in three distinct ways. First, the Modi government's plan to enforce jointness among the three services in a 'top-down' way has largely been unsuccessful, largely due to lack of consensus among the three services. Second, under Modi, national-security bureaucracy has become significantly centralised in the Prime Minister's Office with a diminished role of the Cabinet Committee on Security (CCS) and concomitant empowerment of the National Security Council (NSC) system. Third, at least on paper the Modi government has pushed for significant reforms of the army whose revenue expenditure has become a significant liability to its combat potential.

Jointness among the three services has proved to be one of the most elusive goals in Indian defence policy. No other long-standing debate captures this better than the establishment of a Chief of Defence Staff (CDS) who would be the head of the three services and associated establishments and serve as the single-point military advisor to the government. The 2001 GoM had suggested the establishment of a CDS, following the experience of the early phase of the Kargil conflict where the air force and the army found themselves unable to coordinate their response. (Incidentally, the lack of coordination between these two services was also apparent during the 1965 India-Pakistan War.[30])

The recommendations of the 2011 Naresh Chandra Committee included a reaffirmation of the 2001 GoM recommendation, albeit with a change in nomenclature—instead of recommending that the government appoint a CDS, they suggested the creation of the position of a Permanent Chairman of the Chiefs of Service Staff Committee (PCCOSC).[31] Establishment of a PCCOSC would be a significant improvement over the existing system of a *rotating* Chairman of the Chiefs of Staff Committee whereby the senior-most of the three chiefs assumes the position and it is not a merit-based political appointment. Crucially, unlike the office of the CDS or PCCOSC, the existing system is consensus-driven, derided as 'warfare by committee'. The rotating chairman cannot impose his decision on the other two chiefs lacking, as he does, the legal authority to do so.

One of the first big military-reforms agenda announced by Modi's first Defence Minister, Manohar Parrikar, was the establishment of yet another committee to examine the lacunae in the Indian Armed Forces, led by Lieutenant General (Retd.) D.B. Shekatkar. Whether the Shekatkar Committee recommended the creation of a CDS is unknown given that its recommendations remain classified. Shekatkar himself was cryptic in this regard, noting that while 'India needs a Chief of Defence Staff [...] his role, responsibilities and accountability have to be defined as per Indian requirements and Ministry of Defence should not directly adopt a western model.'[32] In any event the final recommendations adopted by the government in 2018 pertained to mundane *army-specific* reforms.[33] Meanwhile, the services are more than happy to let the government take the blame for the failure to establish a CDS or PCCOSC, noting that there is consensus within the three services on the issue and that they have recommended the Ministry of Defence to this effect.[34] Despite having the electoral mandate to institute this significant piece of military reforms, the Modi government has failed to do so for reasons that remain unclear.

Another elusive quest for jointness is that of 'theatre commands'—integrated geographical commands of the three services lead by a single commander. Proposals of integrated commands include the establishment of a 'Western Theatre Command' that would be responsible for combat with Pakistan, a 'Northern Theatre Command' for China-related contingencies, and an 'Eastern Theatre Command' tasked with dealing with Bangladesh and Myanmar.[35] (Presumably, the existing tri-service A&NC will work with the Eastern and Northern Theatre Commands as well as focus on the eastern Indian Ocean at large, while the Strategic Forces Command will be independent depending, as it does, solely on civilian-political guidance.) Creation of theatre commands is not simply a matter of emulating the People's Liberation Army which established a similar structure in 2016 as part of broad reforms aimed at enhancing joint warfighting capabilities.

Take the example of close air support (CAS) for land-based operations, including implementing a proactive limited-aims strategy. The official 2012 doctrine of the Indian Air Force downplays the role of air assets for CAS noting that 'limited air assets' should not be 'frittered away in penny packets'.[36] Meanwhile the Indian Army does not possess fixed-wing air assets of its own, depending on the air force for CAS. The establishment of integrated theatre commands would remove the conflicting attitude of the two services when it comes to CAS: the theatre commander will not have to depend on the air force's acquiescence when it comes to allocation of air assets for combat tasks. (Under the existing system it is the *air* commander who will have 'the final authority to decide on the employment of air assets keeping the overall air situations in mind'.[37]) It is therefore not surprising that the IAF is widely seen within the three services as the principal obstacle when it comes to the establishment of theatre commands.[38] However, it is important to note that without a CDS or even a PCCOSC, theatre commands are a non-starter, the fundamental issue being that in event of war the theatre commanders will not know which of the three chiefs to report to, the existing rotating chairman of COSC bearing no substantive authority.

Like many other reform issues—and not just related to the military—

there was considerable early excitement that the Modi government would move quickly to establish integrated theatre commands.[39] Instead, the actual progress has been extremely modest. In March 2018, the Modi government took the first step towards establishment of such commands by instituting a statutory rule that 'an officer from any one service can now "exercise direct command" over personnel from the other two services'.[40] The apparent motivation for this decision was to strengthen the strategically-important A&NC which, ironically, did not deserve a single mention in the army-centric JDIAF. Another demonstrative step the Modi government has taken to enhance tri-service coordination is to establish a Defence Cyber Agency, a Defence Space Agency and a Special Operations Division, all of which will draw personnel from the three services. However, under the proposed arrangement, these three new entities will report to the rotating Chairman of COSC[41] and therefore be plagued with all the problems that result from the lack of a permanent head of the COSC. As always, the fundamental step to enhance jointness is from the top, through the establishment of a single legally-empowered head of all three military services. Short of this, proliferation of tri-service agencies gives the illusion of jointness without adding substance.

In the absence of institutional structures to enhance jointness and military effectiveness, the Modi government has sought to work around it by significantly enhancing the powers of the National Security Council (NSC) system and that of the NSA. It has also diminished the importance of the Cabinet Committee on Security (CCS). Three instances illustrate the diminution of the CCS under Modi. First, for almost a sixth of his five-year tenure, Modi did not have a full-time Defence Minister with the Finance Minister wearing both hats. Second, while planning response to the Pathankot attack in January 2016—the first high-profile terror attack in Modi's tenure—the CCS was not convened, with the NSA assuming overall responsibility.[42] Third, while examining military options as response to the 2016 Uri attacks, other than the Defence Minister he did not consult the rest of the CCS.[43]

On the other hand, Modi has significantly empowered the NSA and the Secretariat of the NSC (NSCS) with the budget of the latter seeing a significant increase, standing at more than Rs 3 billion in the 2018-19 budget year.[44] The reconstituted board of external experts that advises the NSC system, the National Security Advisory Board (NSAB), is also much more focused and staffed predominantly by former defence, intelligence, and foreign office personnel—in distinction to the NSAB of the previous governments which included economists, social scientists, and other academic experts. Insiders also point to the increasing interest of the PMO in managing and shaping the agenda of government-funded defence think-tanks.[45]

However, it is Modi's empowerment of NSA Ajit Doval that has been the most consequential element of his focus on the NSC system. Rivalled only by Brajesh Mishra (former Prime Minister Atal Bihari Vajyapee's Principal Secretary and India's first NSA), Doval has played an outsized role in determining the trajectory and implementation of India's security policies. When the Modi government, in 2018, announced the formation of a Defence Planning Committee (DPC) to 'facilitate a comprehensive and integrated planning for defence matters', it put him at its helm making him the 'de-facto CDS'.[46] Parallelly, when the Modi government brought back the Vajpayee-era Strategic Policy Group (SPG) to life, it did so by replacing the Cabinet Secretary with the NSA as its head.[47] While the impact of such moves on civil-military relations and civilian bureaucratic politics remains to be seen, and any future non-Modi government could quickly overturn these arrangements, the emergence of the NSA as a single-most important non-elected actor in Indian defence policy could help mitigate some of the structural problems alluded to earlier in this section by removing persistent infighting and bottlenecks.

That said, the role of the DPC and SPG in the overall management of India's national security is still to be understood in detail. For one, reports suggest that the DPC will guide defence acquisition by aligning it with both budgetary constraints as well as strategic objectives. India already has one mechanism to develop long-horizon plans that inform defence acquisitions—the LTIPP. The Ministry of Defence also has a Defence Acquisition Council (DAC) which, in principle, links service requirements with acquisitions. It is not known whether the DPC mechanism would either supersede or augment both LTIPP and DAC or be an independent function altogether. When the SPG was reconstituted in 2018, the government noted it 'shall be the principal mechanism for inter-ministerial coordination and integration of relevant inputs in the formulation of national security policies'.[48] While DPC and SPG memberships are at the secretarial-level, whether the (re)introduction of these mechanisms marks further diminution of the Cabinet-level CCS, principally the office of the Defence Minister, also remains to be seen.

The last set of reforms that the Modi government has announced pertains to the Indian Army. It is a well-known fact that the skewed revenue expenditure to capital expenditure ratio (in favour of the former) has hampered capital acquisitions and depleted combat effectiveness. For example, one analysis noted that the costs of raising the mountain divisions against China may have led to the 'flatlining' of the army's capital budget.[49] The Indian Army's skewed 'tooth-to-tail' ratio (essentially the number of non-combatant personnel that support one combat soldier) as well as its bloated numerical strength are problems that have been well discussed over the years. Finally, the changing nature of India's strategic environment demands that the Indian Army remains nimble, agile and swift. In order to address these issues, Indian Army Chief General Bipin Rawat recently advanced a set of innovative proposals to restructure his service with the principal military objective being dismantling existing large division-sized forces into 'integrated battle groups' that can swiftly mobilise and execute objectives.[50] This is in consonance with the recent decision to freeze the raising of the mountain strike corps—expensive and large formations whose maintenance cut into the army's expenditure.[51] However, it remains to be seen whether the incumbent government in 2019 will actually approve Rawat's suggestions, given the political costs involved.

Capabilities

Unlike ideation and management, acquisition of new capabilities is the most lacklustre element of Modi's defence policy. And a large part of the problem lies with budgetary allocations and priorities as well as other domestic political considerations. In the Indian context, social-sector spending will always outweigh defence priorities due to extant socio-economic realities. Put simply, India is a poor country that seeks to be a strong state. The tension between the two will remain unreconcilable for a long time to come. Be that as it may, military expenditure (both as a percentage of government expenditure as well as GDP) has steadily fallen over the past three decades as India's economy has grown significantly (see **Figure 1** below).[52]

Figure 1: Indian Military Expenditure

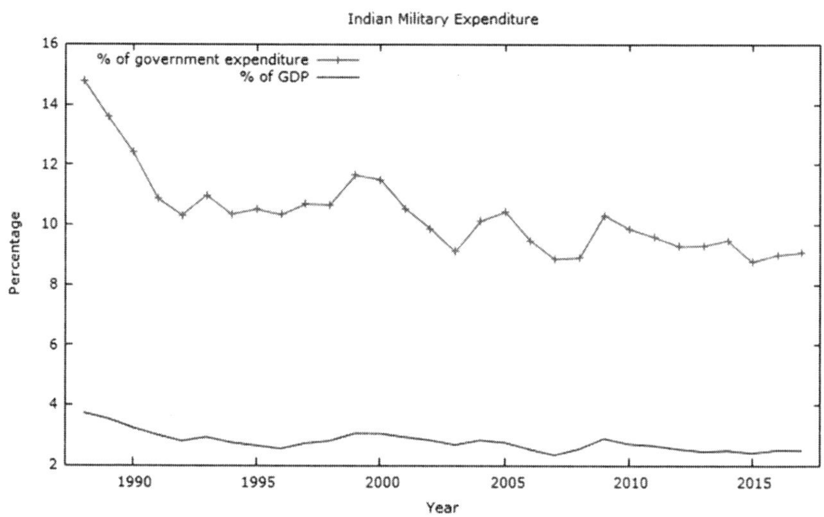

Note: figure; author; data source: SIPRI

In the 2018-19 defence budget (which does not include defence pensions or miscellaneous yet significant Ministry of Defence expenses) 67 per cent of the allocation went to revenue expenditure (mostly salaries of armed forces personnel) while 33 per cent went to capital expenditure. That budget allocated Rs 74,224 crore to capital acquisitions which is much lesser than defence pensions in the MoD budget standing at Rs1,08,853 crore.[53] The inter-services allocations continue to remain skewed with the army commanding 55 per cent of the defence budget, the air force 23 per cent, and the navy 15 per cent.[54] Most alarmingly, that year the share of defence budget in GDP was 1.49 per cent—the lowest since the 1962 war with China.[55] One direct consequence of the pathologies of the defence budget is the worrying state of war-wastage reserves as highlighted both by successive reports of the Comptroller and Auditor General (CAG) as well as by a report tabled by the 2018 Parliamentary Standing Committee on Defence (PSCOD).

The latest (2018) CAG report noted that 50 per cent of ammunitions reserve was at a 'critical level' meaning that they would not last for more than 10 days of intense warfare.[56] The 2018 PSCOD report noted that 'Indian Army has accumulated huge deficiencies of weapons, stores and ammunition as adequate attention was lacked, both in terms of policies and budget to modernise the aging armoury'.[57] In fact, the alarming state of reserves of basic arms and ammunitions became clear when, in the run-up to the cross-LoC strikes of 2016, India had to make emergency purchases of ammunition from Russia to meet any contingency.[58] The Modi government's 2017 decision to grant powers to the army to directly buy certain critical weapons spares and ammunition is a welcome albeit ad-hoc step.[59]

If the composition of defence spending remains one albatross around the neck of Indian military preparedness, the failure to establish an indigenous defence manufacturing base remains another. Between 2008-12 and 2013-17, India was the world's biggest arms importer, with imports increasing by 24 per cent. To compare this to China's in the same period, its imports *decreased* by 19 per cent.[60] (While between 2009-13 and 2014-18, India's position marginally improved—it became the *second* largest arms importer in the world—analysts have noted that this was due to delay in deliveries of orders already placed.[61]) The 2014 BJP manifesto had promised to promote defence manufacturing in India both for domestic use as well as exports. And true to this commitment, soon after coming to office Modi flagged off a 'Make-in-India' campaign that was to *inter alia* also boost domestic defence manufacturing. Despite relaxing conditions on foreign direct investment in defence on coming to office (beyond the pre-existing automatic approval for investments up to 49 per cent by a foreign firm in an Indian defence company), the Modi government only attracted a measly Rs 1.17 crore between April

2014 and December 2017.[62] Modi's defence 'Make in India' agenda has almost completely been unfulfilled. Political pressures also continue to hamper the case of big-ticket defence manufacturing in India. For example, in 2017 American aerospace major Lockheed Martin committed to shifting its entire production line, as well as transfer technology, of the single-engine F-16 Block 70 fighter jets and manufacture them in India (with the Tata group) *only* if it won the bid to sell 110 such aircrafts to the Indian Air Force.[63] Riders like this can turn the issue of defence manufacturing with foreign investments into a highly-sensitive issue subject to international as well as domestic politics.

Inexorably tied with the establishment of an indigenous defence-industrial base, the Modi government has not shown marked interest in acquiring new weapons and platforms. Instead, he has been content with showcasing capabilities of systems approved by previous governments, such as dramatically announcing the country's ASAT prowess through the March 2019 test—something analysts had suspected India has had as early as 2011.[64] The scorecard is correspondingly modest. Defence acquisition continues to remain hobbled with domestic politics. In 2014, the Modi government agreed to procure the Spike-MR, Man-Portable Anti-Tank Guided Missiles from Israel, only to scrap it in 2017 in favour of a similar weapon to be developed by the Defence Research and Development Organisation (DRDO).[65] When it became clear that DRDO will not be able to deliver the indigenous missiles in time—as is the case in many other instances —the Modi government backtracked on its previous backtracking, finally agreeing to purchase the Spike missiles as a 'stop gap' solution in 2018.[66] Meanwhile, the Israeli media was quick to point out the domestic pressures that have shaped the ebb-and-flow in the Spike saga.[67]

Another example of how domestic politics continues to hobble defence acquisitions is the ongoing controversy around the Rafale MMRCA. Without getting into the merits of the arguments on both sides, it is important to note two collateral casualties of the issue. One, following the uproar on the Rafale acquisitions, the Modi government rejected a Russian proposal to partner with the Adani group to make the third generation of the AK-47 assault rifles in India.[68] Had the proposal been accepted, it would have been a significant boost to the 'Make-in-India' campaign and attracted more private-sector players to defence manufacturing. Two, as India plans to build and induct a third aircraft career, *INS Vishal*, in the 2020s, Dassault Aviation (the manufacturer of Rafale) is said to have pitched a naval variant of the MMRCA to the Indian Navy.[69] If the controversy around the air force's acquisition of the Rafale continues, it will most likely colour the Navy's selection decision irrespective of the technical merits either way.

It is in the front of naval capabilities that Modi's India has made modest progress in acquiring new capabilities. In 2016, India entered into a contract to acquire four Krivak-III stealth frigates from Russia, finalising the deal for two of them in 2018.[70] In 2018, India agreed to grant Israel the bid to manufacture the naval variant of the long-range surface-to-air Barak-8 missile system.[71] The naval Barak-8 will consolidate the Indian Navy's denial strategy in the Indian Ocean region. Notably, in December 2018, the Indian Navy inaugurated an intelligence fusion centre tasked with monitoring sea traffic in the Indian Ocean region.[72] As both traditional and non-traditional security challenges abound in the Indian Ocean, the fusion centre is certain to integrate India's (and partners') maritime domain awareness efforts in the region.

The Road Ahead

The picture that emerges from the preceding analysis is that of a lost opportunity. Despite a massive electoral mandate—which freed him from the compulsions of coalition politics—Modi has largely underperformed when it comes to defence policy. The lacklustre performance of his government becomes stark when compared to his early promises. To be fair, political compulsions (domestic, international, as well as bureaucratic) have often stood between what Modi set out to achieve and what he could. Recognising these persistent factors when it comes to defence policy, the tasks before the incoming government are clear.

First, it must *develop* India's conventional military strength. While the issue of acquisition of capabilities is evident—especially for air dominance—the new government also must pay attention to enhancing jointness and interoperability within the three services. The so-called 'Revolution in Military Affairs' demands that different forces work jointly in a network-centric environment. It is unclear to what extent the Indian Army, Air Force and Navy can do so at the moment. The new government must also focus on force projection in the Indian Ocean region, and the larger Indo-Pacific in general. This will necessarily involve recalibration of the defence budget and a larger allocation for the navy (at the expense of streamlining the army's spending). The new government must also focus on intelligence reforms and threat-environment awareness. It is a matter of no small concern that 10 years since the Mumbai 26/11 attacks, the proposed nationwide intelligence integration network (NATGRID) is yet to be operational.

Second, it must *reform* the military bureaucracy. As the American experience shows, inter-services rivalry can only be tamed if reforms to enhance jointness are introduced as a matter of law—top-down. Modi has squandered the opportunity to introduce a Goldwater-Nichols-type legislation that would have comprehensively reformed the military bureaucracy, much in the same way that Ronald Reagan did in 1986. If the next government does indeed have a clear electoral mandate it should introduce legislation that streamlines and integrates the Indian national-security establishment instead of resorting to ad-hoc fixes like the current government. A related issue is that of reorienting the Indian Army away from its counter-insurgency functions in Jammu and Kashmir. Armies, no matter how efficient or well-equipped, have a poor record of being policemen—again, as the American experience has demonstrated.

Finally, the new government must *mainstream* asymmetric capabilities. Despite paying lip service to the importance of new next-generation technologies—whether they relate to electronic warfare, artificial intelligence, drones, hypersonic weapons, synthetic biology, or quantum technologies—the Indian defence establishment is yet to embark on a systematic evaluation of the same in terms of assessing their use in India's own *sui generis* strategic environment. India has a rich scientific and technological base; the new government must ideate innovative ways to integrate the work of civilian scientists and technologists with national-security priorities. These new technologies, of course, will not be panacea to all contingencies, useful as they would be principally to counter China's own capabilities. In order to deal with Pakistan, the new government must reprioritise covert and sub-conventional options.

NOTES

1 S. Jaishankar, 'India Wants to be a Leading Power Rather than Just a Balancing Power.' *The Wire*, 15 July 2015, https://thewire.in/diplomacy/india-wants-to-be-a-leading-power-rather-than-just-a-balancing-power ; Ajit Doval, 'State Security, Statecraft and Conflict of Values,' Lalit Doshi Memorial Lecture, Mumbai, 4 August 2015.

2 While India rhetorically endorses the Indo-Pacific construct, significant obstacles remain when it comes to New Delhi operationalising this notion. For a discussion of these obstacles, see Harsh V. Pant and Abhijnan Rej, 'Is India ready for the Indo-Pacific?' *The Washington Quarterly*, Vol. 41, no. 2 (2018): pp. 47-61. On a sceptical view of the notion itself from a former senior Indian official, see: Shivshankar Menon, 'China-US Contention Has Opened Up Space for Other Powers, Including India,' *The Wire*, 24 December 2018, https://thewire.in/diplomacy/china-us-contention-has-opened-up-space-for-other-powers-including-india

3 Rajesh Rajagopalan, 'India now controls the escalation ladder,' *Observer Research Foundation Expert Speak*, 5 October 2016, https://www.orfonline.org/expert-speak/india-now-controls-the-escalation-ladder

4 Manoj Joshi, 'The politics of surgical strikes,' *The Tribune India*, 11 December 2018, https://www.tribuneindia.com/news/comment/the-politics-of-surgical-strikes/696434.html.

5 'China building helipads, other infra in Doklam area: Nirmala Sitharaman,' *The Economic Times*, 5 March 2018, https://economictimes.indiatimes.com/news/defence/china-building-helipads-other-infra-in-doklam-area-nirmala-sitharaman/articleshow/63173347.cms

6 Suhasini Haidar and Dinakar Peri, 'Not time yet for Australia's inclusion in Malabar naval games,' *The Hindu*, 22 January 2019, https://www.thehindu.com/news/national/not-time-yet-for-australias-inclusion-in-malabar-naval-games/article26058080.ece

7 This is a template taken from the United States military. See: 'Doctrine for the Armed Forces of the United States: Joint Publication 1,' *Joint Chiefs of Staff*, 25 March 2013 Incorporating Change 1, 12 July 2017, https://www.jcs.mil/Portals/36/Documents/Doctrine/pubs/jp1_ch1.pdf

8 Manoj Joshi, 'Higher Defence Management: Evolution and Reform,' in *Military Strategy for India in the 21st Century*, ed. Lt Gen A.K. Singh and Lt Gen B.S.

Nagal (New Delhi: Centre for Land Warfare Studies/Knowledge World Publishers, 2019): p. 266.

[9] Col S. A. Rehman, 'Jointsmanship: The IDS way,' undated, 3 http://ids.nic.in/art_by_offids/Jointmanship%20-%20The%20IDS%20Way%20%20 by%20 Col%20SA%20Rehman.pdf (accessed 6 October 2017). For further corroboration that IDS had indeed forwarded such a strategy to the NSA, see Laxman K. Behera, 'Defence Planning in India,' *Journal of Defence Studies* 4, no. 3 (2010): P.130.

[10] 'Group-of-Ministers Report on National Security, 2001,' hosted at the Vivekananda International Foundation, accessed January 27, 2019, https://www.vifindia.org/sites/default/files/GoM%20Report%20on%20National%20Security.pdf: 98.

[11] India's former Indian Secretary Shyam Saran at Observer Research Foundation, New Delhi, 27 September 2017 at the launch of his book, *How India Sees the World: Kautilya to the 21st Century.*

[12] Nitin Gokhale, 'Indian National Security Strategy Crystallising at a Fast Pace,' *Bharat Shakti*, 16 August 2018, https://bharatshakti.in/indian-national-security-strategy-crystallising-at-a-fast-pace/

[13] For a discussion of the importance of the NSS for defence modernization and budget allocation, see Amit Cowshish, 'Distortions in the Discourse on Modernization of Armed Forces,' *Journal of Defence Studies*, Vol.8, no. 3 (2014): pp. 10-11.

[14] Ankit Panda, 'India's 2017 Joint Armed Forces Doctrine: First Takeaways,' *The Diplomat*, 28 April 2017, https://thediplomat.com/2017/04/indias-2017-joint-armed-forcesdoctrine-first-takeaways/; Anit Mukherjee, 'Joint Doctrine for Armed Forces: The Single-Service Syndrome,' *The Hindu*, 9 May 2017, http://www.thehindu.com/opinion/op-ed/joint-doctrine-of-armed-forcesthe-single-service-syndrome/article18410953.ece; Sudharshan Srikhande, 'Joint Doctrine of the Indian Armed Forces – Wholly Informational, Hardly Doctrinal,' *The Wire*, 8 May 2017, https://thewire.in/133347/joint-doctrineindian-armed-forces-wholly-informational-hardly-doctrinal; Srinath Raghavan, 'Defence policy has to be a joint effort between civilians and the military,' *Hindustan Times*, 11 May 2017, http://www.hindustantimes.com/columns/defence-policy-has-to-be-a-joint-effort-between-civilians-and-themilitary/story-55KtLiHsr63 M1buTG7li 3N.html.

[15] For a detailed analysis of the JDIAF, see: Abhijnan Rej and Shashank Joshi, 'India's Joint Doctrine: A Lost Opportunity,' ORF Occasional Paper No. 139 (New Delhi: Observer Research Foundation: 2018), https://www.orfonline.org/wp- content/uploads/2018/01/ORF_Occasional_Paper_Joint_Doctrine.pdf.

[16] Gen Bipin Rawat, the Indian Army Chief, has at least on one occasion publicly claimed the supremacy of his service. See: Dinakar Peri, 'Army supremacy has to be maintained: Army Chief Bipin Rawat,' *The Hindu*, 6 September 2017, https://www.thehindu.com/news/national/despite-nuclear-weapons-threat-of-two-front-war-is-real-army-chief-bipin-rawat/article19630592.ece.

[17] Rej and Joshi, *India's Joint Doctrine*, 10.

[18] Ibid, (n. 13).

[19] Sandeep Unnithan, 'Battle of the Bulge: Bipin Rawat's radical plan to restructure army,' *India Today*, 12 January 2019, https://www.indiatoday.in/magazine/cover-story/story/20190121-battle-of-the-bulge-1427715-2019-01-12

[20] Joy Mitra, 'India's Land Warfare Doctrine 2018: Hoping for the Best, Preparing for the Worst,' *The Diplomat*, 3 January 2019, https://thediplomat.com/2019/01/indias-land-warfare-doctrine-2018-hoping-for-the-best-preparing-for-the-worst/

[21] See, for example, Yogesh Joshi and Frank O'Donnell, *India in Nuclear Asia: Evolution of Regional Forces, Perceptions and Policies* (Hyderabad: Orient Black Swan, 2018): pp. 165-196.

[22] 'Election Manifesto 2014,' Bharatiya Janata Party, https://www.bjp.org/images/pdf_2014/full_manifesto_english_07.04.2014.pdf, 39. (accessed 27 January 2019)

[23] Manjeet Singh Negi, 'Manohar Parrikar makes bizarre nuclear statement, his ministry says personal opinion,' *India Today*, 10 November 2016, https://www.indiatoday.in/india/story/manohar-parrikar-nuke-statement-defence-minister-surgical-strike-351393-2016-11-10

[24] One prominent proponent of re-examination of India's nuclear doctrine is former Strategic Forces Command Chief Lieutenant General B.S. Nagal. See: in B.S. Nagal, 'India's Nuclear Doctrine and Strategy,' in *Military Strategy for India in the 21st Century*, ed. Lt Gen A.K. Singh and Lt Gen B.S. Nagal (New Delhi: Centre for Land Warfare Studies/Knowledge World Publishers, 2019): pp. 195-224.

[25] Toby Dalton and George Perkovich, *India's Nuclear Options and Escalation Dominance* (Washington, DC: Carnegie Endowment for International Peace, 2016): pp. 2.

[26] Sujan Dutta, 'India's S-400 advantage: IAF in Delhi can shoot down Pakistani missile near Amritsar,' *The Print*, 5 October 2018, https://theprint.in/security/indias-s-400-advantage-iaf-in-delhi-can-shoot-down-pakistani-missile-near-amritsar/129639/

[27] Angad Singh and Abhijit Iyer-Mitra, 'Rafale procurement process has been clumsy, but is it crooked?,' *The Economic Times*, 27 November 2017, https://economictimes.indiatimes.com/blogs/et-commentary/rafale-procurement-process-has-been-clumsy-but-is-it-crooked/ For more background on Rafale as an air vector, see Robert Beckhusen, 'Why India Wants France's Dassault Rafale Fighter Jet: They Can Carry Nuclear Weapons,' *The National Interest*, 21 September 2016, https://nationalinterest.org/blog/the-buzz/why-india-wants-frances-dassault-rafale-fighter-jets-they-17777

[28] Rajat Pandit, 'Nuclear submarine INS Arihant completes patrol, country's N-triad operational,' *The Times of India*, 6 November 2018, https://timesofindia.indiatimes.com/india/as-nuclear-sub-arihant-returns-after-first-deterrence-patrol-indias-nuclear-triad-complete/articleshow/66515624.cms

[29] For more on this strategy, see: Rajesh Rajagopalan, 'Expanding India's nuclear options,' *Observer Research Foundation Expert Speak,* 10 January 2017, https://www.orfonline.org/expert-speak/expanding-indias-nuclear-options/

[30] Joshi, 'Higher Defence Management,' 258.

[31] For a discussion of how the positions of CDS and PCCOSC are different, see: Harsha Kakkar, 'Midway to a CDS,' *Observer Research Foundation Expert Speak,* 11 December 2018, https://www.orfonline.org/expert-speak/midway-cds-46134/

[32] Gaurav C Sawant, 'India needs chief of defence staff, but don't ape the west, says Lt Gen Shekatkar's report,' *India Today,* 27 December 2016, https://www.indiatoday.in/mail-today/story/shekatkar-committee-chief-of-defence-staff-defence-ministry-indian-armed-forces-manohar-parrikar-lt-gen-shekatkar-359673-2016-12-27

[33] 'Recommendations of Shekatkar Committee,' *Press Information Bureau of the Government of India,* 3 January 2018, http://pib.nic.in/newsite/PrintRelease.aspx?relid=175241

[34] Dinakar Peri, 'Services agree on Permanent Chair,' *The Hindu,* 3 December 2018, https://www.thehindu.com/news/national/services-agree-on-permanent-chair/article25656447.ece

[35] Shishir Gupta, 'Government set to usher greatest overhaul of India's military structure,' *Hindustan Times,* 14 February 2017, https://www.hindustantimes.com/india-news/government-set-to-usher-greatest-overhaul-of-india-s-military-structure/story-8RS9ylPnLXDkCxd8rkWVZP.html

[36] '2012 Basic Doctrine of the Indian Air Force,' Official Website of the Indian Air Force, 62, accessed 26 October 2017, http://indianairforce.nic.in/pdf/Basic%20Doctrine%20of%20the%20Indian%20Air%20Force.pdf

[37] '2012 Basic Doctrine of the Indian Air Force,' 61

[38] Rahul Singh, 'Navy says IAF is against joint theatre commands,' *Hindustan Times,* 3 December 2018, https://www.hindustantimes.com/india-news/navy-says-iaf-is-against-joint-theatre-commands/story-5q7Ukqmb4iN1ZDpl38XxJM.html

[39] Gupta, 'Government set to usher greatest overhaul of India's military structure', n. 35.

[40] Rajat Pandit, 'Govt moves on integrated theatre commands; amends rules to bring three forces under a single leadership,' *The Times of India,* 19 March 2018, https://timesofindia.indiatimes.com/india/govt-moves-on-integrated-theatre-commands-amends-rules-to-bring-three-forces-under-single-leadership/articleshow/63358296.cms

[41] Sudhi Ranjan Sen, 'India to set up 3 new agencies, including cyber and space, to boost defence capabilities,' *Hindustan Times,* 16 October 2018, https://www.hindustantimes.com/india-news/india-to-set-up-3-new-agencies-including-cyber-and-space-to-boost-defence-capabilities/story-umuS4UOs Davc0MhHkUjuWN.html

[42] Nitin A. Gokhale, *Securing India the Modi Way: Pathankot, Surgical Strikes and More* (New Delhi: Bloomsbury, 2017), p. 62.

43 Gokhale, *Securing India the Modi Way*, p. 35.

44 Nitin A. Gokhale, 'India's National Security is being transformed,' *Rediff.com*, 22 October 2018, https://www.rediff.com/news/column/indias-national-security-is-being-transformed/20181022.htm

45 Conversations with senior serving and former researchers in one such institution. Details withheld to protect sources.

46 Laxman K. Behera, 'Creation of Defence Planning Committee: A Step towards Credible Defence Preparedness,' Institute of Defence Studies and Analyses Comment, 19 April 2018, https://idsa.in/idsacomments/creation-of-defence-planning-committee-lkbehera-190418

47 Bharti Jain, 'Ajit Doval replaces cabinet secy as head of 'strategic policy group,' *The Economic Times*, 9 October 2018, https://timesofindia.indiatimes.com/india/ajit-doval-replaces-cabinet-secy-as-head-of-strategic-policy-group/articleshow/66126976.cms

48 'Strategic Policy Group reconstituted, Ajit Doval is Chairman,' *The Hindu*, 10 October 2018, https://www.thehindu.com/news/national/strategic-policy-group-reconstituted-ajit-doval-is-chairman/article25175468.ece

49 Shane Mason, *Military Budgets in India and Pakistan: Trajectories, Priorities, Risks* (Washington DC: Stimson Center, 2016): p. 19, https://www.stimson.org/sites/default/files/file-attachments/Military-Budgets-India-Pakistan-Trajectories-Priorities-Risks-Oct2016.pdf.pdf

50 Sudhi Ranjan Sen, 'Integrated Battle Groups now a reality as Indian Army braces for sweeping changes in combat strategy,' *Hindustan Times*, 14 October 2018, https://www.hindustantimes.com/india-news/integrated-battle-groups-now-a-reality-as-indian-army-braces-for-sweeping-changes-in-combat-strategy/story-Oh8ectf0Hj7DlvzSEJTXRJ.html; Sandeep Unnithan, 'Battle of the Bulge'.

51 Sujan Dutta, 'Indian Army puts Mountain Strike Corps aimed at China in cold storage,' *The Print*, 12 July 2018, https://theprint.in/security/indian-army-puts-mountain-strike-corps-aimed-at-china-in-cold-storage/82319/

52 A clarification on a confusing point: 'Government expenditure,' per SIPRI methodology, includes *all* government spending (central + state + municipal etc). In that methodology, 'military expenditure' is taken to be the budget of the Ministry of Defence (= defence budget + pensions + miscellaneous Ministry of Defence expenses) but *also includes* certain Ministry of Home 'expenditure on the paramilitary forces of the Border Security Force, the Central Reserve Police Force, the Assam Rifles, the Indo-Tibetan Border Police and, from 2007 the Sashastra Seema Bal.' For further details, see: 'Sources and Methods,' SIPRI, https://www.sipri.org/databases/milex/sources-and methods#sources (accessed 29 January 2019). To see the breakdown of the 'miscellaneous MoD expenses' head, see 'Ministry of Defence, Demand No. 19, Ministry of Defence (Misc.),' https://www.indiabudget.gov.in/budget2017-2018/ub2017-18/eb/sbe19.pdf

53 Laxman K. Behera, 'Defence Budget 2018-19: The Imperative of Controlling Manpower Cost,' Institute for Defence Studies and Analyses Comment, 2

February 2018, https://idsa.in/issuebrief/defence-budget-2018-19-controlling-manpower-cost-lkbehera-020218

54 Ibid.

55 Ibid; D. K. Singh, 'Is India ready for a two-front war? Our MPs don't think so,' *The Print*, 11 June 2018, https://theprint.in/security/indias-defence-budget-is-the-lowest-since-the-1962-war-with-china-mps-raise-alarm/68511/

56 'CAG pulls up Defence Ministry on ammunition management in Army,' Economic Times, July 11, 2018, https://economictimes.indiatimes.com/news/defence/cag-pulls-up-defence-ministry-on-ammunition-management-in-army/articleshow/47204599.cms

57 'Demand for Grants (2018-19), Forty First Report of the Standing Committee on Defence,' *Lok Sabha Secretariat*, March 2018, http://164.100.47.193/lsscommittee/Defence/16_Defence_41.pdf

58 Shishir Gupta, "Military priority is to have adequate inventory for 30-day war," *Hindustan Times*, 8 May 2018, https://www.hindustantimes.com/india-news/military-priority-is-to-have-adequate-inventory-for-30-day-war/story-zJOh1hnmCpoCvTNb4GI1kO.html

59 'Army Gets Special Powers To Buy Ammo, Spares In Emergency Situations,' *NDTV*, 13 July, 2017, https://www.ndtv.com/india-news/army-gets-special-powers-to-buy-ammo-spares-in-emergency-situations-1724040

60 'Trends in International Arms Transfer, 2017,' *SIPRI Fact Sheet*, 6 March 2018, https://www.sipri.org/sites/default/files/2018-03/fssipri_at2017_0.pdf

61 'Global arms trade: USA increases dominance; arms flows to the Middle East surge, says SIPRI,' *Stockholm International Peace Research Institute*, 11 March 2019, https://www.sipri.org/media/press-release/2019/global-arms-trade-usa-increases-dominance-arms-flows-middle-east-surge-says-sipri

62 Manish Kumar Jha, 'The Long And Winding Road To Make In India,' *Business World*, 21 August 2018, http://www.businessworld.in/article/The-Long-And-Winding-Road-To-Make-In-India/21-08-2018-158251/; Dinakar Peri, '100% FDI in defence: What does it mean?,' *The Hindu*, 20 June 2016, https://www.thehindu.com/news/national/100-FDI-in-defence-What-does-it-mean/article14433877.ece

63 Manu Pubby, 'Lockheed Martin teams up with Tata to make F-16 Fighters in India,' *The Economic Times*, updated 14 July 2018, https://economictimes.indiatimes.com/news/defence/lockheed-signs-pact-with-tata-to-make-f-16-planes-in-india/articleshow/59219549.cms; Tarun Shukla, 'Tata, Lockheed Martin partner to make F-16s in India,' *Mint*, 20 June 2017, https://www.livemint.com/Industry/rxh8UAHH0Hr0HoiCENXurM/Tata-Lockheed-Martin-partner-up-to-make-F16s-in-India.html

64 Dinakar Peri, 'Successful anti-satellite missile test puts India in elite club,' *The Hindu*, 27 March 2019, https://www.thehindu.com/news/national/successful-anti-satellite-missile-test-puts-india-in-elite-club/article26657024.ece

65 Sushant Singh, 'Ministry of Defence scraps $500 million Israeli missile deal, wants DRDO to make in India,' *The Indian Express*, 20 November 2017, https://

indianexpress.com/article/india/ministry-of-defence-scraps-500-million-israeli-missile-deal-wants-drdo-to-make-in-india-4945571/

66 Dinakar Peri, 'India looks to procure Spike missiles,' *The Hindu*, 23 September 2018, https://www.thehindu.com/news/national/india-looks-to-procure-spike-missiles/article25021894.ece

67 Shrenik Rao, 'Modi's Missile Dilemma: Why India Keeps Spiking, and Reviving, a Massive Israeli Arms Deal,' *Haaretz*, 13 June 2018, https://www.haaretz.com/opinion/.premium-modi-s-missile-dilemma-why-india-is-spiking-a-huge-israeli-arms-deal-1.6173373

68 'India rejects Russia's proposal to partner with Adani Group to make AK-103 rifles,' *Business Today*, 4 September 2018, https://www.businesstoday.in/current/policy/india-rejects-russia-proposal-partner-adani-group-ak103-rifles/story/281992.html

69 Ajit Kumar Dubey, 'Indian Navy plans to acquire its third aircraft carrier for a whopping Rs 1.6 lakh crore,' *India Today*, 15 January 2018, https://www.indiatoday.in/mail-today/story/indian-navy-plans-to-acquire-its-third-aircraft-carrier-for-a-whopping-rs-1-6-lakh-crore-1144836-2018-01-15

70 Vivek Raghuvanshi, 'India signs $950 million contract with Russia to buy two stealth frigates,' *DefenseNews*, 30 October 2018, https://www.defensenews.com/naval/2018/10/30/india-signs-950-million-contract-with-russia-to-buy-two-stealth-frigates/

71 'From Russia's S-400 to Israel's Barak-8 missiles: How India is fortifying its defence,' *The Times of India*, 25 October 2018, https://timesofindia.indiatimes.com/india/from-russias-s-400-to-israels-barak-8-missiles-how-india-is-fortifying-its-defence/articleshow/66362137.cms

72 Dinakar Peri, 'Gurugram centre to monitor Indian Ocean Region coastline,' *The Hindu*, 22 December 2018, https://www.thehindu.com/news/national/gurugram-centre-to-monitor-indian-ocean-region-coastline/article25808944.ece

2

Defence Modernisation and Production: Enduring Challenges

Kapil Patil

A long-standing refrain among the Indian strategic analysts and thinkers has been the lack of National Security Strategy (NSS) that can harness the instrument of military power in support of the country's long-term political objectives.[1] Owing to lack of such strategy, India's defence modernisation has long suffered from ad-hocism and impinged on its ability to plan and prepare for the future wars. The Indian policymakers have been traditionally criticised for according low priority to issues of strategy and concurrent military modernisation. The decades of political neglect are further compounded by bureaucratic inefficiencies and the absence of inter-service consultations which often manifests itself in mismatched priorities between needs of integrated war-fighting and the acquisition of new weapons and technologies. As a consequence, the defence planning and modernisation in India have been widely criticised as archaic and ineffective to guarantee its safety against uncertain and unpredictable security challenges.[2] This state of affairs was expected to change significantly in the aftermath of the 1999 Kargil War, which led the National Democratic Alliance (NDA) Government under Prime Minister Atal Bihari Vajpayee to introduce systematic reforms from 1999 to 2004.[3] The successor UPA governments, however, failed to carry out any major structural reforms in Indian defence even though the country experienced rapid deterioration in its security environment due to Pak-sponsored terrorism, the spread of radical extremism, and the rise of militarily assertive China.[4]

In this backdrop, the historic electoral mandate of the Bharatiya Janata Party (BJP) in the 2014 general elections raised high expectations for infusing new life to reforms and military modernisation. The expectations were mainly galvanised by the promises made by the BJP in its election manifesto which, in principle, promised to 'address the issue of reforms... modernise armed forces, and increase the R&D (Research and Development) in defence, with a goal of developing indigenous defence technologies and fast-tracking of defence purchases'.[5] In line with the electoral promises, the BJP government led by Prime Minister Narendra Modi has enacted a number of reforms in the areas of higher defence organisation, military restructuring, procurement policy, etc. and several new measures are on the cards. Therefore, an assessment of what has been achieved in the past five years and what remains on the reform agenda is in order. The chapter, therefore, examines two inter-related questions: To what extent the Modi government has succeeded in implementing reforms as part of its electoral promise; and what are the remaining challenges in India's defence modernisation? In exploring the aforesaid questions, the chapter will analytically examine the Modi government's approach to defence reforms; identify its key achievements; and the challenges that remain before the country in the area of military modernisation. The chapter mainly argues that defence reforms and modernisation under the Modi government have gained significant pace compared to the previous United Progressive Alliance (UPA) government. The Modi government has not only addressed a number of long-standing issues including those relating to the morale and welfare of the military personnel but also introduced major institutional changes which are expected to bring about a structural shift in India's strategic planning and outlook. However, in view of the complex challenges facing the country, it is imperative to move swiftly and complete many of the pending reforms in the areas of military modernisation. Given the inherently dynamic nature of military change, a more forceful enactment of reforms would go a long way in eliminating structural flaws in India's national security framework and secure its core strategic interests in the turbulent world order.

Defence Reform: An Unfinished Agenda

Over the past two decades, India has witnessed a raging debate among policymakers, analysts and military practitioners about the nature and scope of reforms required in military planning and modernisation.[6] The debate is mainly in continuation of systematic structural adjustment measures which India undertook in the aftermath of the 1999 Kargil conflict. Post Kargil, two important committees set-up by government, namely the Kargil Review Committee (KRC) and the Committee of Group of Ministers (GoM) called for a thorough review and reorganisation of India's national security management system.[7] In particular, the KRC made many important observations on different aspects of national security and in accordance with its recommendations; the then government of Prime Minister Atal Bihari Vajpayee introduced many far-reaching reforms in line with the key recommendations of these committees. The reforms brought many notable changes in India's overall higher defence management, integrated planning, budgetary measures, acquisitions, intelligence coordination, border management, internal security and so on. For instance, pointing to the need for infusing greater synergy among the three services, the GoM report recommended the creation of several tri-service organisations.[8] These included the creation of Headquarters Integrated Defence Staff (HQ IDS), the Andaman and Nicobar Command, the Strategic Forces Command, the Defence Intelligence Agency (DIA), etc.[9]

The creation of HQ IDS with representation from all the three services has been the most important institutional measure and since its creation, it embarked upon the process of conducting long-term perspective planning for defence. The HQ-IDS formulated 15-year Long-Term Integrated Perspective Plan (LTIPP) for 2012-2027 which was approved by the Defence Acquisition Council (DAC) in 2012.[10] The perspective planning process within the HQ IDS was further streamlined with the formulation of new Defence Planning Guidelines (DPG).[11] Unlike in the past, the perspective planning in accordance with the new guidelines started taking into account an integrated view of the threat environment and outlines the roadmap of strategic alternatives, potential technologies, and industrial capabilities required by the armed forces. The creation of HQ IDS has also improved the coordination among the three services in the areas of joint planning, intelligence sharing and military exercises which were frequently neglected in the past.[12] Additionally, the GoM report's recommendations ushered in many structural changes in India's defence acquisition system. In 2001, the government opened up the defence sector for private participation and subsequently introduced a number of enabling measures for boosting innovation and industrial competitiveness of the Indian defence firms.[13] The Defence Procurement Procedure (DPP) which was formally introduced in 2002 has been subsequently revised in 2005, 2008, 2009, 2011, 2013, and more recently in 2016.[14] A defence offset policy was also enacted with the intent of fostering Indian firms into global supply chains as per the recommendations of the Kelkar Committee.[15]

Notwithstanding such changes, a number of issues have lingered on in the form of troubled civil-ministry relations, lack of national security strategy, weak integrated planning, resource constraints, and so on. The KRC in its report had sharply criticised the organisational inertia in both military and civilian bureaucracies which perpetuated an inefficient national security management system over the past many decades. Also, the troubled civil-military relations between the Ministry of Defence (MoD) and the three services on a number of critical policy issues have considerably weakened the functioning of India's overall defence apparatus. The reforms introduced after 2001 only partially addressed these issues and the complete overhaul of the national security systems envisioned by the KRC members remained a distant dream. For instance, a key recommendation of the KRC and GoM report for the appointment of the Chief of Defence Staff (CDS) and to oversee the issues of integrated planning and jointness in military operations has been kept in abeyance owing to lack of political consensus among successive governments in the past.[16] In the absence of an overarching military authority, much of the approach to planning and military modernisation has remained silo-based. As a result, defence planning in India suffers from lack of an integrated approach that can optimally leverage the scarce financial and technological resources to achieve higher military effect.

Furthermore, the continuing separation of the service headquarters from the Ministry of Defence (MoD) remains a major bone of contention in the area of inter-agency planning and coordination. To review some of these issues a decade after the reforms introduced by KRC and GoM reports, the UPA II government constituted yet another committee under the chairmanship of former Cabinet Secretary Naresh Chandra in 2010. Amidst the lack of political will for appointing the CDS, the Naresh Chandra Committee recommended the creation of a Permanent Chairman, Chiefs of Staff Committee (COSC). The Buy Indian-IDDM category is a first of its Permanent Chairman, Chiefs of Staff Committee (COSC) was, nevertheless, perceived to be insufficient for creating a unified structure for joint warfare and operational coordination.[17] Also, the committee's suggestion for increased cross-posting of military officers to key executive positions in the MoD to minimise the separation between MoD and the three service headquarters have been met with scepticism. It remains unknown to what extent this proposal has been implemented and its impact on achieving greater synergy between the MoD and services.[18] The agenda of integrated military planning and coordination thus remained incomplete even a decade after MoD embarked upon systemic reforms. The existing Chiefs of Staff Committee (COSC) which works on a consensus basis reportedly faces serious difficulties in the distribution of scarce resources among the services and within the different arms of individual service. In the absence of an overarching authority to vet defence plans, the service headquarters propose acquisitions as per their respective war-fighting doctrines and as such LTIPP merely combines such disparate demands for weapons and equipment without any overarching strategic logic attached to it.[19] For such reasons, the demand for appointment of CDS continues to resonate even though the previous UPA governments were highly apathetic to the idea.

Additionally, the Naresh Chandra Committee recommended the creation of a new Special Operations, Aerospace and Cyber Command and called for a China-centric national security strategy.[20] On the acquisition front, it suggested the creation of an Advanced Projects Agency on the lines of Defence Advanced Research Projects Agency (DARPA) under the aegis of the Scientific Adviser.[21] Although the then UPA government was fully apprised of the threat from a militarily assertive China, it failed to usher in any major change by way of a coherent national security strategy, doctrines, military plans, and capabilities. The policy indecisiveness during much of the UPA II government was evident in its inability to implement any major recommendations of the Naresh Chandra Committee. Further, many crucial acquisitions of new weapons and platforms remained mired in bureaucratic red tape despite much-trumpeted reforms in the procurement policy during the UPA II government. As a result, the task of defence reforms and modernisation remained incomplete during the UPA governments, and it was left to the successor governments to carry forward the mantle of reforms.

Carrying Forward the Mantle of Reforms

In 2014, the election manifesto of the Bharatiya Janata Party (BJP) promised to implement radical reforms in India's national security system. The BJP's manifesto accused the Congress-led United Progressive Alliance (UPA) government of 'suffering from major policy paralysis' and 'surrendering India's core interests' which are manifested in 'intrusions inside the LAC (Line of Actual Control), loss of squadrons of combat aircraft by the air force, witnessing of a series of accidents by the navy, leading to a loss in its combating capability built over many decades, communal riots, Maoist attacks, increase in incidence of Pakistan-backed terror groups in India, and illegal immigration across the eastern border.'[22] In response to such challenges, the BJP manifesto, among others, promised strong measures to strengthen India's military preparedness by (a) addressing the issue of reforms with regard to defence equipment, support services, organisational reforms; (b) modernising armed forces, increasing the R&D in defence, boosting indigenous defence technologies and fast-tracking of defence purchases; (c) addressing the increasing shortage of manpower in defence in a time-bound manner; (d) ensuring greater participation of the armed forces in the decision-making process of the Ministry of Defence; (e) dealing with cross-border terrorism with a firm hand, including improved border management, and periodical reviews; (f) improving military justice, by reforming Armed Forces Tribunals (AFT), etc.[23] The BJP government thus promised to be far more decisive on defence and national security issues and to proactively deal with many important issues of immediate and long-term significance.

Expectedly, among the major decisions taken early in its tenure, the Modi government approved the One Rank, One Pension (OROP) scheme, and the construction of a National War Memorial in New Delhi.[24] By agreeing to these long-standing demands, the Modi government not only gained support from the community of ex-servicemen who had long agitated for equality in the disbursement of pensions but also reiterated the commitment of his government to national security issues. Secondly, at the time of assuming office, India's military preparedness was quite dismal owing to acute shortage of arms and ammunition, fighter jets, submarines and warships, combat helicopters, artillery guns, etc. Taking cognisance of such crucial shortfalls, the Defence Acquisition Council (DAC) approved several big-ticket acquisitions within a year of Modi assuming office. Cumulatively, the DAC has approved acquisition deals worth over Rs 100,000 crore within a year. Also, among the deals pending from the previous government, the MoD moved swiftly to terminate the long-running contracts like the purchase of 126 Medium Multi-Role Combat Rafale jets for the IAF and announced the direct purchase of 36 Rafale jets in flyaway condition from France in a government-to-government deal.[25] The decisions on Avro replacement programme and Kamov helicopters, with the involvement of the Indian industry, has significantly helped India's aerospace ecosystem.[26] In addition to fast-tracking defence acquisitions, the Modi government made important moves to restructure the military and pursue systematic modernisation.

a) Rebalancing Allocations

While addressing the Combined Commanders Conference in December 2015, Prime Minister Modi remarked that 'at a time when major powers are reducing their forces and relying more on technology, we are still constantly seeking to expand the size of our forces. Modernisation and expansion of forces at the same time is a difficult and unnecessary goal. We need forces that are agile, mobile and driven by technology, not just human valour.'[27] The Prime Minister's sentiments were also echoed by the then Defence Minister Manohar Parrikar who not only called for slashing the Army's flab without adversely affecting its combat capabilities but also to equip them with latest military hardware by streamlining the procurement process and stimulating greater involvement of India's private sector in defence production.[28] In recent years, India's decision to expand the military manpower in the eastern sector by raising a new mountain strike corps has caused a significant spike in the revenue expenditure. The rise in revenue expenditure has come at the cost of a declining capital expenditure which, in turn, adversely impacted the Indian Army's plans for technological upgradation. The shrinking of defence capital expenditure to merely 25 per cent have made it necessary to cut down military manpower without affecting its war-fighting capability. The MoD, therefore, set up a committee under the chairmanship of Lt Gen (Retd.) D.B. Shekatkar to rebalance defence allocations between revenue and capital expenditure and to recommend measures to rationalise manpower ratios without affecting its combat capabilities.[29] In this context, the Shekatkar Committee made several key recommendations to rebalance the defence expenditure and enhance combat capabilities of military forces. After the Shekatkar Committee submitted its report to the government in December 2016, the MoD has reportedly accepted 65 out of 99 recommendations of the committee and these are currently at various stages of implementation.[30] The most far-reaching outcome of this exercise is to downsize the new mountain strike corps from its sanctioned strength of 90,000 to 35,000 troops in the eastern sector.[31]

b) Procurement Reforms & Make in India Initiative

Defence production and procurement is another important area which has been accorded high priority by the Modi government early in its tenure. The reforms in these areas were mainly guided by Prime Minister Modi's 'Make in India' vision which aims to transform India into a global manufacturing hub.[32] The reforms in defence industrial policy thus sought to leverage the country's large capital expenditure to not only increase the share of indigenous industry in defence acquisitions but also improve the overall design and innovation competitiveness of the Indian industry. Accordingly, in 2015 the MoD set up a committee under the chairmanship of former Home Secretary Dhirendra Singh to incorporate goals of 'Make in India' into India's Defence Procurement Procedure (DPP) and to revamp the procurement policy framework. Unlike many other reports, the MoD decided to make the Dhirendra Singh Committee report public which triggered a widespread public debate on how MoD can push 'Make in India' goals into India's existing policy framework.[33] One of the key recommendations of the Dhirendra Singh Committee report is the establishment of a strategic partnership model wherein select public and private sector giants would be nominated by the MoD for building technological capabilities in the areas of major platforms—aircraft, helicopters, warships, armoured vehicles, weapons systems etc.—by involving them in major 'Buy and Make' and Government-to-Government contracts.[34]

Similarly, the MoD also enacted a number of enabling measures for fostering greater interface between MoD and the industry. The new Defence Procurement Policy 2016 (DPP-2016) was released by the MoD in May 2016 which incorporates the new policy category called 'Buy Indian-Indigenously Designed, Developed and Manufactured (IDDM)'. The Buy Indian-IDDM category is a first of its kind preferential procurement policy measure aimed at targeting indigenous product innovations in the Indian industry.[35] By granting preference to indigenously designed and developed equipment as opposed to those assembled using foreign design and intellectual property rights (IPRs), the IDDM policy tool seeks to provide early market access to indigenously designed systems and technologies. The Buy Indian-IDDM thus strongly reflects Prime Minister Modi's 'Make in India' vision which aims to foster indigenous value addition by the Indian industry. Additionally, the DPP 2016 includes a simplified 'make' procedure that seeks to promote R&D and commercialisation projects by the Indian industry.[36] Furthermore, a revised offset policy has also been notified for acquisitions above Rs 2,000 crore. The DPP 2016, however, failed to inspire confidence among industry for its inability to cut red tape and the resultant delay caused in the acquisition of vitally needed equipment.

Also, despite outlining the process for implementing the Strategic Partnership (SP) model in the 2016 DPP, to this day, not a single contract under the SP model has been awarded. Instead, the MoD continues to rely on time-intensive tendering procedures which cause significant delays in user-trials, contract negotiations and delivery of platforms. In 2015, the MoD also appointed another committee under the chairmanship of former Petroleum Secretary Vivek Rae to study 'the setting up of a Defence Procurement Organisation in the Government of India'. Although the Committee has submitted its report to the government, little is known about government's decision to set-up the new defence procurement organisation as per its core recommendations.[37] Also, it remains unknown whether the MoD was willing to carry out major structural changes in the country's existing procurement system by creating an entirely new organisation as practised in countries like Canada, South Korea and Israel. Besides several reforms in the procurement policy as a demand-side instrument of industrial policy, in recent years, the government also paid considerable attention to R&D spending as a supply-side instrument of innovation and industrial development. The defence R&D system in India is mainly dominated by public sector labs under the aegis of Defence Research and Development Organisation (DRDO) whereas private sector spending on defence R&D is virtually non-existent. To stimulate R&D activities by the private sector, in 2016, MoD launched the scheme of Defence Innovation Fund (DIF) along with the list of 'Make in India' projects to be undertaken by the Indian industry. These schemes seek to award grants to wide-ranging R&D institutions, academia and industry including MSMEs, start-ups and even individual innovators to pursue innovative development and technology commercialisation.[38] The R&D procurement and commercialisation, however, remains much smaller than what is needed for the successful promotion of 'Make in India' objectives. Overall the lack of dynamism in the DRDO laboratories along with missing industrial innovation eco-system presents a serious challenge for India to build a sound defence industrial base.

c) Defence Planning Committee & New Institutional Reforms

Achieving synergy, integration, and jointness among the MoD and military services has been one of the highly contested issues in India's defence policy framework. In the Combined Commanders Conference, Prime Minister Modi called on senior military commanders to reform their 'beliefs, doctrines, objectives and strategies.' He remarked that—'We have been slow to reform the structures of our armed forces... we should promote jointness across every level of our armed forces... Jointness at the top is a need that is long overdue.'[39] In the past, however, the prevalence of silo-based approach among the individual services has signicantly limited their scope for developing an integrated approach to inter-agency planning and preparation. This is further compounded by the physical separation of service headquarters from the MoD headquarters which led to lack of strategic guidance to military planning and capability augmentation among the three services. Addressing these issues has proven to be quite challenging despite several recommendations of successive committees to reform India's higher defence organisation. In 2018, the Modi government made a decisive move in this direction by setting up a permanent Defence Planning Committee (DPC) under the aegis of the National Security Advisor (NSA).[40] Although established just a year before Modi government completing the five-year term in office, the DPC aims to enhance India's ability to improve institutional coordination and undertake long-term planning and thinking.

The DPC, in principle, provides a much-needed institutional framework for pursuing effective defence planning and force structuring. Set up as a permanent body, the DPC is intended to 'facilitate comprehensive and integrated planning for defence matters'. According to defence expert, Laxman Behara, the DPC is the "vital component of defence preparedness, which was conspicuously missing in the new institutional set-up created in the wake of the Kargil Conflict."[41] The

DPC's core mandate involves delineation of clear political goals and to efficiently mobilise resources for harnessing military as an instrument of national power. The DPC is thus expected to play a vital role in providing an overarching strategy and vision for Indian's defence planning. Comprising of the Chairman of the Chiefs of Staff Committee, three Service Chiefs, and the Defence, Expenditure and Foreign Secretaries, the committee aims to leverage the cross-domain expertise to resolve some of the long-standing issues in military planning and civil-military relations. Four sub-committees have been appointed under DPC to draft reports on 'national security strategy, international defence engagement strategy, roadmap to build a defence manufacturing ecosystem, strategy to boost defence exports, and priority capability development plans'.[42] On all of these issues, the DPC provides a unified structure to monitor progress and implementation. Also as part of the restructuring, two additional positions of Deputy National Security Advisors, as opposed to just the National Security Advisor in the earlier structure, have been created. More importantly, it has now been reported that under DPC the 'National Security Strategy' document has also been finalised. Although the govenrment is unlikely to make the strategy document public any time soon, its finalisation is significant for steering the direction of India's defence modernisation. The creation of DPC, arguably the most important defence reform in decades, is thus likely to have a far-reaching consequence in the way defence planning and preparedness is carried out in India.

Defence Modernisation: Challenges Ahead

Over the past four-and-half years, India has seen systematic efforts under the Modi government to reform the country's defence planning and management system. While the Modi government has shown strong political commitment to creating new overarching structures and practices, there are also many bonafide concerns about the nature of reforms and restructuring of the Indian military. For instance, with the creation of the DPC, the NSA has now come to play the role of a de-facto CDS. However, many fear that this will further skew the balance in India's civil-military relations by concentrating large decision-making power in the hands of the civilian bureaucracy.[43] While the DPC is expected to play an important role in integrated planning and coordination, the government must try to address the concerns of the military as considerable powers are now vested in the hands of national security bureaucracy which could make it less accountable and immune to accepting external policy inputs regarding the appointment of CDS in future.[44] For systematic reforms and modernisation, a healthy public debate and a synergistic civil-military partnership consisting of right-minded individuals is an essential prerequisite. The DPC must, therefore, be made more broad-based and consult cross-section of experts on matters of comprehensive national security. It must make every effort to bridge the existing gap between the MoD and services headquarters and ensure greater coordination through cross-postings as envisaged by the Naresh Chandra Committee.

Secondly, for any modernisation effort to be successful, the government must aim at bringing about structural transformation by making appropriate institutional changes and committing requisite resources. On this count, India's defence reforms and modernisation agenda faces several constraints which the Modi government has failed to address effectively irrespective of its earnest intentions. Among other, this mainly includes the government's inability to commit sufficient resources for military modernisation.[45] India's growing revenue expenditure on account of salaries and pensions has put considerable pressure on the defence budget to pursue systematic modernisation efforts. Although the proposed rationalisation of military manpower by downsizing the army's strength to 1.5 lakh personnel as proposed by the Shekatkar Committee is expected to save up to Rs 7,000 crore a year in revenue expenditure, there is clearly a strong case for increasing the share of defence capital expenditure to enable rapid modernisation of the Indian military.

Thirdly, the announcement of new reforms alone is unlikely to bring the desired change and what India fundamentally requires in the words of former Central Army Commander, Lt Gen (Retd.) Anil Chait is the 'forceful implementation of deliverable policies that are currently under preparation'.[46] This is mainly so given the continuing resistance among the civilian bureaucracy to implement reforms earnestly. Many civilian bureaucrats, for instance, remain in favour of maintaining a status-quo instead of pursuing systematic military restructuring. The lack of knowledge and specialisation on the issues of military modernisation and procurement significantly limit their ability to support radical reforms in the defence sector. Similarly, while the Modi government has approved the creation of a number of new joint commands such as Cyber, Space, Special Forces, etc., it has paid scant attention to promoting integration among the existing commands. The military's opposition to integrated planning and preparation has come at the cost of improving the country's overall military effectiveness and efficiency in planning. The logic of bureaucratic expansion and increased opportunities for upward mobility incidentally trump over core strategic interests that military services should uphold. The DPC should, therefore, focus on completing the pending reforms and ensure that appropriate balance exists in civil-military relations.

Fourth, the DPC should also monitor the implementation of reforms in the existing defence procurement framework to better reflect the priorities of 'Make in India' initiative. Notwithstanding India's historic preference for indigenous development of major platforms and weapons systems, the preference of military services for state-of-the-art foreign technologies and systems has always placed Indian defence production system at a serious disadvantage. The procurement policy's preference to 'Make in India' categories thus merely remain on paper and in reality most of the acquisitions occur through the import route which brings India a dubious reputation as world's largest arms importer. Such policy contradictions are unlikely to do justice to India's ambition to emerge as a defence manufacturing hub.

Finally, defence planning in India, over the past two decades, has been affected by the existence of highly fluid strategic environment along with changing profiles of threat and shifting power equations. Furthermore, the Revolution in Military Affairs (RMA) due to rapid advances in technology has made the weapons systems become obsolete at a fast rate. This has significantly reduced the time required for adapting to future changes and to acquire new weapons systems needed by the military services. Owing to such dynamic change and grave strategic uncertainty, effective defence planning calls for improving coordination among various arms of the government and ensuring greater synergy between national defence and development plans. The lack of such synergy in the past has put the country at a serious disadvantage vis-a-vis its regional adversaries.[47] With systematic reforms carried out over the past two decades, much seems to have changed in India's national security system. Although it is premature to expect a rapid change from various structural adjustments, measures undertaken by the Modi government in the past few years, its candid acknowledgment of the problem and earnest effort to address them has brought a welcome change. While the Modi government has moved in the right direction on many complex and contentious issues, the future will depend upon how the modernisation agenda is taken to its logical conclusion through a cohesive National Security Strategy.

Conclusion

Historically, the issues of defence planning and modernisation have been long neglected by Indian policy-makers at the detriment of country's overall defence preparedness. This has not only led to ad-hocism in decision-making but also adversely affected the ability of Indian forces to prepare for future threats and challenges. Although reforms undertaken in the aftermath of the Kargil War were expected to reform India's defence institutional structure and make it more adaptable to emerging threats, the pace of reforms has been very slow with tardy implementation. In this context, the Modi government has introduced many far-reaching changes to India's defence policymaking structures by streamlining the domain of defence policy, planning, procurement process, and military restructuring. Several committees appointed by the Modi government have identified the gaps in the country's planning and institutional structures and recommended measures to bring a procedural change.

Overall, the reforms are expected to streamline defence planning and make the process more responsive in order to deal effectively with the rapidly changing geostrategic and regional security environment. With these changes, it can thus be surmised that India is gradually learning to harness its military resources in service of her long-term political objectives.

NOTES

[1] Stephen P. Cohen & Sunil Dasgupta, *Arming without aiming: India's military modernization* (Washington DC: Brookings Institution Press, 2013); B. R. Nayar & T. V. Paul, *India in the World Order: Searching for Major-power Status* (New Delhi: Cambridge University Press, 2003); Deepa Ollapally, 'India: The Ambivalent Power in Asia,' International Studies, *Sage Journals*, Vol. 48, Issue 3-4 (2011): pp. 201-222; Also see, G.K. Tanham, *Indian Strategic Thought: An Interpretive Essay* (Santa Monica, CA: Rand Corporation, 1992).

[2] Arun Prakash, 'India's Higher Defence Organisation: Implications for National Security and Jointness,' *Journal of Defence Studies*, Vol 1, No. 1 (2007): p. 24.

[3] S. Singh, 'Atal Bihari Vajpayee and national security: Daring leap, step by step,' *The Indian Express*, 17 August 2018, https://indianexpress.com/article/india/atal-bihari-vajpayee-on-national-security-daring-leap-step-by-step-5310834/

[4] H. Irfan, 'The mixed legacy of defence minister A.K. Antony,' *DNA*, 13 December 2013, https://www.dnaindia.com/india/report-the-mixed-legacy-of-defence-minister-ak-antony-1934037; S. Unnithan, 'Worst Defence Minister Ever.' *India Today*, 7 March 2014, https://www.indiatoday.in/magazine/special-report/story/20140317-ak-antony-defence-minister-scams-upa-ii-800422-2014-03-07

[5] Bharatiya Janata Party, 'Ek Bharat, Shreshtha Bharat: Sabka Saath, Sabka Vikas'—Election Manifesto 2014.

[6] Vinod Misra, Ed., *Core Concerns in Indian Defence and the Imperatives for Reforms* (New Delhi: Pentagon Press, 2014).

[7] Kargil Review Committee Report at http://nuclearweaponarchive.org/India/KargilRCA.html & GoM Report on National Security, at https://www.vifindia.org/sites/default/files/GoM%20Report%20on%20National%20Security.pdf

[8] Lt Gen Prakash Katoch, 'New Tri-Service Commands,' *Indian Defence Review*, 22 August 2015, http://www.indiandefencereview.com/news/new-tri-service-commands/

[9] 'Tri-service integrated command in place,' *The Hindu*, 29 September 2001, https://www.thehindu.com/2001/09/30/stories/0230000f.htm

[10] Amit Cowshish, 'Technology Perspective and Capability Roadmap 2013', *The Institute for Defence Studies & Analyses*, 2 July 2013, https://idsa.in/idsacomments/TechnologyPerspectiveandCapabilityRoadmap2013_acowshish_020713

[11] Gurmeet Kanwal, 'Holistic look at the reforms needed for effective and sustainable Capability Development,' *South Asia Defence & Strategic Review*, Vol 9, Issue 1 (Mar - Apr 2015): pp. 16, http://www.defstrat.com/defence-reforms-capability-development-planning-and-decision-making-need-improvement

[12] Vinod Anand, 'Integrating the Indian Military: Retrospect and Prospect,' *Journal of Defence Studies*, IDSA, Vol 2, Issue 2 (Winter 2008): pp. 19-40.

[13] A. Didar Singh, 'In defence of private participation,' *The Hindu Business Line*, 7 February 2014, https://www.thehindubusinessline.com/opinion/in-defence-of-private-participation/article22995575.ece

[14] 'Much-awaited Defence Procurement Procedure with "Make in India" focus to be out soon,' *Press Trust of India*, 11 July 2018, https://economictimes.indiatimes.com/news/defence/much-awaited-defence-procurement-procedure-with-make-in-india-focus-to-be-out-soon/articleshow/50231974.cms

[15] 'Defence Offset Guidelines', *Ministry of Defence*, 2012, https://mod.gov.in/sites/default/files/revised-guidelines.pdf

[16] Gurmeet Kanwal, 'Where is India's Chief of Defence Staff?' *The Economic Times*, 27 September 2018, https://economictimes.indiatimes.com/news/defence/where-is-indias-chief-of-defence-staff-/articleshow/65975999.cms?from=mdr

[17] Rajneesh Singh, 'Chairman Chiefs of Staff Committee: A Midway Solution', *Institute for Defence Studies & Analyses*, 7 August 2012, https://idsa.in/idsacomments/ChairmanChiefsofStaffCommitteeAMidwaySolution_RajneeshSingh_070812

[18] Gurmeet Kanwal, 'Agenda for the new Defence Minister,' *Indian Defence Review*, 2 December 2014, http://www.indiandefencereview.com/news/agenda-for-the-new-defence-minister/

[19] Shekhar Sinha, 'Role of integrated defence staff in defence procurement', *Bharat Shakti*, 30 December 2015, https://bharatshakti.in/role-of-integrated-defence-staff-in-defence-procurement/

[20] Nitin Gokhale, 'Naresh Chandra Task Force's Report on National Security: An Appraisal,' *Vivekananda International Foundation*, 16 July 2012, at https://www.vifindia.org/article/2012/july/16/naresh-chandra-task-force-s-report-on-national-security-an-appraisal

[21] Josy Joseph, 'Set up agency to steer defence R&D, recommends Naresh Chandra Task Force on national security,' *TNN*, 25 July 2012, https://timesofindia.indiatimes.com/india/Set-up-agency-to-steer-defence-RD-recommends-Naresh-Chandra-Task-Force-on-national-security/articleshow/15133875.cms

[22] See, BJP election manifesto (n 5).

[23] Ibid, BJP election manifesto (n 5).

[24] Implementation of One Rank One Pension, *Press Information Bureau*, 6 April 2016, http://pib.nic.in/newsite/PrintRelease.aspx?relid=138646; Cabinet approves construction of National War Memorial, *Press Information Bureau*, 7 October 2015, http://pib.nic.in/newsite/mbErel.aspx?relid=128493

[25] Dinakar Peri, 'Military modernisation picks up pace,' *The Hindu*, 19 May 2015, https://www.thehindu.com/news/national/military-modernisation-picks-up-pace/article7220791.ece

[26] Ibid.

[27] 'Prime Minister Narendra Modi at Combined Commanders Conference on board INS Vikramaditya at Sea,' *Press Information Bureau*, 15 December 2015, http://pib.nic.in/newsite/PrintRelease.aspx?relid=133265

[28] Rajat Pandit, 'Army's non-operational flab will be cut: Parrikar', *TNN*, 23 May 2015, https://timesofindia.indiatimes.com/india/Armys-non-operational-flab-will-be-cut-Parrikar/articleshow/47391311.cms

[29] Shravan Nune, 'Union Government constituted DB Shekatkar Committee on defence spending,' *Jagran Josh*, 23 May 2016, https://www.jagranjosh.com/current-affairs/union-government-constituted-db-shekatkar-committee-on-defence-spending-1463995875-1

[30] Sandip Dighe, 'Key recommendations ignored by defence ministry: Shekatkar panel', *TNN*, 8 November 2017, https://timesofindia.indiatimes.com/city/pune/key-recommendations-ignored-by-defence-ministry-shekatkar-panel/articleshow/61558168.cms

[31] Pradip R. Sagar, 'Army on diet,' *The Week*, 29 October 2018, https://www.theweek.in/theweek/current/2018/10/27/army-on-diet.html

[32] 'PM launches "Make in India" global initiative,' *Press Information Bureau*, 25 September 2014, http://pib.nic.in/newsite/PrintRelease.aspx?relid=110017

[33] 'Committee of Experts for Amendment to DPP-2013 including formulation of policy framework,' *Ministry of Defence*, July 2015, https://mod.gov.in/dod/sites/default/files/Reportddp.pdf

[34] 'Strategic Partnership in Defence Sector,' *Press Information Bureau*, 17 March 2017, http://pib.nic.in/newsite/PrintRelease.aspx?relid=159486

[35] 'Defence Procurement Policy,' *Press Information Bureau*, Ministry of Defence, 24 March 2017, http://pib.nic.in/newsite/PrintRelease.aspx?relid=159864

[36] 'Simplified "Make-II": Major Steps Towards "Make in India" in Defence Production,' *Press Information Bureau*, Ministry of Defence, 17 January 2018, http://pib.nic.in/newsite/mbErel.aspx?relid=175681

[37] Rajat Pandit, 'Govt to set up specialised defence procurement organisation,' *TNN*, 15 May 2017, https://timesofindia.indiatimes.com/india/govt-to-set-up-specialised-defence-procurement-organisation/articleshow/58675462.cms

[38] 'Defence Innovation Organisation,' *Press Information Bureau*, Ministry of Defence, 21 July 2017, http://pib.nic.in/newsite/PrintRelease.aspx?relid=168797

[39] See 'PM Modi at Combined Commanders Conference', n.27

[40] 'NSA-headed committee for higher defence management,' *The Hindu*, 19 April 2018, https://www.thehindu.com/news/national/nsa-headed-committee-for-higher-defence-management/article23599248.ece

[41] Laxman K. Behera, 'Creation of Defence Planning Committee: A Step towards Credible Defence Preparedness', *Institute for Defence Studies and Analyses*, 19 April 2018, https://idsa.in/idsacomments/creation-of-defence-planning-committee-lkbehera-190418

[42] Col Arun Kumar, 'Defence Planning Committee', *Defence ProAC Magazine*, http://www.defproac.com/?p=7122

[43] Lt Gen D.S. Hooda, 'Gap in Civil-military Relations Will Only Grow with Creation of Defence Planning Committee', *News18*, 13 November 2018, https://www.news18.com/news/opinion/gap-in-civil-military-relations-will-only-grow-with-creation-of-defence-planning-committee-writes-lt-gen-ds-hooda-1937513.html

[44] Brig S.K. Chatterji, 'Defence Planning Committee is not enough to fight security challenges. India needs a chief of defence staff,' *dailyO*, 31 May 2018, https://www.dailyo.in/politics/defence-planning-committee-chief-of-defence-staff-defence-ministry-modi-government-ajit-doval-nsa-nirmala-sitharaman/story/1/24559.html

[45] Manu Pubby, 'Defence spending slips when NDA is in power, Rs 11,595 crore unspent,' *The Economic Times*, 11 July 2018, https://economictimes.indiatimes.com/news/defence/defence-spending-slips-when-nda-is-in-power-rs-11595-crore-unspent/articleshow/51216838.cms?from=mdr

[46] Dinkar Peri, 'Military modernisation picks up pace,' (n.25).

[47] Harsh V. Pant, 'Defence reforms get a fillip, but more needs to be done urgently', *Observer Research Foundation*, 15 January 2019, https://www.orfonline.org/research/defence-reforms-get-a-fillip-but-more-needs-to-be-done-urgently-47358/

3

Maritime Security and India: India as a Regional Security Provider

Tuneer Mukherjee

INDIA is geographically predicated to be a maritime nation. The long-tapered peninsula with water on three sides renders India's participation in regional maritime affairs not a matter of choice but one of compulsion. Yet, despite the 7,500-km-long coastline, India's security agenda has traditionally been dominated by continental engagements.[1] Frequent border skirmishes with Pakistan and China, along with cross-border terrorism and domestic left-wing extremism, have kept successive governments occupied in building a robust army.[2] Most Indian administrations have therefore made continental security dynamics a focus of their national security strategy, relegating maritime security affairs to the tertiary pedestal.[3] However, over the years this has changed. Factors such as piracy, maritime terrorism, humanitarian assistance and disaster relief, growing naval capacities of adversaries like China and Pakistan, along with India's desire to possess a robust sea-based nuclear deterrent, have all convinced policymakers in India to focus on maritime security and naval strategy in a more concerted manner.[4] The changing contours of Asian security with an increased focus on maritime power have furthered this change in track. India has been compelled to expand the scope of its maritime security apparatus, and the five-year tenure of the Narendra Modi government serves as evidence of this reorganisation.

The Modi government has attempted to accentuate India's status as a stakeholder in regional maritime security and outlined plans to build a modern navy to fulfil that role. He understands that as India realises its strategic niche, maritime security will be key to securing India's economic and political future. Considering this evolving security agenda, the chapter attempts to discern developments made in the maritime security space under the leadership of Narendra Modi. The analysis is coalesced around two major dimensions: political and naval. The political part of the analysis introspects the measures taken by the Modi government in furthering India's maritime security role. While, the naval portion of the analysis is centred around the Indian Navy and its future strategies on force-structuring and acquisition. The chapter as a whole attempts to deduce how geopolitical formulations in synchronisation with naval modernisation can fulfil India's ambition to be a 'net security provider in the Indian Ocean'.

India's Evolving Maritime Security Agenda

In recent times, two incidents have changed how India perceives maritime security, and consequently have gone on to shape India's approach to the maritime domain. The first was the terrorist attacks of 2008 in Mumbai (also known as the 26/11 attacks).[5] The attacks perpetrated by 10 armed terrorists who came to Mumbai via sea from Pakistan exposed the weakness of India's coastal security architecture.[6] The attacks served as a grim reminder to policymakers in New Delhi that offshore maritime security is crucial to India's internal security.

Since the attacks, the coastal security architecture has received substantial attention from successive governments.[7] The reforms that began after the 26/11 attacks encapsulated a broad range of security measures and have included 'capacity augmentation of maritime security agencies for surveillance and patrol of the nation's maritime zones; enhanced technical surveillance of coastal and offshore areas; establishment of mechanisms for inter-agency coordination; increased regulation of activities in the maritime zones; and integration of the fishing and coastal communities'.[8] Significantly, the existing Coastal Security Scheme (2005) was upgraded and now involves a three-tier security arrangement, with the Indian Navy, the Coast Guard and the marine police jointly tasked with safeguarding India's maritime zones.[9] At the apex level, the National Committee for Strengthening Maritime and Coastal Security (NCSMCS), headed by the Cabinet Secretary, began coordinating all matters related to coastal security.[10] The attacks also led to an increased emphasis on the country's offshore electronic surveillance capacity. The reforms initiated under Manmohan Singh, India's then Prime Minister, led to the setting up of the Information Management and Analysis Centre (IMAC), a data dissemination and aggregation centre for coastal security sensors.[11] IMAC, which became operational in 2014, now serves as the nodal centre of the National Command Control Communications and Intelligence Network (NC3I Network).[12] The NC3I is tasked to assist the forces involved in coastal defence with maritime domain awareness (MDA). Modi's regime has significantly enhanced this setup by provisioning a radar chain called 'Coastal Surveillance Network (CSN) comprising of chain of static sensors having radar, Automatic Identification System (AIS), Long Range Identification and Tracking (LRIT), day/night cameras, and communication systems.'[13] Going forward, future governments need to frequently upgrade these systems and, if necessary, formulate a new CSS. A nation of India's stature cannot afford the repeat of a terrorist attack from the sea.

The second and more recent incident that moulded India's approach to maritime security was the docking of Chinese submarines in the Port of Colombo in 2014.[14] The presence of Chinese naval assets in the Indian Ocean was not a new occurrence at that time. Both surface and submersible forces belonging to the People's Liberation Army Navy (PLAN) had routinely been present in the Indian Ocean.[15] But the likely logistical support provided to these assets from an Indian Ocean island country so close to the Indian homeland greatly altered India's strategic calculus. In the aftermath of the incident, India vociferously opposed the presence of Chinese naval assets in Sri Lanka.[16] Colombo acceded to this request later, but PLAN assets to this day continue to ply the Indian Ocean in increasing numbers, validating India's security predicament vis-à-vis Beijing's growing maritime prowess.[17] Tackling this security threat will be central to any future Indian maritime security agenda.

The Indian Navy has repeatedly asserted that it closely monitors

Chinese naval activity in the region and has a variety of anti-submarine assets to counter any malicious action.[18] The Manmohan Singh government upheld this rationale and built maritime connections with nations in the region judiciously.[19] However, from 2010 onwards, China's naval actions in the South China Sea and the East China Sea have turned increasingly bellicose.[20] The reclamation of islands in the South China Sea and its subsequent militarisation pose serious questions about the true motive of China's naval expansion.[21] Beijing's patronage network in the Indian Ocean Region (IOR) further complicates the scenario for New Delhi.[22] India under Modi has addressed this by astutely weaving together new security partnerships with prominent maritime nations such as Japan, Indonesia, the United States, France etc.[23] Given, the present gap in material capabilities between the PLAN and the Indian Navy, this could be India's best policy in the short-term. In the long-term, however, India needs to develop material capabilities to meet its security requirements.

India's Maritime Resolution: Net Security Provider in the Indian Ocean

Prime Minister Manmohan Singh had famously remarked in 2013 that 'India sought to assume its responsibility for stability in the Indian Ocean Region and was well-positioned, therefore, to become a net provider of security in its immediate region and beyond'.[24] Modi picked up from where Prime Minister Singh left off and undertook an active role in maturing India's maritime connections with the rest of the world while simultaneously expanding the reach of the Indian Navy. This aspiration to provide security for the wider maritime commons best encapsulates India's evolving maritime security agenda. The question then arises, what entails being 'a net security provider'? Ideally, a net security provider in the IOR would be one that guarantees the freedom of navigation and commerce in the region, provides quick humanitarian assistance and disaster relief, assists in patrolling of territorial waters, provides modern naval assets and technologies to partner nations, and most importantly, guards against any entity that threatens the security of the maritime commons.

The naval solution of the puzzle can be drawn from the maritime security strategy document titled 'Ensuring Secure Seas', released by the Indian Navy in 2016.[25] Largely seen as a document that transcends different political changes in New Delhi, the new naval doctrine relayed India's strategic roadmap to the world. It aims to transform India from a 'brown water navy' that operates in territorial waters to a 'blue water navy' capable of executing coordinated manoeuvres on the high seas. The document outlines the blueprint for India to become a 'blue water navy', and positions future acquisitions and force-structuring around two aircraft carrier task forces (CTFs) prioritising sea-control.[26] Indian naval planners have focused on developing, 'three Carrier Battle Groups (CBGs), each centred on an aircraft carrier with multi-mission escort and support ships, with integral anti-air, anti-surface and anti-submarine warfare capabilities'.[27]

Accordingly, the capital asset acquisition programme followed this rationale. Aircraft carriers were prioritised, and naval aviation units were considered for key upgrades. India planned to move into theatre-level operational readiness with these changes and conducted multiple multinational maritime exercises in the IOR, namely Malabar and Milan.[28] The Malabar exercise widened India's operational domain as far as the Western Pacific.[29] Additionally, the Theatre Level Readiness and Operational Exercise (TROPEX) in 2017 demonstrated that the Navy's primary offensive objective had shifted from guarding against Pakistan to countering China.[30] As the Indian Navy undertakes such long distance multi-faceted missions, longer 'sea legs' and operational cycles along with extended air reach and logistical support have become a key requirement.[31] Consequently, the Indian Navy's intelligence, surveillance and reconnaissance (ISR) capabilities have been considered for modern upgrades. The launch of the Rukmini GSAT satellite in 2013 has aided the ability of Indian naval assets to connect with each other and cover activities from the Strait of Malacca in the east to the Strait of Hormuz in the west.[32] Going forward, the navy needs to simultaneously achieve the arduous task of maintaining off-shore security of the homeland while extending India's maritime domain awareness (MDA) to key choke points in the Indian Ocean. The goal is to always maintain the 'home field advantage' afforded by the Indian Ocean. The Indian Navy reoriented its fleet mission pattern to suit these objectives and currently has seven permanent 'mission-based deployments (MBD)'.[33] (See Table 1).

Name of Mission-Based Deployments (MBD) Area of Focus

Table 1: List of the Indian Navy's Permanent Mission Base Deployments with their geographic scope[34]

MALDEP	Strait of Malacca
NORDEP	North Bay of Bengal – Andamans, Bangladesh & Myanmar
ANDEP	North Andamans to South Nicobar
GULDEP	North Arabian Sea, Strait of Hormuz, Gulf of Persia
POGDEP	Anti-Piracy patrolling in Gulf of Aden
CENDEP	Maldives and Sri Lanka
IODEP	Southern Indian Ocean, Mauritius, Seychelles, Madagascar

Correspondingly, to realise the 'net security provider' tag, India needs a fresh approach to geopolitical engagements in order to move beyond the traditional subcontinental neighbourhood. Modi's first policy step as leader was to reach out to the heads of state of South Asian Association for Regional Cooperation (SAARC) nations and consolidate neighbourhood relations.[35] Unfortunately for Modi, his 'Neighbourhood First' policy was not entirely successful. Furthermore, during the same time, Beijing undertook a multi-faceted maritime outreach to nations in India's own backyard.[36] As realised over the next few years, China undertook massive port development projects in countries like Pakistan, Sri Lanka, Bangladesh and Myanmar, while also offering transfer of naval equipment to these countries.[37] The Modi government realised it had to expand its scope beyond the neighbourhood to counter China, and started seeing the wider Indian Ocean Region (IOR) as a suitable arena to showcase its 'region of influence'.

The first measure of this approach came in the form of 'Project Mausam'.[38] Largely a cultural initiative, it provides an idea of how Prime Minister Modi observed the maritime geography. By promoting India's own rendition of maritime linkages in the Indian Ocean, New Delhi acknowledges the sea lines of communication (SLOCs) significant to India, and at the same time, provides a loose normative alternative to Beijing's '21st Century Maritime Silk Road'.[39] India essentially attempted to link its western theatre of operations with the eastern half to achieve a unitary maritime outlook. This approach achieved the dual objective of countering Chinese influence in the immediate neighbourhood while also providing the administration the ability to escape rigorous subcontinental political dynamics by wading into broader maritime security outlines.

The first notable development in this new approach came in the form of the 'Act East' policy.[40] Coined by External Affairs Minister Sushma Swaraj while on a diplomatic visit to Hanoi,[41] it is essentially an upgrade of the existing 'Look East' policy formulated by the administration of P.V. Narasimha Rao in the early 1990s to improve relations with Southeast Asian countries and its umbrella organisation the Association of Southeast Asian Nations (ASEAN).[42] The 'Act East' policy further expands India's outreach in the eastern Indian Ocean and the Western Pacific and envisions cooperation and engagement with both Southeast Asian and Northeast Asian states.[43] The policy identified key players in the region and sought to build cooperation frameworks with them. Resultantly, defence cooperation with countries such as Japan, Vietnam, Singapore, Republic of Korea, Australia and Indonesia was enhanced.[44] The aim is to establish naval presence in the eastern Indian Ocean and the Western Pacific and establish control over the Strait of Malacca on the side of the Andaman Sea. Intertwining, with this approach towards the east, Prime Minister Modi has also attempted to institute a common maritime security framework in the Bay of Bengal through the Bay of Bengal Initiative for Multi-Sectoral Technical and Economic Cooperation (BIMSTEC).[45] Securing the Bay of Bengal is crucial to India's net security provider agenda in the IOR. Further, it also consolidates India's control over its territorial seas. To this end, the Prime Minister has repeatedly outlined plans to develop naval facilities on the Andaman and Nicobar Islands which constitute 30 per cent of India's Exclusive Economic Zone (EEZ).[46] A revamp of the naval command in the Andamans would help establish Indian naval influence in both the Bay of Bengal and in Southeast Asia.[47]

Generally, islands have formed a key plank of Prime Minister Modi's intensified maritime policy engagement. In the Southern Pacific, the conception of the Forum for India–Pacific Islands Cooperation established Modi's foreign policy credentials and extended India's maritime engagement beyond the Indian Ocean to island nations in the Pacific.[48] Closer to home, the Prime Minister while visiting Seychelles and Mauritius, postulated his vision for the Indian Ocean via the acronym 'SAGAR (Ocean in Hindi)—Security and Growth for All in the Region.'[49] Modi visualised an Indian Ocean island community that depended on India for maritime security and thereby allowed Indian surveillance assets to operate from their territory. Modi essentially built upon the diplomatic groundwork laid down by the previous administration of Manmohan Singh and sought to expand the Trilateral Cooperation on Maritime Security (TMSC) between India, the Maldives and Sri Lanka (IO-3) to include the Seychelles and Mauritius (IO-5).[50] Such a framework would also allow India to expand the coverage of its coastal surveillance network setup under IMAC.

Similarly, Modi has also courted African nations like Madagascar and Mozambique to support India's role as a security provider in the region.[51] Piracy around the Gulf of Aden has been a concern for India, and maritime cooperation with African nations help the Indian Navy fulfil its anti-piracy missions.[52] Ergo, as the Indian Navy plies to become a major force east of Red Sea, India, under Modi, has initiated a concerted maritime policy framework towards West Asia. The primary strategic aim is to secure key SLOCs and have assured passage through important Western Indian Ocean choke points—Strait of Hormuz in the Gulf of Persia and the Bab-el-Mandeb strait in the Gulf of Aden.[53] West Asia provides more than 65 per cent of India's energy supplies and is also home to more than seven million Indian migrants.[54] This necessitates unhindered access to the waters of the region. Prime Minister Modi during his tenure has pursued closer strategic cooperation in the maritime arena with Gulf Cooperation Council (GCC) nations and established fruitful relationships with Arab nations such as the UAE, Oman and Qatar.[55] This has further solidified maritime contacts and has given new direction to India's effort to link its western operating theatre with its eastern counterpart. Furthermore, Indian governments have been compelled to carry out multiple civilian rescue operations from affected areas in West Asia and North Africa suffering from continuous civil conflict and political turmoil.[56] Such humanitarian assistance and disaster relief (HADR) operations have continued to take place under Modi and the Indian Navy continues to value its security role in this region.[57]

Iran represents another test case of Modi's maritime security framework in the region. India has signed an agreement to develop two berths of the Chabahar port in south-eastern Iran and further solidified this by the establishment of the tripartite agreement with Afghanistan and Iran to develop a transport corridor from Chabahar to Afghanistan.[58] Given such crucial commercial interests, the need for India to have a consistent naval presence in the Western Indian Ocean cannot be emphasised enough. Consequently, in its bid to enhance its MDA in these waters, India has initiated cooperation with the US Central Command (CENTCOM) and has plans to deploy a defence attaché at the United States Naval Forces Central Command (NAVCENT) in Bahrain.[59]

India under Modi has become more self-confident in asserting its security principles, and maritime security is the best example of this transformation. On the campaign trail for the 2014 general elections, Modi assured the electorate of a more robust security architecture. And even though, at that time, he did not indicate a specific agenda to improve India's maritime security apparatus, in the following five years he has devoted considerable time and focus to solidifying India's maritime connections. There is considerable continuity in policy frameworks established by previous administrations, but Prime Minister Modi has also realised that he can leverage the maritime domain as a platform to express his larger worldview by defining a clear strategy and direction for Indian foreign policy. Challenges remain and there is lot to be desired for India to be truly secure in the maritime arena, yet Modi's term as Prime Minister is a good starting point for the future of maritime security issues in India, and attests to India's role as a 'net security provider in the Indian Ocean'.

Balancing Security Ambitions: Reimagining the Indo-Pacific

India faces multiple security challenges, but none more prominent than the acute security dilemma emanating from a bellicose China. On the continental front, the border standoff in the Doklam plateau in 2017 between Indian and Chinese armed forces demonstrated that Beijing is on the 'change the status quo' path in the region.[60] Additional to its increased maritime presence in the Indian Ocean, China is also financing and constructing the China-Pakistan Economic Corridor (CPEC) that traverses through disputed territories of Gilgit-Baltistan.[61] It is evident from these developments that New Delhi's security in the future will be threatened by Chinese actions. While the Modi government has assuaged some of the prevalent tensions at the informal summit with President Xi Jinping in 2018 at Wuhan, India needs to remain guarded against any Chinese encroachment of its strategic space.[62] Reimagining India's maritime space in a manner that balances its security equations in the region is key to this realisation.

Building upon such consternations, New Delhi under Modi adopted the Indo-Pacific framework and its accompanying maritime dynamics. The idea to link security interests of the Indian and the Pacific maritime theatres have been doing the rounds for a while, but India has been reluctant to embrace the concept. This changed with the reinvigoration of the Quadrilateral Security Dialogue (Quad) in 2017.[63] Albeit, consultations were held at the level of junior officials between India, the US, Japan and Australia on the sidelines of the East Asian Summit in Manila in November 2017.[64] What came out of it was a loose framework on how to deal with issues pertaining to the maritime commons and the concept of a 'Free and Open Indo-Pacific' was born.[65] The consultative mechanism has since then become regularised and is aiming to expand to include like-minded nations.[66]

Interestingly, the first rendition of the Quad was initiated in 2008 during the first term of Manmohan Singh.[67] The initiative, however, quickly lost relevance due to concern among the nations that it was being perceived as a containment policy against Beijing.[68] The fear of a potential backlash from China due to closer military cooperation between the group, also meant that the Malabar naval exercise would be limited in the future and not feature nations such as Singapore and Australia, who were a part of the 2007 edition in the Bay of Bengal. The situation has practically reversed since then, and instead of the Quad nations appearing belligerent, it is China that has normatively and materially threatened the rules-based order in the Indo-Pacific region. China's construction of artificial islands in the South China Sea, and subsequent militarisation of them, displays a blatant disregard for the security of the maritime space. Moreover, through its connectivity platform—the Belt and Road Initiative (BRI), Beijing has implicitly pronounced its interest in shaping a Sino-centric Asian order.[69]

India remains far off from counteracting the BRI or sustaining a permanent counter-theatre presence in the Western Pacific. Modi has realised this predicament partially and taken a realist view of things. Options remain open for India to offset Chinese influence in the geopolitical space, both internally and externally. In order to keep itself engaged in the future discourse of maritime security of Asia, and keep the strategic pressure on China, the 'Free and Open Indo-Pacific' framework offers India an avenue to balance these security dynamics. During Modi's tenure as Prime Minister, India has also engaged with established naval nations such as Japan, Indonesia, the US, Australia and France to initiate new avenues of maritime security cooperation.[70] Coordinated deliberations in the maritime space with such countries afford India the opportunity to maintain its geopolitical foothold in the Indian Ocean at a time when strategic calculations are changing.

Among these nations, the most prominent progress has been achieved with the US. While, Indo-US strategic relations have followed an upward trajectory since the 2008 nuclear deal, it is under Modi that this relationship found new meaning in the maritime space.[71] After years of reluctance, India finally signed the foundational military agreements LEMOA (Logistics Exchange Memorandum of Agreement) and COMCASA (Communications Compatibility and Security Agreement), opening the gateway for joint operability with the US.[72] The growing maritime engagement with the US is another corroboration of the cold calculations New Delhi is making in the maritime domain to maintain its stronghold on SLOCs in the Indian Ocean.

Contrastingly, Prime Minister Modi has refrained from positioning India in an anti-China stance and prefers to keep his options open. His speech at the 2018 Shangri-La Dialogue was a notable demonstration of this design. He posited the 'Indo-Pacific' construct as open and inclusive, he made it clear that 'India does not see the Indo-Pacific region as a strategy or as a club of limited members. Nor as a grouping that seeks to dominate. And by no means… as directed against any country'.[73] In effect, Modi has pursued 'strategic autonomy' on one end and 'strategic hedging' on the other. A hedging strategy allows Modi to build India's maritime capabilities and engage in security cooperation with like-minded partners in the Indo-Pacific without directly confronting China. And the principle of 'strategic autonomy' allows India leeway to engage any nation in a partnership arrangement without giving a perception that it is aligned to a particular worldview. This approach could well become a mainstay in India's maritime security agenda for future administrations. However, rather than solely relying on security partnerships, India needs to proactively modernise its naval capabilities.

Modernising the Navy

Behind India's maritime benefactorship in the Indian Ocean and its ambitions to be a balancer in the security dynamics of Asia, lies the true stakeholder of India's sea power—the Indian Navy. The current strength of the navy lacks the force to implement the wide-ranging visions that the present government has outlined in its 'Security Provider' agenda over the last five years. Maritime security encompasses anti-piracy, humanitarian assistance and disaster relief, protection of offshore asserts, assured passage through SLOCs etc. Doubts persist over the capabilities of the navy's 140-odd warships and submarines to fulfil these multiple simultaneous roles in the long-term.[74] As per the navy's roadmap, it is expected to increase its naval strength to 200 warships (including submarines) and 400 naval aviation units by 2027.[75] However, given the current rate of shipbuilding in India under the 'Make in India' initiative and the Indian Naval Indigenisation Plan (INIP) 2015-30, both purported under the government of Narendra Modi, it is projected that India will fall short of meeting the navy's needs in the prescribed timeline.[76] India for such reasons has habitually relied on foreign procurement of naval assets to meet its needs.[77] Data shows that India's budgetary allocation for the modernisation of the navy has gone down during Modi's tenure in office. India requires around Rs 1.8 lakh crore over the next 10 years for its fleet expansion plan but has not invested that amount annually between 2014 and 2019.[78] Unless this trajectory is reversed, India's maritime security agenda will remain dominated by maritime partnerships rather than actual naval power.

In addition, the operating conditions of the Navy's existing vessels are well below par. Ranging from insufficient refitting facilities to longer operational cycles and sparse logistical support, Indian naval vessels are stretched beyond capacity to fulfil their multi-faceted MBDs.[79] A striking example of this is the present state of India's submarine fleet. India currently operates 14 conventional submarines and 2 nuclear submarines. However, both nuclear submarines—INS *Arihant* and INS *Chakra*—have encountered accidents in the past few years.[80] The incapacitation of the *Arihant*, India's only operational Ship Submersible Ballistic Nuclear (SSBN) asset after an accident effectively invalidated the sea-leg of India's nuclear triad and second-strike capabilities for a long time. The accidents involving the *Arihant* and the *Chakra* follow a long list of submarine accidents that have become routine in the Indian Navy.[81] In November 2018, when the *Arihant* completed its first deterrence patrol, Modi was quick to hail it as a momentous achievement and remarked that India's 'nuclear triad was complete'.[82] However, multiple analysts have expressed their doubts regarding the authentic status of the Indian Navy's sea-borne nuclear force.[83] The Modi government needs to pay more attention to such finer details that constitute India's maritime security apparatus.

Another example of India's ostensible naval power is its aircraft carrier programme. As mentioned before, the Indian Navy's future force-

Table 2: India Defence Budget—Naval Fleet Modernisation Expenditure (2014–2019)[84]

Financial Year	*Total Budget Estimate for Naval Modernisation (Rs in crore)**	*% Increase in Current Year over Previous Year (Budget Estimate)*	*Total Budget Estimate for Naval Fleet Modernisation (Rs in crore)**	*% Increase in Current Year over Previous Year (Budget Estimate)*
2018–2019	19,927	6.3	10,300	-6.6
2017–2018	18,749	-12.1	11,023	-11.6
2016–2017	21,323	-12.2	12,467	-22.3
2015–2016	24,283	5.9	16,050	27.6
2014–2015	22,941	-2.29	12,576	6.4

Note: *Figures are approximate

projection is based around CTFs and CBGs. Therefore, for India to fulfil this strategic imperative, it needs to acquire two additional aircraft carriers in the earliest possible time-frame to add to its flagship vessel—INS *Vikramaditya*. Until now, multiple delays have kept on postponing the commissioning of its indigenously-built aircraft carrier (IAC-1) INS *Vikrant*.[85] The third aircraft carrier (IAC-2) or INS *Vishal*, that was initially planned to be a nuclear-powered supercarrier also continues to be in the planning stage and has seen little tangible progress despite a partnership with the US under the Joint Working Group on Aircraft Carrier Technology Cooperation (JWGACTC).[86] The situation in other variations of surface combatants is similar and need multiple rounds of swift acquisition. Yet, the budgetary allocation of the Modi government for the navy's capital acquisition programme has remained incongruous over the past five years.

Nuclearisation of the navy is another significant requirement for India to realise its maritime security goals. The Bhabha Atomic Research Centre (BARC) that has produced indigenous reactors for naval units, has not yet been able to come up with a high-powered corrosive resistant reactor suitable for longer 'sea-legs'. The fact that future nuclear submarines being produced in India may face the same problem defeats the intended purpose of a nuclear triad. Similarly, regarding an indigenous nuclear reactor for an aircraft carrier, BARC told the navy that the process would take 15-20 years so that the nuclear reactor has all features to protect the aircraft from the corrosive and dynamic marine environment.[87]

Presently, India has only produced a 190-megawatt (MW) reactor based on Russian designs which have been commissioned to INS *Arihant*.[88] Since INS *Vishal* would require a reactor capable of generating at least 500 MW, India will have to develop a brand new, miniaturised reactor.

Most importantly, for India to keep its date with its ambitious maritime security agenda, it needs to start venturing into the domain of unmanned and autonomous vessels, and artificial intelligence supported communication frameworks and battle management systems.[89] At a time when major navies have their own research and development agencies to innovate new advances in naval technologies, India's own Defence Research and Development Organisation (DRDO) has fallen well short of providing India's naval assets with the cutting-edge technology and equipment that are gradually becoming commonplace in naval warfare.[90] Lately, the Prime Minister and his coterie have realised the potential of AI-based technology in military operations, but how far that percolates down to the naval domain remains a question.[91] A bright spot lies in the fact that the US has been willing to supply to India advanced naval equipment such as the Sea Guardian drones.[92] However, this further demonstrates the continued inability of India to indigenously produce modern naval assets. During Manmohan Singh's tenure as Prime Minister, India overly relied on Russia for advanced assets, as evidenced by the procurement of old Russian vessels—the INS *Vikramaditya* (formerly Admiral Gorshkov) and INS *Chakra* (formerly K-152 Nerpa).[93] Similarly, in the coming years, over-dependence on American equipment transfers might become a trend. The political establishment in New Delhi needs to realise that it has to provide the Indian Navy with appropriate tools if it wants to fulfil its maritime security agenda. Operational difficulties may also arise due to the inconsistency in systems between the different types of vessels procured from different nations.

Conclusion: Evaluating the Current Government in Maritime Security

India's present maritime security policy is a representation of its growing stature as a naval power. Modi's enthusiasm for across the seas diplomacy, stretching from the South Pacific to the Western Indian Ocean, has made cooperation in the maritime arena a cornerstone of India's outreach to the world. Retrospectively, it can be said that maritime security is central to many of the foreign policy actions that encapsulate Modi's doctrine of foreign policy. Nothing better constructs New Delhi's worldview as it steps up operations from 'brown' territorial waters to the 'blue' waters of the high seas. However, an ambiguously hostile China keeps Indian naval strategy on the edge as the pressure to enter a maritime connectivity race with Beijing hangs on the horizon. Modernising present capabilities and developing new technologies also remain a key challenge.

Any incoming administration after the 2019 general elections needs to get a better grasp of this evolving agenda and make the right manoeuvres. Maritime security has never been an election issue because the electorate, like the political parties in India, has always been captivated by continental security problems. Now, as India expands the scope of its foreign policy, maritime policy will be crucial for India's economic, energy and social security. Under Modi, India has undertaken a massive port development scheme titled Sagarmala. The Sagarmala Project is envisioned to develop 14 major ports across the coastline along with accompanying coastal economic zones (CEZs). Multiple lines of multi-modal transport corridors are also being planned under the project to connect neighbouring landlocked countries like Nepal and Bhutan to the sea lanes of international trade. Funding for the project has been sparse till now but is expected to pick up in the next five to seven years. Developing the coastal economy will make maritime security an even more important area of governance.

While coalescing all this together, is what defines India's maritime security strategy, India's future as a naval power depends on its political leadership. The tenure of the Modi government has demonstrated India's will to engage with the idea of being a maritime force of the twenty-first century but is only in its initial stages. For India to progress further, it needs to fast track its acquisitions in order to meet its political promises. India needs to hone its maritime relationships with regional powers, and project influence in its immediate neighbourhood. Only after a sustained period of focus on India's naval capacities and relationships, can India realise its tryst with geography as an effective modern day maritime power.

NOTES

1 David Scott, 'The Indian Ocean as India's Ocean,' in *The Oxford Handbook of Indian Foreign Policy,* ed. David M. Malone Et al., (Oxford University Press, 2015); Walter Ladwig III, 'Drivers of Indian Naval Expansion' in *Rise of The Indian Navy: Internal Vulnerabilities, External Challenges,* ed. Harsh V. Pant, Corbett Centre for maritime policy studies, (Burlington, VA: Ashgate, 2012).

2 David Scott, 'The Indian Ocean as India's Ocean,' in *The Oxford Handbook of Indian Foreign Policy,* ed. David M. Malone Et al., (Oxford University Press, 2015); C. Raja Mohan, *Samudra Manthan: Sino-Indian Rivalry in the Indo-Pacific,* (Carnegie Endowment for International Peace, 2015); Walter Ladwig III, 'Drivers of Indian Naval Expansion' in *Rise of The Indian Navy: Internal Vulnerabilities, External Challenges,* ed. Harsh V. Pant, Corbett Centre for maritime policy studies, (Burlington, VA: Ashgate, 2012).

3 Arun Prakash, 'The Rationale and Implications of India's Growing Maritime Power' in *India's Contemporary Security Challenges,* ed. Michael Kugelman, (Washington DC: Woodrow Wilson International Center for Scholars, 2011).

4 Walter Ladwig III, 'Drivers of Indian Naval Expansion' in *Rise of The Indian Navy: Internal Vulnerabilities, External Challenges,* ed. Harsh V. Pant, Corbett Centre for maritime policy studies, (Burlington, VA: Ashgate, 2012).

5 'Officials quit over India attacks,' *BBC News,* 29 November 2008, http://news.bbc.co.uk/2/hi/south_asia/7756068.stm

6 'Slain navigator of Porbandar trawler was imprisoned in Pak,' *The Economic Times,* 30 November 2008, https://economictimes.indiatimes.com/news/politics-and-nation/slain-navigator-of-porbandar-trawler-was-imprisoned-in-pak/articleshow/3777132.cms

7 'India's coastal security better post 26/11 but chinks remain (Five Years After 26/11),' *Business Standard,* 25 November 2013, https://www.business-standard.com/article/news-ians/india-s-coastal-security-better-post-26-11-but-chinks-remain-five-years-after-26-11-113112500541_1.html; 'Measures to enhance Coastal Security,' *Press Information Bureau,* Ministry of Defence, Government of India, 5 March 2018, http://pib.nic.in/newsite/PrintRelease.aspx?relid=176953

8 'Measures to enhance Coastal Security,' *Press Information Bureau,* Ministry of Defence, Government of India, 5 March 2018, http://pib.nic.in/newsite/PrintRelease.aspx?relid=176953; 'Initiatives to Strengthen Coastal Security,' *Integrated Headquarters of Ministry of Defence (Navy),* Government of India, https://www.indiannavy.nic.in/content/initiatives-strengthen-coastal-security

9 Abhijit Singh, 'Why India's coastal security project is still a work in progress,'

Observer Research Foundation, 25 November 2016, https://www.orfonline.org/expert-speak/why-indias-coastal-security-project-is-still-a-work-in-progress/

10 'Initiatives to Strengthen Coastal Security,' Integrated Headquarters of Ministry of Defence (Navy), Government of India, https://www.indiannavy.nic.in/content/initiatives-strengthen-coastal-security

11 'India's coastal security better post 26/11 but chinks remain (Five Years After 26/11),' *Business Standard*, 25 November 2013, https://www.business-standard.com/article/news-ians/india-s-coastal-security-better-post-26-11-but-chinks-remain-five-years-after-26-11-113112500541_1.html

12 'Raksha Mantri Shri Manohar Parrikar Inaugurates IMAC, a Navy-CG Joint Operations Centre,' Indian Navy, Ministry of Defence, Government of India, https://www.indiannavy.nic.in/content/raksha-mantri-shri-manohar-parrikar-inaugurates-imac-navy-cg-joint-operations-centre; 'Initiatives to Strengthen Coastal Security,' Integrated Headquarters of Ministry of Defence (Navy), Government of India, https://www.indiannavy.nic.in/content/initiatives-strengthen-coastal-security

13 'Measures to enhance Coastal Security,' *Press Information Bureau*, Ministry of Defence, Government of India, 5 March 2018, http://pib.nic.in/newsite/PrintRelease.aspx?relid=176953

14 Shihar Aneez and Ranga Sirilal, 'Chinese submarine docks in Sri Lanka despite Indian concerns,' *Reuters*, 2 November 2014, https://in.reuters.com/article/sri-lanka-china-submarine/chinese-submarine-docks-in-sri-lanka-despite-indian-concerns-idINKBN0IM0LU20141102

15 'China flexes muscle in Indian Ocean, Navy concerned,' *The Times of India*, 13 May 2013, https://timesofindia.indiatimes.com/india/China-flexes-muscle-in-Indian-Ocean-Navy-concerned/articleshow/20032323.cms

16 Shihar Aneez and Ranga Sirilal, 'Sri Lanka rejects Chinese request for submarine visit: Sources,' *Reuters*, 11 May 2017, https://www.reuters.com/article/us-sri-lanka-china-submarine/sri-lanka-rejects-chinese-request-for-submarine-visit-sources-idUSKBN1871P9

17 Sandeep Unnithan, 'Exclusive: We can match China in the Indian Ocean region, says Navy chief Sunil Lanba,' *India Today*, 17 November 2018, https://www.indiatoday.in/magazine/interview/story/20181126-we-can-match-china-in-the-indian-ocean-region-admiral-sunil-lanba-1388904-2018-11-17

18 Ibid.

19 David Scott, 'The Indian Ocean as India's Ocean,' in *The Oxford Handbook of Indian Foreign Policy*, ed. David M. Malone Et al., (Oxford University Press, 2015); Sarabjeet Singh Parmar, 'Maritime Security in the Indian Ocean: An Indian Perspective,' *Journal of Defence Studies*, Institute for Defence Studies and Analyses, Vol. 8, No. 1(January–March 2014): pp. 49–63, https://idsa.in/system/files/8_1_2014_MaritimeSecurityintheIndianOcean.pdf

20 'East China Sea Tensions: Approaching A Slow Boil,' *Asia Maritime Transparency Initiative*, Center for Strategic and International Studies, 14 April 2016, https:/

/amti.csis.org/east-china-sea-tensions/; 'China's New Spratly Island Defenses,' *Asia Maritime Transparency Initiative*, Center for Strategic and International Studies, 13 December 2016, https://amti.csis.org/chinas-new-spratly-island-defenses/; Tuneer Mukherjee, 'China's naval power and national prestige,' *Observer Research Foundation*, 8 March 2018, https://www.orfonline.org/expert-speak/china-naval-power-national-prestige/

21 Ibid.

22 Tuneer Mukherjee, 'China's Maritime Quest in the Indian Ocean: New Delhi's Options,' *The Diplomat*, 24 April 2018, https://thediplomat.com/2018/04/chinas-maritime-quest-in-the-indian-ocean-new-delhis-options/

23 Dhruva Jaishankar, 'A Confluence of Two Strategies: The Japan–India Security Partnership in the Indo-Pacific,' in *India and Japan: Assessing the Strategic Partnership*, ed. Rajesh Basrur and Sumitha Narayanan Kutty, (Palgrave Macmillan, 2018); 'India-Indonesia Joint Statement during visit of Prime Minister to Indonesia,' Ministry of External Affairs, Government of India, 30 May 2018, https://www.mea.gov.in/bilateral-documents.htm?dtl/29932/IndiaIndonesia+Joint+Statement+during+visit+of+Prime+Minister+to+Indonesia+May+30+2018; 'India-France Joint Statement during State visit of President of France to India,' *Press Information Bureau*, Prime Minister's Office, Government of India, 10 March 2018, http://pib.nic.in/newsite/PrintRelease.aspx?relid=177251; Ankit Panda, 'Strategic Trade Authorization: A Fillip for India's "Major Defense Partner" Status with the US,' *The Diplomat*, 1 August 2018, https://thediplomat.com/2018/08/strategic-trade-authorization-a-filip-for-indias-major-defense-partner-status-with-the-us/

24 Vinay Kumar, 'India well positioned to become a net provider of security: Manmohan Singh,' *The Hindu*, 23 May 2013, https://www.thehindu.com/news/national/india-well-positioned-to-become-a-net-provider-of-security-manmohan-singh/article4742337.ece

25 'Ensuring Secure Seas: Indian Maritime Security Strategy,' Integrated Headquarters, Ministry of Defence (Navy), Government of India, 2015, https://www.indiannavy.nic.in/sites/default/files/Indian_Maritime_Security_Strategy_Document_25Jan16.pdf

26 Ibid.

27 Ibid.

28 Prashanth Parameswaran, 'The Real Significance of India's MILAN Navy Exercise,' *The Diplomat*, 28 February 2018, https://thediplomat.com/2018/02/the-real-significance-of-indias-milan-navy-exercise/; Prashanth Parameswaran, 'The Malabar Exercise: An Emerging Platform for Indo-Pacific Cooperation?' *The Diplomat*, 12 June 2016, https://thediplomat.com/2016/06/the-malabar-exercise-an-emerging-platform-for-indo-pacific-cooperation/; Pragya Pandey, 'Malabar 2017: Trilateral Naval Exercise Concludes Amid India-China Standoff,' *The Diplomat*, 19 July 2017, https://thediplomat.com/2017/07/malabar-2017-trilateral-naval-exercise-concludes-amid-india-china-standoff/

29 'IN Ships arrive Guam to participate in Ex-Malabar 2018,' *Press Information*

Bureau, Ministry of Defence, Government of India, 7 June 2018, http://pib.nic.in/newsite/PrintRelease.aspx?relid=179862

30 Franz-Stefan Gady, 'Indian Navy Practices Sinking Chinese Subs in Largest-Ever Military Exercise,' *The Diplomat*, 10 February 2017, https://thediplomat.com/2017/02/indian-navy-practices-sinking-chinese-subs-in-largest-ever-military-exercise/

31 'Ensuring Secure Seas: Indian Maritime Security Strategy,' Integrated Headquarters, Ministry of Defence (Navy), Government of India, 2015, https://www.indiannavy.nic.in/sites/default/files/Indian_Maritime_Security_Strategy_Document_25Jan16.pdf

32 'What is GSAT-7 Rukmini?' *The Indian Express*, 5 July 2017, https://indianexpress.com/article/what-is/india-rukmini-gsat-7-satellite-china-indian-ocean-region-sikkim-standoff-4736318/

33 R.S. Vasan, 'Indian Navy's 'CAMPING' Expeditions in the Indian Ocean Region,' *National Maritime Foundation*, 6 April 2018, http://www.maritimeindia.org/View%20Profile/636585847056911533.pdf; Sujan Dutta, '"Alphabet soup" of Navy missions dots Indian Ocean,' *The New Indian Express*, 1 April 2018, http://www.newindianexpress.com/thesundaystandard/2018/apr/01/alphabet-soup-of-navy-missions-dots-indian-ocean-1795343.html

34 Ibid.

35 'Narendra Modi invites all SAARC heads to swearing-in,' *India Today*, 21 May 2014, https://www.indiatoday.in/india/story/narendra-modi-invites-saarc-heads-to-swearing-in-193881-2014-05-21

36 'India, Modi and the neighbourhood,' *Gateway House*, 25 August 2014 https://www.gatewayhouse.in/india-modi-and-the-neighbourhood/; Tuneer Mukherjee, 'China's Maritime Quest in the Indian Ocean: New Delhi's Options,' *The Diplomat*, 24 April 2018, https://thediplomat.com/2018/04/chinas-maritime-quest-in-the-indian-ocean-new-delhis-options/; Suhasini Haider, 'Neighbourhood first?' *The Hindu*, 1 December 2018, https://www.thehindu.com/opinion/lead/neighbourhood-first/article25637451.ece; Vinay Kaura, 'Grading India's Neighborhood Diplomacy,' *The Diplomat*, 1 January 2018, https://thediplomat.com/2017/12/grading-indias-neighborhood-diplomacy/

37 Tuneer Mukherjee, 'China's Maritime Quest in the Indian Ocean: New Delhi's Options,' *The Diplomat*, 24 April 2018, https://thediplomat.com/2018/04/chinas-maritime-quest-in-the-indian-ocean-new-delhis-options/

38 'Project Mausam,' *Press Information Bureau*, Ministry of Culture, Government of India, 24 July 2017, http://pib.nic.in/newsite/PrintRelease.aspx?relid=168923

39 Akhilesh Pillalamarri, 'Project Mausam: India's Answer to China's "Maritime Silk Road",' *The Diplomat*, 18 September 2014, https://thediplomat.com/2014/09/project-mausam-indias-answer-to-chinas-maritime-silk-road/

40 'Time to Change "Look East Policy" to "Act East Policy": Sushma Swaraj,' *NDTV*, 25 August 2014, https://www.ndtv.com/india-news/time-to-change-look-east-policy-to-act-east-policy-sushma-swaraj-653063; Amitav Acharya, *India's 'Look*

East' Policy in The Oxford Handbook of Indian Foreign Policy, ed. David M. Malone Et al., (Oxford University Press, 2015).

41 Ibid.

42 Amitav Acharya, *India's 'Look East' Policy* in The Oxford Handbook of Indian Foreign Policy, ed. David M. Malone Et al., (Oxford University Press, 2015).

43 V. K. Singh, 'Act East Policy,' *Press Information Bureau*, Ministry of External Affairs Government of India, 23 December 2015, http://pib.nic.in/newsite/PrintRelease.aspx?relid=133837

44 'India and Republic of Korea: A Vision for People, Prosperity, Peace and our Future,' Ministry of External Affairs, Government of India, 10 July 2018, https://mea.gov.in/bilateral documents.htm?dtl/30041/India+and+Republic+of+Korea+A+Vision+for+People+Prosperity+Peace+and+our+Future; David Brewster, 'Australia's quest for maritime domain awareness in the Indian Ocean,' *Journal of the Indian Ocean Region*, Vol. 14, No. 3 (October 2018): pp. 296-314; 'Joint statement by Smt. Nirmala Sitharaman, Minister of Defence of the Republic of India and Dr Ng Eng Hen, Minister for Defence of the Republic of Singapore,' *Press Information Bureau*, Ministry of Defence, Government of India, 29 November 2017, http://pib.nic.in/newsite/PrintRelease.aspx?relid=173945; 'India-Indonesia Joint Statement during visit of Prime Minister to Indonesia,' Ministry of External Affairs, Government of India, 30 May 2018, https://www.mea.gov.in/bilateraldocuments.htm?dtl/29932/IndiaIndonesia+Joint+Statement+during+visit+of+Prime+Minister+to+Indonesia+May+30+2018; 'India-Vietnam Joint Statement during State Visit of President to Vietnam,' Ministry of External Affairs, Government of India, 21 November 2018, https://www.mea.gov.in/bilateral-documents.htm?dtl/30615/IndiaVietnam_Joint_Statement_during_State_Visit_of_President_to_Vietnam; 'India-Japan Vision Statement,' Ministry of External Affairs, Government of India, 29 October 2018, https://www.mea.gov.in/bilateral-documents.htm?dtl/30543/IndiaJapan_Vision_Statement

45 'First meeting of the BIMSTEC National Security Chiefs,' Ministry of External Affairs, Government of India, 21 March 2017, https://mea.gov.in/press-releases.htm?dtl/28193/First_meeting_of_the_BIMSTEC_National_Security_Chiefs_March_21_2017

46 Darshana Baruah, 'Andaman and Nicobar as India's smart islands,' *The Economic Times*, 18 October 2017, https://economictimes.indiatimes.com/blogs/et-commentary/andaman-and-nicobar-as-indias-smart-islands/; Jeff Smith, 'Andaman and Nicobar Islands: India's Strategic Outpost,' *The Diplomat*, 18 March 2014, https://thediplomat.com/2014/03/andaman-and-nicobar-islands-indias-strategic-outpost/

47 David Brewster, 'Glug, glug, glug: India's interest in unsinkable aircraft carriers,' *The Interpreter*, Lowy Institute, 20 June 2018, https://www.lowyinstitute.org/the-interpreter/glug-glug-glug-india-interest-unsinkable-aircraft-carriers; Darshana Baruah, 'The Andaman And Nicobar Islands: India's Eastern Anchor In A Changing Indo-Pacific,' *War on the Rocks*, 21 March 2018, https://

warontherocks.com/2018/03/the-andaman-and-nicobar-islands-indias-eastern-anchor-in-a-changing-indo-pacific/

48 'Prime Minister's remarks at Pacific Island Leaders Meeting,' Ministry of External Affairs, Government of India, 19 November 2014, https://mea.gov.in/outoging-visit-detail.htm?24279/Prime+Ministers+remarks+at+Pacific+Island+Leaders+Meeting+November+19+2014; Balaji Chandramohan, 'India's Strategic Expansion in the Pacific Islands,' *The Diplomat*, 13 June 2018 https://thediplomat.com/2018/06/indias-strategic-expansion-in-the-pacific-islands/

49 'Prime Minister's Remarks at the Commissioning of Offshore Patrol Vessel (OPV) Barracuda in Mauritius,' Ministry of External Affairs, Government of India, 12 March 2015, https://mea.gov.in/outoging-visit-detail.htm?24912/Prime+Ministers+Remarks+at+the+Commissioning+of+Offshore+Patrol+Vessel+OPV+Barracuda+in+Mauritius+ March+12+2015

50 David Scott, 'The Indian Ocean as India's Ocean,' in *The Oxford Handbook of Indian Foreign Policy*, ed. David M. Malone Et al., (Oxford University Press, 2015).

51 'India-Madagascar Joint Statement during the State Visit of President to Madagascar,' Ministry of External Affairs, Government of India, 14 March 2018 https://www.mea.gov.in/bilateral-documents.htm?dtl/29666/India Madagascar_Joint_Statement_during_the_State_Visit_of_President_to_Madagascar_March_1415_2018; 'Joint Press Statement on Visit to Mozambique by Minister of State for External Affairs, Gen (Dr) V.K. Singh (Retd.),' Ministry of External Affairs, Government of India, 14 February 2018, https://www.mea.gov.in/bilateral-documents.htm?dtl/29486/Joint_Press_Statement_on_Visit_to_Mozambique_by_Minister_of_State_for_External_Affairs_GenDr_VK_Singh_Retd_February_1213_2018

52 David Scott, 'The Indian Ocean as India's Ocean,' in *The Oxford Handbook of Indian Foreign Policy*, ed. David M. Malone et al., (Oxford University Press, 2015); Abhijit Singh, 'Evaluating India-Africa Maritime Relations,' *The Diplomat*, 29 October 2015, https://thediplomat.com/2015/10/evaluating-india-africa-maritime-relations/

53 'Ensuring Secure Seas: Indian Maritime Security Strategy,' Integrated Headquarters, Ministry of Defence (Navy), Government of India, 2015.

54 Abhijnan Rej and Tuneer Mukherjee, 'Whither India in the Indo-Pacific?' Italian Institute for International Political Studies, 4 June 2018 https://www.ispionline.it/en/pubblicazione/whither-india-indo-pacific-20688

55 Kallol Bhattacherjee, 'India, UAE to deepen strategic ties, counter terror,' *The Hindu*, 11 February 2018, https://www.thehindu.com/news/national/indias-ties-with-uae-much-more-than-that-of-buyer-seller-says-pm-modi/article22720865.ece; 'India-Qatar Joint Statement during the visit of Prime Minister to Qatar,' Ministry of External Affairs, Government of India, 5 June 2016, https://www.mea.gov.in/bilateral-documents.htm?dtl/26870/IndiaQatar_Joint_Statement_during_the_visit_of_Prime_Minister_to_Qatar; 'India and Oman agree for deeper maritime security,' *Financial Express*, 27

September 2018, https://www.financialexpress.com/defence/india-and-oman-agree-for-deeper-maritime-security/1328764/

56 David Scott, 'The Indian Ocean as India's Ocean,' in *The Oxford Handbook of Indian Foreign Policy*, ed. David M. Malone Et al., (Oxford University Press, 2015); Abhijit Singh, 'The Indian Navy's humanitarian impulse,' *Live Mint*, 14 June 2017, https://www.livemint.com/Opinion/5yMHIeapeZianzdanLf9JN/The-Indian-Navys-humanitarian-impulse.html?utm_source=scroll &utm_medium =referral &utm_campaign=scroll

57 'Ensuring Secure Seas: Indian Maritime Security Strategy,' Integrated Headquarters, Ministry of Defence (Navy), Government of India, 2015; Abhijit Singh, 'The Indian Navy's humanitarian impulse,' *Live Mint*, 14 June 2017, https://www.livemint.com/Opinion/5yMHIeapeZianzdanLf9JN/The-Indian-Navys-humanitarian-impulse.html?utm_source=scroll&utm_medium=referral&utm_campaign=scroll

58 'India, Iran and Afghanistan sign Chabahar port agreement,' *Hindustan Times*, 24 May 2016, https://www.hindustantimes.com/india/india-iran-afghanistan-sign-chabahar-port-agreement/story-2EytbKZeo6zeClpR8WSuAO.html

59 Shishir Gupta, 'Soon, India defence attaché at US navy Bahrain command,' *Hindustan Times*, 21 March 2018, https://www.hindustantimes.com/india-news/soon-india-defence-attache-at-us-navy-bahrain-command/story-iTGPB5sLbOlod11MlprWjI.html

60 Michael Safi, 'Chinese and Indian troops face off in Bhutan border dispute,' *The Guardian*, 6 July 2017, https://www.theguardian.com/world/2017/jul/06/china-india-bhutan-standoff-disputed-territory

61 Gurmeet Kanwal, 'Pakistan's Gwadar Port: A New Naval Base in China's String of Pearls in the Indo-Pacific,' Center for Strategic and International Studies, 2 April 2018, https://www.csis.org/analysis/pakistans-gwadar-port-new-naval-base-chinas-string-pearls-indo-pacific

62 'India-China Informal Summit at Wuhan,' Ministry of External Affairs, Government of India, 28 April 2018, https://mea.gov.in/press-releases.htm?dtl/29853/IndiaChina_Informal_Summit_at_Wuhan

63 Tanvi Madan, 'The Rise, Fall, And Rebirth Of The "Quad",' *War on the Rocks*, 16 November 2017, https://warontherocks.com/2017/11/rise-fall-rebirth-quad/

64 Ibid.

65 Mark Valencia, 'What Does a 'Free and Open Indo-Pacific' Actually Mean?' *The Diplomat*, 30 March 2018, https://thediplomat.com/2018/03/what-does-a-free-and-open-indo-pacific-actually-mean/; Tanvi Madan, 'The Rise, Fall, And Rebirth Of The "Quad",' *War on the Rocks*, 16 November 2017, https://warontherocks.com/2017/11/rise-fall-rebirth-quad/

66 Jason Koutsoukis, 'Shared concern about China's rise helped the Quad come together,' *The Print*, 17 November, 2018, https://theprint.in/economy/shared-concern-about-chinas-rise-helped-the-quad-come-together/150689/

67 Tanvi Madan, 'The Rise, Fall, And Rebirth Of The "Quad",' *War on the Rocks*, 16 November 2017, https://warontherocks.com/2017/11/rise-fall-rebirth-quad/

68 Tanvi Madan, 'The Rise, Fall, And Rebirth Of The "Quad",' *War on the Rocks*, 16 November 2017, https://warontherocks.com/2017/11/rise-fall-rebirth-quad/ ; Jim Yardley and Somini Sengupta, 'Two Giants Try to Learn to Share Asia,' *The New York Times*, 13 January 2008, https://www.nytimes.com/2008/01/13/world/asia/13singh.html; Siddharth Varadarajan, 'Chinese demarches to 4 nations,' *The Hindu*, 14 June 2007, https://www.thehindu.com/todays-paper/tp-international/Chinese-demarches-to-4-nations/article14777267.ece; Brendan Nicholson, 'China warns Canberra on security pact,' *The Age*, 15 June 2007, https://www.theage.com.au/national/china-warns-canberra-on-security-pact-20070615-ge54v5.html

69 'China has a vastly ambitious plan to connect the world,' *The Economist*, 26 July 2018, https://www.economist.com/briefing/2018/07/26/china-has-a-vastly-ambitious-plan-to-connect-the-world; James Kynge, 'China's Belt and Road difficulties are proliferating across the world,' *The Financial Times*, 9 July 2018, https://www.ft.com/content/fa3ca8ce-835c-11e8-a29d-73e3d454535d; 'China unveils action plan on Belt and Road Initiative,' The State Council of the People's Republic of China, 28 March 2015, http://english.gov.cn/news/top_news/2015/03/28/content_281475079055789.htm

70 'Joint Strategic Vision of India-France Cooperation in the Indian Ocean Region,' Ministry of External Affairs, Government of India, 10 March 2018, https://www.mea.gov.in/bilateral-documents.htm?dtl/29598; 'Shared Vision of India-Indonesia Maritime Cooperation in the Indo-Pacific,' Ministry of External Affairs, Government of India, 30 May 2018, https://www.mea.gov.in/bilateral-documents.htm?dtl/29933/Shared_Vision_of_IndiaIndonesia_Maritime_Cooperation_in_the_IndoPacific; 'India, Australia maritime cooperation to cover piracy, terrorism,' *The Times of India*, 6 April 2019, https://timesofindia.indiatimes.com/city/visakhapatnam/india-australia-maritime-cooperation-to-cover-piracy-terrorism/articleshow/68746055.cms; 'India-Japan Vision Statement,' Ministry of External Affairs, Government of India, 29 October 2018, https://www.mea.gov.in/bilateral-documents.htm?dtl/30543/IndiaJapan_Vision_Statement; Abhijit Singh Et al., 'The new India-US partnership in the Indo-Pacific: Peace, prosperity and security,' *Observer Research Foundation*, 19 January 2018, https://www.orfonline.org/research/new-india-united-states-partnership-indo-pacific-peace-prosperity-security/

71 Ashley J. Tellis, 'Narendra Modi and U.S.–India Relations,' Carnegie Endowment for International Peace, 1 November 2018, https://carnegieendowment.org/2018/11/01/narendra-modi-and-u.s.-india-relations-pub-77861

72 Varghese K. George, 'India, US sign military logistics pact,' *The Hindu*, 30 August 2016, https://www.thehindu.com/news/international/India-US-sign-military-logistics-pact/article14598282.ece; Jeff Smith, 'COMCASA: Another Step Forward for the United States and India,' *The Diplomat*, 11 September 2018, https://thediplomat.com/2018/09/comcasa-another-step-forward-for-the-united-states-and-india/

[73] 'Prime Minister's Keynote Address at Shangri La Dialogue,' Ministry of External Affairs, Government of India, 1 June 2018, https://www.mea.gov.in/Speeches-Statements.htm?dtl/29943/Prime+Ministers+Keynote+Address+at+Shangri+La+Dialogue+June+01+2018

[74] 'Defence Minister takes note of key shortfalls in Navy,' *The Hindu*, 27 October 2017, https://www.thehindu.com/news/national/defence-minister-takes-note-of-key-shortfalls-in-navy/article19927152.ece

[75] Zachary Keck, 'Watch Out, China: India's Navy Wants 200 Warships,' *The National Interest*, 15 July 2015, https://nationalinterest.org/blog/the-buzz/watch-out-china-indias-navy-wants-200-warships-13340

[76] 'Indian Naval Indigenisation Plan (INIP) (2015-2030),' Directorate of Indigenisation, Integrated Headquarters of Ministry of Defence (Navy), Government of India, 2016, https://ddpmod.gov.in/sites/default/files/INIP%20(2015-2030).pdf; Abhijit Singh, 'Future technologies for the Indian Navy,' *Observer Research Foundation*, 23 February 2017, https://www.orfonline.org/expert-speak/future-technologies-for-the-indian-navy/#_ftn3; Vivek Raghuvanshi, 'Indian Navy's modernization plans in jeopardy,' *Defense News*, 20 April 2017, https://www.defensenews.com/naval/2017/04/20/indian-navy-s-modernization-plans-in-jeopardy/

[77] 'India Submarine Import and Export Behavior,' *NTI*, 30 September 2015, https://www.nti.org/analysis/articles/india-submarine-import-and-export-behavior/; 'US approves sale of 24 MH 60 Romeo Seahawk helicopters to India for $2.4 bn,' *The Economic Times*, 3 April 2019, https://economictimes.indiatimes.com/news/defence/us-approves-sale-of-24-mh-60-romeo-seahawk-helicopters-to-india-for-usd-2-4-bn/articleshow/68698990.cms; Vivek Raghuvanshi, 'India signs $3 billion contract with Russia for lease of a nuclear submarine,' *Defense News*, 8 March 2019, https://www.defensenews.com/global/asia-pacific/2019/03/08/india-signs-3-billion-contract-with-russia-for-lease-of-a-nuclear-submarine/; 'Gorshkov deal finalised at USD 2.3 billion,' *The Hindu*, 10 March 2010, https://www.thehindu.com/news/national/Gorshkov-deal-finalised-at-USD-2.3-billion/article16554605.ece

[78] See Table 2; Vivek Raghuvanshi, 'Indian Navy's modernization plans in jeopardy,' *Defense News*, 20 April 2017, https://www.defensenews.com/naval/2017/04/20/indian-navy-s-modernization-plans-in-jeopardy/

[79] Harsh V. Pant ed., *Rise of The Indian Navy: Internal Vulnerabilities, External Challenges*, Corbett Centre for maritime policy studies, (Burlington, VA: Ashgate, 2012).

[80] Josy Joseph, 'Russia seeks Rs125 crore to carry out repairs on INS Chakra,' *The Hindu*, 13 February 2018, https://www.thehindu.com/news/national/russia-seeks-125-crore-to-carry-out-repairs-on-ins-chakra/article22735617.ece; Dinakar Peri and Josy Joseph, 'INS Arihant left crippled after "accident" 10 months ago,' *The Hindu*, 8 January 2018, https://www.thehindu.com/news/national/ins-arihant-left-crippled-after-accident-10-months-ago/article22392049.ece

[81] Ajai Shukla, 'The sinking feeling over Indian navy,' *Al Jazeera*, 6 March 2014, https://www.aljazeera.com/indepth/opinion/2014/03/sinking-feeling-over-indian-navy-20143665414242983.html; Sruthi Gottipati, 'Indian navy chief quits after submarine accident,' *Reuters*, 26 February 2014, https://www.reuters.com/article/us-india-submarine-resign/indian-navy-chief-quits-after-submarine-accident-idUSBREA1P11T20140226

[82] 'Prime Minister felicitates crew of INS Arihant on completion of Nuclear Triad,' *Press Information Bureau*, Prime Minister's Office, Government of India, 5 November 2018, http://pib.nic.in/PressReleseDetail.aspx?PRID=1551894

[83] Abhijit Singh, 'INS *Arihant*: A step closer to a credible "Triad" but not quite there yet,' *Observer Research Foundation*, 8 November 2018, https://www.orfonline.org/expert-speak/ins-arihant-a-step-closer-to-a-credible-triad-but-not-quite-there-yet-45449/; Manoj Joshi, 'INS *Arihant*'s deterrence patrol: More hype than necessary,' *Observer Research Foundation*, 6 November 2018, https://www.orfonline.org/expert-speak/ins-arrogant-deterrence-patricks-more-hype-than-necessary-45427/

[84] Laxman K. Behera, 'Defence Budget 2018-19: The Imperative of Controlling Manpower Cost,' Institute for Defence Studies and Analyses, 2 February 2018, https://idsa.in/issuebrief/defence-budget-2018-19-controlling-manpower-cost-lkbehera-020218; Laxman K. Behera, 'India's Defence Budget 2017-18: An Analysis,' Institute for Defence Studies and Analyses, 3 February 2017, https://idsa.in/issuebrief/india-defence-budget-2017-18_lkbehera_030217; Laxman K. Behera, 'All About Pay and Perks: India's Defence Budget 2016-17,' Institute for Defence Studies and Analyses, https://idsa.in/issuebrief/pay-and-perks-india-defence-budget-2016-17_lkbehera_030315; Laxman K. Behera, 'India's Defence Budget 2015-16,' Institute for Defence Studies and Analyses, 2 March 2015, https://idsa.in/issuebrief/IndiasDefenceBudget2015-16_lkbehera_020315; Laxman K. Behera, 'India's Interim Defence Budget 2014-15: An Appraisal,' Institute for Defence Studies and Analyses, 23 February 2014, https://idsa.in/idsacomments/IndiasInterimDefenceBudget2014-15_lkbehera_230214

[85] Dinakar Peri, 'Navy confident of commissioning aircraft carrier Vikrant in two years,' *The Hindu*, 19 January 2018, https://www.thehindu.com/news/national/navy-confident-of-commissioning-aircraft-carrier-vikrant-in-two-years/article22474986.ece; Rajat Pandit, 'India without aircraft carrier for 8 months,' *The Times of India*, 27 July 2016, https://timesofindia.indiatimes.com/india/India-without-aircraft-carrier-for-8-months/articleshow/53407213.cms; Sudhi Ranjan Sen, 'Indian aircraft carrier: More costly, already delayed,' *NDTV*, 20 November 2018, https://www.ndtv.com/india-news/indian-aircraft-carrier-more-costly-already-delayed-505119; Huma Siddiqui, 'Navy unlikely to expand aircraft carrier fleet in next 15 years,' *Financial Express*, 20 July 2017, https://www.financialexpress.com/india-news/navy-unlikely-to-expand-aircraft-carrier-fleet-in-next-15-years/770553/

[86] Ajai Shula, 'Navy drops cherished dream of nuclear-powered aircraft carrier,' *Business Standard*, 27 October 2017, https://www.business-standard.com/

article/current-affairs/navy-drops-cherished-dream-of-nuclear-powered-aircraft-carrier-117102700031_1.html; Huma Siddiqui, 'Navy unlikely to expand aircraft carrier fleet in next 15 years,' *Financial Express*, 20 July 2017, https://www.financialexpress.com/india-news/navy-unlikely-to-expand-aircraft-carrier-fleet-in-next-15-years/770553/; Zachary Keck, 'India's Navy Has a Problem: An Aircraft Carrier Shortage,' *The National Interest*, 11 July 2018, https://nationalinterest.org/blog/buzz/indias-navy-has-problem-aircraft-carrier-shortage-25481

87 Ajai Shula, 'Navy drops cherished dream of nuclear-powered aircraft carrier,' *Business Standard*, 27 October 2017, https://www.business-standard.com/article/current-affairs/navy-drops-cherished-dream-of-nuclear-powered-aircraft-carrier-117102700031_1.html

88 Ajai Shula, 'Navy drops cherished dream of nuclear-powered aircraft carrier,' *Business Standard*, 27 October 2017, https://www.business-standard.com/article/current-affairs/navy-drops-cherished-dream-of-nuclear-powered-aircraft-carrier-117102700031_1.html; Abhijit Singh, 'INS *Arihant*: A step closer to a credible "Triad" but not quite there yet,' *Observer Research Foundation*, 8 November 2018, https://www.orfonline.org/expert-speak/ins-arihant-a-step-closer-to-a-credible-triad-but-not-quite-there-yet-45449/

89 Tuneer Mukherjee, 'Securing the maritime commons: The role of artificial intelligence in naval operations,' *Observer Research Foundation*, 16 July 2018, https://www.orfonline.org/research/42497-a-i-in-naval-operations-exploring-possibilities-debating-ethics/

90 Ibid.

91 Ibid.

92 'Indian Govt Seals Sea Guardian Drones Procurement Deal With US,' *The Quint*, 21 December 2017, https://www.thequint.com/news/india/india-to-get-sea-guardian-drones-procurement-deal-with-us

93 'Gorshkov deal finalised at USD 2.3 billion,' *The Hindu*, 10 March 2010, https://www.thehindu.com/news/national/Gorshkov-deal-finalised-at-USD-2.3-billion/article16554605.ece; Vivek Raghuvanshi, 'India signs $3 billion contract with Russia for lease of a nuclear submarine,' *Defense News*, 8 March 2019, https://www.defensenews.com/global/asia-pacific/2019/03/08/india-signs-3-billion-contract-with-russia-for-lease-of-a-nuclear-submarine/; 'Russia hands over Nerpa attack submarine to India,' *NDTV*, 31 December 2011, https://www.ndtv.com/india-news/russia-hands-over-nerpa-attack-submarine-to-india-570766

4

India's Evolving Space Programme and Policy: A Story of Rising Ambitions

Rajeswari Pillai Rajagopalan and Vidya Sagar Reddy

INDIA'S space programme has achieved some impressive feats in the last few years. The Indian Space Research Organisation (ISRO) has had a number of successes: the Mars mission in September 2014, the launch of 104 satellites on a single Polar Satellite Launch Vehicle (PSLV) rocket in February 2017, the launch of the 100th Indian satellite in January 2018, the launch of geostationary satellite, GSAT-6A (although communications with the satellite was lost) on the 12th flight of the Geosynchronous Satellite Launch Vehicle, GSLV-F08 in March 2018, the launch of GSAT-29 using GSLV Mk III in November 2018, are all substantial achievements for ISRO. These launches also demonstrate the increasing sophistication and reliability of the Indian rockets as well as the maturing Indian satellite fabrication capabilities.

Nevertheless, on the space policy front, India has been somewhat lagging. Even though ISRO has released certain sector-specific policies such as for remote sensing and satcom (satellite communication), the requirement for an overarching space policy is real. India traditionally approached space from a social and developmental perspective, but there is a growing set of requirements in the national security context, and India's policy approach has to be broadened to include these as well. Traditionally, these requirements were not given much attention even though technology pursuit and demonstration would have obvious security spin-offs and should have been important considerations for India. India's INSAT (Indian National Satellite System), Indian Remote Sensing (IRS) satellites and Cartosat series are evidence of this consideration. On the importance of technology demonstration, Dr Vikram Sarabhai, father of India's space programme, had said, 'We are convinced that if we are to play a meaningful role nationally, and in the community of nations, we must be second to none in the application of advanced technologies to the real problems of man and society.'

With ISRO having achieved several impressive feats, India must now focus on developing a holistic approach to space. An open space policy can bring India several benefits, both from an internal and external perspective. ISRO had prepared a draft Space Activities Bill, 2017 which is a step in the right direction. The bill, once introduced in Parliament and approved, would establish a regulatory mechanism that will carry out authorisation and licensing of space activities. The legislation will also provide for liability in case of damage due to space activities of a licensee, and a risk sharing mechanism by which the government is able to determine the quantum of liability to be assumed by the licensee.[1] While the draft bill is a useful step, India should become more innovative in combining the different functions of space to have an overarching space policy in the open.

However, two key steps taken by the Modi government combining space with India's foreign policy and strategic interests are worth noting. Firstly, the induction of the Foreign Secretary into the Space Commission is a strategic decision, implying that space is no more just a scientific programme but one that would develop and evolve in relation to the growing strategic and national security dynamics. Secondly, Modi's announcement in 2014 of a South Asia satellite as a gift to the South Asian neighbourhood was the realisation of a long pending objective. Modi has also invited the South Asian neighbouring countries to make full utilisation of the Indian navigation system, the Indian Regional Navigation Satellite System (IRNSS). South Asian countries also stand to benefit from the IRS programme that will offer enormous assistance in the context of urban planning, disaster warning and mitigation. These policies are clearly in line with Modi's 'neighbourhood first' approach that will strengthen India's standing in the region.

This chapter outlines key developments relating to India's space programme and policy in the last five years under Prime Minister Modi. Of course, the Indian space programme is decades old and has received strong support from successive governments. On the other hand, since 2014, ISRO has also achieved several milestones, beginning with the Mars Orbiter Mission and testing of the indigenous cryogenic engine for its GSLV rockets to demonstrate the Reusable Launch Vehicle (RLV) technology and is currently working on the human space mission to be launched in 2022. The chapter has examined each of these initiatives in detail and provides a prescriptive approach to how ISRO should also focus on developing its policy and institutional framework.

Mars Mission

As the Indian space programme took shape, interplanetary missions such as mission to Mars were not part of the initial thinking. Neither India's first Prime Minister Jawaharlal Nehru nor the father of India's space programme Dr Vikram Sarabhai imagined India to pursue such missions. On the contrary, Dr Sarabhai had stated that India did 'not have the fantasy of competing with the economically advanced nations in the exploration of the moon or the planets or manned space-flight'.[2] Nevertheless, India's attempt to launch a mission to the red planet is a sign of the times, the competition and race that is gripping Asia, even in the outer space domain. After a journey of 300 days from Earth, Mangalyaan, the Indian spacecraft for the Mars mission, entered the Martian orbit in September 2014, making India the first Asian country and the fourth globally to achieve this feat. Prime Minister Narendra Modi went on to congratulate the scientists at ISRO and remarked: 'Travelling a mind-boggling distance of more than 650 million, or 65 crore, kilometres, we have gone beyond the boundaries of human enterprise and imagination. We have, accurately navigated our spacecraft, through a route known to very few.'[3] He went on to highlight how 'India is the only country to have succeeded in its very first attempt' and even praised former Prime Minister Atal Bihari Vajpayee's vision that initiated ISRO to do the moon mission—Chandrayaan 1 in 2008. Modi said that it was the successful Chandrayaan mission that pushed India to attempt the Mars mission.

Technologically, the Mars mission was a major accomplishment for the ISRO. The success of the mission demonstrated the technological advancements that India has made especially for deep space communication, navigation-guidance-control of the mission as well as testing the autonomous features to handle contingency situations. As for the scientific objectives of the mission, these included exploring the Martian surface features including the presence of Methane, morphology, mineralogy and Martian atmosphere by using indigenous scientific instruments.[4]

India spent a total of US$74 million for the Mars mission, a tiny fraction of the US$671 million that National Aeronautics and Space Administration (NASA) had spent on MAVEN, its Mars mission, which also reached the Martian orbit a few days earlier. However, there is no comparison between MAVEN and Mars Orbiter Mission (MOM) because the kind of complex payload MAVEN had undertaken was far superior. MOM was primarily a technology demonstration mission and scientific objectives of the mission were secondary to the mission. Hence, MOM had a limited objective of testing the advancements in science and technology whereas MAVEN was primarily a scientific mission putting into play the relatively tried and tested technology. The cost-effective manner of MOM had caught quite some attention. This was possible due to several factors, including a modular approach, giving both cost and schedule gains. The MOM, for instance, used the same PSLV XL, designed with a new trajectory and that helped keep the costs low as against MAVEN, whose launch (on Atlas V rocket) cost itself came to US$187 million.[5] Two, MAVEN had carried a large device with a launch mass of around 2.5 tonnes and MOM, on the other hand, had just over a tonne of launch mass, implying that MAVEN required a much bigger and more expensive launch vehicle. The size of the payload too was significantly different. Given that MOM's payload was small, ISRO was able to use its own PSLV instead of getting it launched on a foreign launcher that would have shot up the expenses.

The successful Mars mission has got ISRO to focus on more exploratory missions to gain a better understanding of the solar system while showcasing India's growing space prowess. In furthering its quest to undertake more inter-planetary missions, ISRO is planning a Venus mission, which is seen as the next ideal candidate in planetary exploration. Given the similarities in size, mass, density and gravity, Venus is generally called the 'twin sister' of the Earth. India will not be the first country to explore Venus—under the Venera series, Russia has undertaken a total of 16 missions between 1961 and 1983.

The first mention of ISRO's potential Venus mission appeared in the budgetary allocations of the Department of Space for 2017-2018. More recently, ISRO announced its plans for the Venus mission in early 2020s where it has also invited international proposals for scientific payloads.[6] The mission will reportedly carry 12 scientific payloads aboard the satellite, including S-Band Synthetic Aperture Radar (SAR), Advanced Radar for Topside Ionosphere and subsurface sounding, Ultra Violet (UV) Imaging Spectroscopy Telescope, Thermal Camera, Cloud Monitoring Camera, Venus Atmospheric Spectro Polarimeter, Airglow photometer and Mass Spectrometer. Prior to this, in 2017, ISRO made a call for space-based experiments proposals from scientists based in India.[7]

Cryogenic Engine and GSLV Programme

The Satellite Instructional Television Experiment (SITE) performed in the 1970s made it clear to India that communications satellites are necessary for realising the stated objective of utilising space technology for economic development. Accordingly, the INSAT programme was conceived. The INSAT-1 series consisting of four satellites was built by Ford Aerospace and three of them were launched from the United States. Like the PSLV which relieved India from launching its remote sensing satellites using foreign launchers, the Geostationary Satellite Launch Vehicle (GSLV) has been conceived for independently accessing the geostationary orbit.

The GSLV rocket is designed with PSLV heritage elements but the upper stage required a cryogenic engine. This engine is a high-end technology available only to a few spacefaring countries such as the United States, Russia and France. Cryogenics is the science of liquefying gases like Hydrogen and Oxygen. Oxygen liquefies at –183°C and Hydrogen at –252.9°C. Hydrogen has low molecular weight and burns with high intensity while oxygen is one of the easily available oxidisers. A cryogenic rocket engine using these liquefied gases provides more thrust for every kilogram of fuel consumed when compared to other propellants, raising the payload capacity of the launch vehicle. The liquefaction process also increases the density of these gases, allowing them to be stored in smaller containers on-board rockets. However, designing a cryogenic engine that can withstand the structural pressure and heat emanating from the combustion of these fuels involves sophisticated engineering and material science and, therefore, the design process is closely guarded.

The realisation of commercial prospects of satellite broadcasting made the geostationary orbit a lucrative market. Western companies began launching multiple series of communications satellites that had promoted the launch vehicle and broadcasting industries. In addition, military communications were augmented from outer space supporting global deployments. As a result, cryogenic engine technology attracted a premium. For example, India had the opportunity in the1970s to buy these engines from France for Rs 1 crore.[8] In the late 1980s, it quoted about Rs 900 crore for a few of these engines. India found the prices offered by France and the US exorbitant when Russia offered to sell two engines along with transfer of technology for Rs 235 crore. In 1990, India and Russia concluded a Rs 750-crore agreement for three cryogenic engines (two built in Russia with ISRO participation and one in India) with the first launch to take place in 1997.[9]

This deal, however, proved to be politically complicated because of the demise of the Soviet Union. The US imposed Missile Technology Control Regime (MTCR) sanctions on India and Russia in 1992 based on the regime's understanding that cryogenic engine technology would improve India's missile technology. As a result, India's access to cryogenic engine technology was blocked despite the technical consideration that these engines were no longer a design choice for building missiles. The

US sanctions and incentives supported the Russian administration to prevail over the supporters of the original deal leading to a new agreement in 1994 where India would buy only the manufactured engines.

Thereafter, India restarted its plan for developing the cryogenic engines indigenously. However, the programme experienced a series of failures delaying India's capability to reach the geostationary orbit independently and, therefore, rely on foreign launch service provider. Between 2001 and 2010, GSLV Mk II flew seven times but only two were successful. Two of the failures in 2006 and December 2010 showed major design flaws in the heritage launch modules with the rocket veering off the predicted trajectory after launch.[10] India's attempt to fly the indigenous cryogenic stage in April 2010 was also unsuccessful. After a gap of almost four years, the indigenously developed cryogenic stage performed successfully on GSLV-D5 in 2014. Since then, it had been performing successfully with the last three launches done in operational mode, although at a low rate of one launch per year. It is yet to obtain the expected launch cadence of two to three per year, as part of the accelerated launch plan of ISRO.[11]

The GSLV Mk II is capable of launching only 2.5 tonnes into the geostationary orbit, an initial target for India. With the satellites mass advancing faster than the capacity of launch vehicles, India's reliance on foreign launch vehicles continued. Recently, the Ariane 5 launched the 5.8-tonne GSAT-11 while the four tonne-capable GSLV Mk III was operationalised in late 2018. It uses CE-20, an advanced cryogenic engine designed and fabricated indigenously. Unlike GSLV Mk II, it had been flying successfully since 2017 and is planned to launch India's second mission to the moon in 2019. The Chandrayaan project was an initiative of geopolitical significance when the then Prime Minister Atal Bihari Vajpayee announced it in 2003 in response to China's announcement earlier that year to undertake human spaceflight.

The GSLV Mk III will be upgraded to launch 6 tonnes in 2021 by replacing the liquid core stage consisting of two Vikas engines with a semi-cryogenic engine and thereafter to 10 tonnes by using a cluster of semi-cryogenic engines.[12] A semi-cryogenic engine uses liquid oxygen and rocket grade kerosene instead of liquid hydrogen as fuel. This reduces design complexities as this blend of kerosene is available in liquid form at room temperature and, therefore, not requiring cooling. With this capability, the GSLV Mk III will also launch India's human spaceflight, which was earlier assigned to GSLV Mk II. The Indian government is supporting the GSLV Mk III by approving funds for 10 of these launch vehicles to be fabricated between 2019 and 2024.[13] The plan will allow ISRO to realise at least two GSLV Mk III launches per year as part of the accelerated launch plan. Moreover, the increase in payload capacity to six tonnes within this five-year plan could close the rocket-satellite gap and, therefore, relieve India from contracting foreign rockets.

However, realising a commercial GSLV Mk III launch could be an ambitious target within the approved plan. The demand for transponders either for commercial or government purposes is increasing and ISRO has already allotted two launches for testing the human spaceflight system and one launch for the actual mission. Therefore, ISRO is left with only seven of these rockets which could be fully allotted for meeting the national requirements. It remains to be seen if India will continue to procure foreign launch services as a result of this or the combination of increasing satellite mass, innovative use of frequency bands and electric propulsion could allow placing the requisite satellites using the remaining launches. ISRO could nevertheless demand additional funds for the GSLV Mk III in its annual budgets over the years to fabricate more of these rockets since the human spaceflight programme had been initiated by the Indian government after the allotment of the funds for the 10 GSLV Mk III rockets. However, ISRO will have to determine if it is capable of fabricating and launching more than two of these rockets per year.

The cryogenic engine development had been a tumultuous period in India's space programme. The cryogenic engine deal with Russia and the subsequent imposition of MTCR sanctions led to deterioration in India-US political relations. The Indian space programme lost valuable time in developing next generation rockets and placing enough transponders over India. Currently, India is still reliant on foreign transponders for its use. Despite the delay, the cryogenic engine development indigenously has made India self-sufficient in a high-end technology relieving it from being dependant on foreign assistance. The operationalisation and allotment of funds make the GSLV Mk III the next workhorse for India realising the domestic needs and foreign policy related objectives.

Reusable Launch Vehicle

The GSLV may not yet be a part of India's share of international commercial launch services industry. The PSLV, on the other hand, is competitive because of its reliability and low cost. The launch of 104 satellites, which are majorly small, and continuous improvements such as the fourth stage re-start capability helped it emerge as a primary choice for small satellite operators.[14] The demand for small satellites had increased exponentially over the last few years because of their relevance for satellite internet, Earth observation, Internet of Things etc. The business models require cheaper, frequent access to low Earth orbit, which the traditional launch vehicles were incapable of. Finding a ride-share with bigger satellites meant delays and inaccessibility to a variety of orbits for small satellites. In this context, India's low-cost PSLV launches became significant. However, the US maintains a ban on the PSLV because of the lack of a Commercial Space Launch Agreement with India. The American small satellite operators could obtain a one-time waiver to launch on the PSLV and the waivers are provided as the US did not possess a dedicated small satellite launch vehicle.

The Falcon rockets operated by SpaceX tried altering this situation. Elon Musk, founder of SpaceX, began developing reusable launch vehicles with the intent to lower the launch costs. In the traditional launch scenario, the launch modules are discarded after a single use. Musk questioned this model with the view that launch vehicles should be built and operated like airplanes, which are used multiple times by refuelling between flights and periodic maintenance. Reusability is not a new idea as the American space shuttles successfully proved this concept. However, the space shuttles failed to keep the cost of access to space low because of lower launch cadence and higher refurbishment costs. Musk, on the other hand, intends to reuse Falcon 9 at least 10 times without and up to a 100 times with refurbishment done under 24 hours. Over a minimum launch cadence, SpaceX is offering 30 per cent reduction on the current price of Falcon 9, which is currently at US$62 million.[15] The cost could be further reduced to US$37 million if the company transfers 100 per cent of the cost savings to its customers. The cost savings attracted satellite companies such as SES to fly on the reusable rockets. Musk intends to retrieve and reuse the upper stage as well as the payload fairings, making the Falcon 9 completely reusable and, therefore, further reduce the launch costs. The Falcon Heavy also used previously flown Falcon 9 core stages.

SpaceX developments in reusable launch technologies had induced similar experiments amongst major launch service providers such as Arianespace, India and China. ISRO began its reusable launch vehicle (RLV) programme in 2016 with the aim to bring down the launch cost to US$2,000 per kg.[16] The government had invested Rs 95 crore into the project and the first experiment of RLV technology demonstrator (RLV-TD) in the shape of a winged body tested the vehicle's performance during re-entry. The hypersonic profile, autonomous mission management and re-entry technologies were successfully flight tested.[17] The hypersonic experiment will be followed by runway landing, scramjet engine test etc. A scramjet absorbs atmospheric oxygen for combustion instead of carrying it onboard reducing the overall weight of the rocket and in turn increasing the payload capacity. It also decreases the turnaround time of the launch vehicle.

The flight proven, scaled up version of RLV-TD is expected to become part of India's future two-stage-to-orbit launch vehicle. The modularity, scramjet and reusable aspects of this launch vehicle allowing a higher launch frequency will make India's launch services economical and reliable in the international launch market. The existing launch vehicles such as PSLV and GSLV could also be made reusable with retrospective application of these technologies.

Space Sciences: Astrosat

Space sciences served as the foundation for India's space programme. Vikram Sarabhai's experiments with cosmic rays and his scientific credentials allowed him to establish ties with a number of leading scientists and international laboratories. This had emerged as an advantage when Thumba Equatorial Rocket Launching Station (TERLS) was being set up in the wake of International Geophysical Year 1957-58. The sounding rockets from the leading spacefaring nations such as the US, France and Russia were transferred to India for investigating cosmic rays and atmospheric phenomena. TERLS was itself later dedicated to the United Nations. The Indian space programme benefited from this activity developing satellite and launch vehicle technologies.[18] With increasing self-reliance in these technologies, investigating space sciences emerged as a fundamental objective of ISRO. In this context, it launched Astrosat in 2015 to study various astronomical objects in multiple wavelengths simultaneously such as stars, black holes etc. and also perform deep field survey of the Universe.[19] Astrosat allows Indian scientists to reduce their dependency on foreign telescopes and spacecraft for observing space. The new data helps original research and also international collaborations.

Astrosat represents a broader trend of India advancing its basic sciences. India became an associate member of European Organization for Nuclear Research (CERN) in 2017 and is supplying components such as the Cryosat to International Thermonuclear Experimental Reactor (ITER).[20] This reactor is being used to experiment with nuclear fusion, a process that sustains the Sun and is expected to reduce carbon emissions on Earth, if successfully adapted. Similarly, Astrosat made India part of an exclusive club of spacefaring nations with own space-based telescopes. For example, the Hubble is a well-known space telescope that has expanded science while capturing hearts and minds. This has the positive effect on space sciences, basic national science education and funding to space research organisations. Moreover, specific space telescopes have become instrumental in identifying distant planets and assessing the probability of presence of water. Based on Astrosat's success and the increasing significance of space telescopes for finding habitable planets, ISRO has decided on the follow-up mission Astrosat 2.

Human Space Mission

Another area that has gained recent attention within the Indian space establishment is the human space mission. Modi in his Independence Day speech to the nation announced that India will launch its first manned space mission by 2022. He also added that as India celebrates the 75th year of its independence, there will be an Indian astronaut aboard Gaganyaan, the Indian manned space vehicle, 'unfurl[ing] the Tricolour in space'.[21] A successful manned mission will assure India a place among the handful of countries that have achieved such a feat. So far, India has a lone astronaut—Rakesh Sharma, an Indian Air Force pilot—who went to space on a Soyuz T-11 for eight days in 1984.

For long, ISRO has held the view that manned missions are not a priority as it brings no major technological spin-offs.[22] Instead, ISRO's focus has always been on space applications with day-to-day relevance in the social and economic growth story of India. There are also many who will raise questions such as the utility of a manned mission and criticise it as driven by prestige than any tangible benefits. While manned space missions may not bring any direct benefits, they are particularly important in the context of rekindling public imagination and get the next generation excited about space and science. Nevertheless, the project will help create around 15,000 jobs in the coming years as the entire programme will depend on technology developed indigenously. In a defensive style, ISRO Chairman Dr K. Sivan proactively defended that Gaganyaan will be a 'national project and not just ISRO's'.[23] The astronauts who will be part of this mission will reportedly undertake many experiments although ISRO has not provided more information as of now.

While manned space missions have not been a priority, ISRO has been engaged in some research for this project. Financial constraints have been a factor for the limited endeavour on this. Back in December 2013, then Vikram Sarabhai Space Centre (VSSC) Director S.

Ramakrishnan had stated that 'it would take 10 years for India to undertake human space flight'.[24] Previous United Progressive Alliance (UPA) government had allocated Rs1.45 billion (US$20.68 million) to undertake pre-launch work.[25] Meanwhile, ISRO has also been developing and testing some of the critical technologies for the mission, using around Rs 600 million from its internal Research and Development (R&D) budget.[26] There is no open information on the budget estimate for the manned mission, but reports citing internal sources indicate it to be around Rs 100 million to 120 million.[27] As done in the case of the Mars mission, ISRO will be using one of the in-house rockets to keep the costs down. Some of the former ISRO officials said the mission could possibly use the GSLV Mk III, which is India's heaviest rocket. Previously, ISRO had used the GSLV Mk III[28] to test an early model of the Crew module in the Crew module Atmospheric Re-entry Experiment (CARE) test in December 2014.[29] This was a test done to validate the operational aspects of the parachute-based deceleration system as well as to study the re-entry aerothermodynamics.

While a few experiments and tests have been done to prepare for the manned mission, there remains a lot to be accomplished in the next three years. Key technological tests to be done in preparation for a manned mission include the Crew Module System, Crew Escape System and Environmental Control and Life Support System (ECLSS). ISRO has tested so far only the Crew Escape System and the Crew module Atmospheric Re-entry Experiment (CARE). In July 2018, ISRO did a successful technology validation of the Crew Escape System, where an emergency escape system, to get the astronauts out of the launch vehicle should there be a launch abort, was tested. Earlier in December 2014, a CARE mission was tested, separating the crew module from the launch vehicle at an altitude of 126 kilometres and a re-entry into the Earth's atmosphere at an altitude of 80 kilometres.[30] Further, according to the latest annual report (2017-18) of the Department of Space, there are many other sub-systems of ECLSS such as Thermal and Humidity Control System (THCS), CO_2 and Odor Removal System (CORS) and Cabin Pressure Control System (CPCS) that are being 'integrated into Cabin Environment

Simulation Chamber simulating the Crew cabin volume and integrated tests are in progress'.[31]

Conclusion

India's space programme began with the social and development challenges in mind, and it must be reiterated that the initial focus has not changed. India is still a developing country and the efforts to uplift the lives of its people using space technologies will continue to be a key driving factor. For instance, the ISRO's focus in developing GSAT-9, GSAT-29, GSAT-11 and GSAT-20 (to be launched later in September 2019) is to enable digital India. These satellites together will provide around 70-100 GB per second data link.[32] Nevertheless, India cannot remain oblivious to the emerging challenges in the security and strategic domains in the Indo-Pacific region. In fact, the changing security dynamics in the broader region will compel India to re-orient its space programme to developing certain military characteristics to its space programme. While militarisation of space is a reality with militaries around the world using space assets for passive military applications, the growing trend with regard to space weaponization is particularly of concern to India.

India's growing space prowess has made it a significant actor in global technological clubs. Technology denial had indeed become a blessing in disguise elevating India's own research and development potential and relieving the nation from dependence on foreign countries. The cryogenic engine technology remains the most discussed aspect of this phenomenon. Denial of this technology had created serious setbacks to India's space programme but that also helped India develop these technologies indigenously, thus deriving many spin-off benefits.

The GSLV Mk II, which had been subject to sanctions, had suffered a series of setbacks. However, the recent launch validated the claim that India now possesses indigenous cryogenic technology, as continuous modifications to the rocket are being successfully flight tested. The biggest impact, however, is on India's next generation launch vehicle GSLV Mk III. This rocket had been flying successfully since inception and made India self-reliant in launching four-tonne satellites. In addition to improvements to these rockets, India is also experimenting with reusable technologies to bring down the launch costs. This also allows India to compete better in the international launch market. In addition to technologies, India is also stressing the importance of space sciences by launching relevant spacecraft such as the Astrosat. Space science has helped India gain mastery in satellite and launch technologies and they are in turn helping advance astronomy and science popularisation.

So, ISRO has come a long way since the first satellite launch in 1975 and the GSLV, the successful Mars mission and the plans for a Venus mission demonstrate the steady growth and sophistication of India's space prowess. Along with the development of the technological wherewithal, ISRO also needs to get proactive in the policy realm. Within the policy spectrum, there is an urgent need for India to provide appropriate space to the private sector so that ISRO can focus on larger, common-interest areas such as space exploration and the private sector can pursue some of the tried and tested programmes such as the PSLV. ISRO must develop a strong regulatory framework, creating a level playing field for the private sector. India's space policy proactivism should also expand to the global governance domain especially as the competition in this global commons is picking up greater traction.

NOTES

1 'Space Activities Bill', Press Information Bureau, Government of India, Department of Space, 12 December 2018, http://pib.nic.in/newsite/PrintRelease.aspx?relid=186315; 'Draft Space Activities Bill, 2017', Government of India, Department of Space, 21 November 2017 http://www.prsindia.org/sites/default/files/bill_files/Draft%20Space%20Activities%20Bill%202017.pdf

2 'Dr Vikram Sarabhai (1963-1971),' Indian Space Research Organisation, https://www.isro.gov.in/about-isro/dr-vikram-ambalal-sarabhai-1963-1971

3 Narandra Modi, 'Text of Prime Minister Shri Narendra Modi's address on the historical success of Mars Orbiter Mission (MOM) in Martian orbit,' 24 September 2014, https://www.narendramodi.in/prime-minister-shri-narendra-modis-address-on-the-historic-successful-insertion-of-mars-orbiter-mission-mom-into-martian-orbit-2866

4 '[PSLC C-25/ Mars Orbiter Mission] Mission Objectives,' Indian Space Research Organisation, https://www.isro.gov.in/pslv-c25-mars-orbiter-mission/mission-objectives

[5] 'NASA Awards Launch Services Contract for Maven Mission,' NASA Science, Mars Exploration Program, 21 October 2010, https://mars.nasa.gov/news/1454/nasa-awards-launch-services-contract-for-maven-mission/

[6] 'Announcement of Opportunity (AO) to international science community for Space-Based Experiments to Study Venus,' Department of Space, Indian Space Research Organisation, https://www.isro.gov.in/sites/default/files/ao_venus.pdf

[7] 'Announcement of Opportunity (AO) for Space-Based Experiments to Study Venus,' Department of Space, Indian Space Research Organisation, https://www.isro.gov.in/announcement-of-opportunity-ao-space-based-experiments-to-study-venus

[8] Nambi Narayanan and Arun Ram, *Ready To Fire: How India and I Survived the ISRO Spy Case* (Bloomsbury India: New Delhi, 2018)

[9] Vasudevan Mukunth, 'U.R. Rao, ISRO Chairman Who Helped India's Space Programme Settle Down,' *The Wire*, 24 July 2017, https://thewire.in/science/ur-rao-isro-aslv-unispace-cryogenic

[10] 'List of GSLV Launches,' Indian Space Research Organisation, https://www.isro.gov.in/launchers/list-of-gslv-launches

[11] 'ISRO Planning At Least Two GSLV-MkII Launches Every Year,' *The Wire*, 10 September 2016, https://thewire.in/space/isro-gslv-mkii-cryogenic

[12] T. Nandakumar, 'ISRO to bank on semi-cryogenic engine for heavy lift rockets,' *The Hindu*, 17 June 2017, https://www.thehindu.com/sci-tech/science/isro-to-bank-on-semi-cryogenic-engine-for-heavy-lift-rockets/article19095367.ece

[13] 'Cabinet approves Continuation Programme for Geosynchronous Satellite Launch Vehicle Mark-III,' Press Information Bureau, 6 June 2018, http://pib.nic.in/newsite/PrintRelease.aspx?relid=179807

[14] 'PSLV Upper Stage Engines (PS4) successfully restarted in space,' Indian Space Research Organisation, https://www.isro.gov.in/pslv-upper-stage-engines-ps4-successfully-restarted-space

[15] Peter B. de Selding, 'SpaceX's reusable Falcon 9: What are the real cost savings for customers?,' *Space News*, 25 April 2016, https://spacenews.com/spacexs-reusable-falcon-9-what-are-the-real-cost-savings-for-customers/

[16] Dennis Jesudasan, 'Indigenous technology demonstrator of reusable launch vehicle tested successfully,' *The Hindu*, 23 May 2016, https://www.thehindu.com/sci-tech/science/india-successfully-launches-reusable-launch-vehicle/article8635448.ece

[17] 'RLV-TD,' Indian Space Research Organisation, 23 May 2016, https://www.isro.gov.in/launcher/rlv-td

[18] 'The Profile,' Vikram Sarabhai Space Centre, http://isrohq.vssc.gov.in/VSSC_V4/index.php/about-isro/genesis

[19] 'Astrosat Mission,' Indian Space Research Organisation, https://www.isro.gov.in/astrosat-0

[20] 'India delivering components for largest fusion energy project,' *The Economic Times*, 27 June 2016, https://economictimes.indiatimes.com/industry/energy/

power/india-delivering-components-for-largest-fusion-energy-project/articleshow/52943379.cms

21 Full Text of PM Modi's Independence Day Speech,' *The Indian Express*, 16 August 2018, https://indianexpress.com/article/india/prime-minister-modi-independence-day-speech-red-fort-5308847/

22 Ajay Sukumaran, 'Satellites Are Our Priority Now, Not Human Space Flight,' An Exclusive Interview with ISRO Chairman A.S. Kiran Kumar, *Outlook India*, 13 July 2017, https://www.outlookindia.com/magazine/story/satellites-are-our-priority-now-not-human-space-flight/299103

23 Vaibhav Tiwari (with inputs from IANS), 'Indian Space Agency's Manned Mission Will Create 15,000 Jobs, Says Chief,' *NDTV*, 15 August 2018, https://www.ndtv.com/india-news/indian-space-agencys-manned-mission-will-create-15-000-jobs-says-chief-1901032

24 'ISRO Gearing Up for Space Capsule Recovery Experiment,' *The Hindu*, 21 December 2013, https://www.thehindu.com/sci-tech/science/isro-gearing-up-for-space-capsule-recovery-experiment/article5484393.ece

25 Chetan Kumar, 'India to launch first manned space mission by 2022: PM Modi,' *The Times of India*, 15 August 2018, https://timesofindia.indiatimes.com/india/india-to-launch-first-manned-space-mission-by-2022-pm-modi/articleshow/65410373.cms

26 Chetan Kumar, 'PM vows to put Indians in space by 2022, Isro begins the long trek,' *The Times of India*, 15 August 2018, https://timesofindia.indiatimes.com/india/pm-vows-to-put-indians-in-space-by-2022-isro-begins-the-long-trek/articleshow/65414878.cms

27 Chetan Kumar, 'India to launch first manned space mission by 2022: PM Modi,' *The Times of India*, 15 August 2018, https://timesofindia.indiatimes.com/india/india-to-launch-first-manned-space-mission-by-2022-pm-modi/articleshow/65410373.cms

28 'Isro readying GSLV-Mark III for human space flight: K. Kasturirangan,' *PTI*, 9 June 2017, https://www.livemint.com/Science/OJPI57NxvOLOVdiSDa0gsK/Isro-readying-GSLVMark-III-for-human-space-flight-K-Kastu.html

29 'Crew module Atmospheric Re-entry Experiment (CARE),' Department of Space, Indian Space Research Organisation, https://www.isro.gov.in/Spacecraft/crew-module-atmospheric-re-entry-experiment-care

30 'Crew module Atmospheric Re-entry Experiment (CARE),' Department of Space, Indian Space Research Organisation, https://www.isro.gov.in/Spacecraft/crew-module-atmospheric-re-entry-experiment-care

31 Annual Report 2017-2018, Government of India, Department of Space, https://www.isro.gov.in/sites/default/files/article-files/node/9805/annualreport2017-18.pdf

32 Pallava Bagla, 'ISRO To Launch 10 Missions In 100 Days, Satellite Internet To Make Debut,' *NDTV*, 20 November 2018, https://www.ndtv.com/science/isro-to-launch-10-missions-in-100-days-satellite-internet-to-make-debut-1950013

5

Countering Terrorism in India: The Challenges of Ad-hoc Policies

Kabir Taneja

COUNTERING terrorism has become the focus point of global security debates over the past two decades. While the problem of terrorism has been plaguing states around the world for a long time now, the United Nations (UN) at its home in New York and the global moral and ethical authority, by design, has been the venue where many countries, including India, tried and failed for years to underline the lingering threats that non-state militant actors posed to the very idea of a nation state. Terrorism has now become the biggest political and security challenge of the twenty-first century.

According to the 2018 Global Terrorism Index, India went up one space from the previous year to number seven in the rankings of countries most affected by terrorism, defeating even Yemen, currently in the grasp of a civil war, which came in at eight.[1] The threat perception was ranked as 'high', shy by just one place to be categorised under the 'very high' bracket where the likes of Iraq, Syria and Pakistan reside. This showcases the linear manner in which the number of terror attacks in India during the past two years have taken place, and the continuity of the same illustrates both the magnitude of the issue, the time frame over which this has escalated and the continuation of lack of institutionalised policies and frameworks to tackle these threats.

Conceptually, of course, non-state militant actors are relatively weak in nature, often working largely in a limited geographical space and political argument, coupled with basic funding, and in most cases, some sort of state backing.[2] While one finds arguments differentiating militancy and terrorism, the means to the end of both remain the same and much of the differentiation is confined to the academic world and not the operational one. The method of studying contemporary terrorism is generally divided into two eras—one after the attacks of 11 September 2001 (often referred to as 9/11) on the United States of America leading to the 'global war on terror' and one that predates 9/11.

The issue of terrorism in the international community has been a point of contention for years, with the definition of 'terrorism' itself—what it stands for and what it entails—being mired in the quagmire of geo-politics and individualistic interests of nation states as state-sponsored terrorism and state-supported militancy became a trusted, low-cost tool of war and instability in many regions. This problem of definitions exists in both the world of realpolitik and academia alike, as policymakers, politicians and researchers attempt to categorise and have a universal guideline to combat terrorism. The fact that much of these debates exclusively revolve around Islamist terrorism has only muddled the processes even further, and the failure of the UN to not just gain consensus but also recognise the challenges every individual or institution faces only compounds the problem. Global efforts to address these concerns can be highlighted by a common saying amongst scholars from this field, that 'one man's terrorist is another's freedom fighter', an argument that helps underline as to why the UN has failed on a mutual definition and why others who do not believe the UN to be non-partisan in these debates either ignore or set up alternative forums.

It is also arguable that the word terrorism is not one-dimensional, and many other political concepts have far too many understandings attached to the term. For example, in the media, acts of terror have often been labelled under various terms that could allow both either dissolving or amplifying the narratives around such an event. During terror strikes in India, foreign media outlets have often been forced to re-evaluate terminologies after public criticism and accusations of double standards for using the term 'terrorist' for certain cases and 'militant', 'gunman' and other such words for certain cases.[3] Newspapers have often used multiple terms to discuss the same event within a single report, showcasing the wide-ranging effects of the issues an undefined political act of violence creates. For example, in November 2018 security forces shot and killed Lashkar-e-Taiba (LeT) commander Naveed Jatt, with media using both 'militant' and 'terrorist' to describe him, showing the ad-hoc use of the terms.

From an Indian context, an official definition of terrorism is consequential to policy formation and implementation. In public discourse, terrorism has been seen, felt and experienced, from the daily degrees of cross-border terror attacks in Kashmir emitting from the state sanctioned policies of Pakistan to create menace in the state and the de facto Line of Control (LoC) to the audacious 2008 Mumbai attacks (26/11). India's counter-terror narratives are far more complex than those faced by Western states, at least in the pre-Islamic State era which began in 2014 and can be seen as a pivotal border before which terrorism was dealt differently and after which many of the traditional approaches in both intelligence and military operations were deemed obsolete and forced to change.

To colour these grey areas further, in Indian public discourse, the term 'terrorism' or 'terrorist' is usually used more in the context of Kashmir, specifically due to the Pakistani state-sponsored cross-border nature of the situation in the state. Despite previous distinctions, 26/11 changed the vocabulary to a more strengthened and clearer format.[4] It is imperative to remember here that there are no set guidelines for the same, and media houses use terminologies on a case-to-case or report-to-report basis (the BBC has set guidelines on use of the word 'terror', which offers an interesting peek into the organisation's approach on trying to differentiate these terms).[5] For example, while the term 'terrorists' is commonly used for cases in Kashmir, other insurgencies such as in the North Eastern states of India, the preferred term is 'militants'. While these two regions have organised narratives now, the far-left insurgencies in Indian states such as Chhattisgarh etc. use only the term 'Naxals' to accommodate their narratives, sifting away from labelling them either terrorists or militants. Here, 'Naxal', named after the region Naxalbari in

West Bengal, has over time become a verb instead, having its own independent identity.

However, defining terror only from the pretext of Kashmir from an Indian perspective could be seen as flawed approach. In India's North East, many states are facing violent insurgency and secessionist movements against the state. Groups such as the United Liberation Front of Assam (ULFA), the National Socialist Council of Nagaland (NSCN) (which is now divided into two factions, discussed later in this chapter) and other smaller factions also add to India's anti-terror narratives and policies, but tend to be overshadowed by the question of Kashmir. The fallacies between terrorism, insurgencies and so on between two domestic landscapes give one a quick idea on how large the challenge of building narratives against terror in the international arena is. This is also a policy crisis India has suffered from. While new agencies to fight terrorism have been developed, specifically in the realms of cybserspace, signal intelligence and so on, their effective utilisation and successful institutional intra-agency quorum still leave much to be desired.[6]

Political scientist Boaz Ganor in his works has divided the need to define both 'terrorism' and 'counter-terrorism' into a set of parameters that play critical roles in moving the discourse towards a set definition. For a 'terrorism' definition, Ganor highlights six levels of action that could be found at the core of an official terminology, legislative action, punitive action, international cooperation, offensive action, actions directed towards terrorism-supporting populations and public relations activity.[7] It is important to note that theology or ideological clarity on terrorism is not necessary to define it, but the act of violence in itself supersedes arguments on the why and the how. The legal frameworks around implicating terrorists today are based on a single country's ideas and laws, which rely more on a state's outlook not just on terrorism but its political aims as well, leaving the terminology at the mercy of various interpretations.

Within India, systems to tackle terror legally have faced tremendous debate and often pushback for the fear of persecution of communities, protecting constitutional liberties while balancing national security concerns. From a legislative point of view, which features heavily in Ganor's approach, India has been both politically and socially at loggerheads on its laws and how to deal with terrorism. The first such instance was witnessed after the assassination of Prime Minister Indira Gandhi in 1984 at the hands of her own Sikh bodyguards, and the ensuing Khalistani terror movement in the state of Punjab. One of the results of this event was the Terrorist and Disruptive Activities (Prevention) Act, or TADA in short. This act was seen, at that time, as an extension of the Emergency era thinking, which saw the suspension of the Indian Constitution between 1975 and 1977 orchestrated by Indira Gandhi, and the intellectual discourse saw the act as a regressive way to counter terrorism which, at that time, was mostly comprised of domestic insurgencies against the state. For example, Section 21 of TADA presumed that the accused were guilty and the defendant had no automatic right to face his or her accuser.[8] By 1994, as many as 76,000 people had been arrested under TADA, with only one per cent of these facing charges. In 1995, under public pressure, the government of then Prime Minister P.V. Narasimha Rao revoked TADA.[9]

Fast forward less than a decade and the threat of terrorism itself had changed, as Islamist terrorism developed a global footprint. After the 2001 attack on the Indian Parliament, a successor to TADA called the Prevention of Terror Act (POTA) was installed. Like TADA, POTA as well faced many hurdles, and was accused of being too sweeping in its mandate, allowing it to be abused by both security agencies and politicians alike. However, it was applied under the BJP-led coalition government of Prime Minister Atal Bihari Vajpayee, but later repealed by the government of Prime Minister Manmohan Singh in 2004, as the Congress party blamed agencies and states for misusing it to arrest high profile political opponents and innocent civilians alike.

The above highlighted challenges are the philosophical debates that are equally important to counter-terror policies as a military or law-enforcement led response. For example, while the crisis in Kashmir has cross-border support for terrorism at the centre of it, domestic grievances and local political and ideological narratives also play a large role.

The Terror—Counter-Terror Divide under Modi

If you don't know where you're going, every road will get you nowhere

—Henry Kissinger

From India's eyes, the word terrorism largely emits from its experiences in Kashmir and the fractured relationship with its nuclear-armed neighbour, Pakistan. Having fought three wars with Pakistan, the latter over the years has perfected the art of using terror as a state policy, cornering India into a state of play where the option of a full-blown conventional war is largely off the table due to the nuclear capabilities of both India and Pakistan. This deterrence, from Indian perspective, was designed to counter the two-front nuclear borders of India, Pakistan on one side and overall the bigger threat, China on the other. The fact that China is Pakistan's biggest supporter and confidante not only helps sustain a narrative around Islamabad's version of 'counter-terrorism' but Beijing's unparalleled support for Pakistan also brings up a significant challenge to India's anti-terror narratives across multilateral platforms.

The 2014 general elections in India were seen as somewhat of a line in the sand, with expected changes in the country's political postures, specifically when national security is concerned. The elections saw the loss of the Indian National Congress (INC), which under the leadership of Prime Minister Manmohan Singh, had been in power since 2004 and got involved in various corruption scandals. The Bharatiya Janata Party (BJP), led by the then Chief Minister of the prosperous state of Gujarat Narendra Modi was viewed as a harbinger of a fresh perspective on national security and capable of responding to Pakistan's threats in a more robust and direct manner than what the Congress had managed, specifically after the 26/11 Mumbai attacks.

The BJP won the elections with a majority in Parliament, not having to rely on smaller parties to support it via a coalition, making such a situation possible for the first time since 1984. The nature of the BJP as a political party, a nationalist-Hindu conglomerate reliant on its *karyakartas* (ground workers) and expected to champion national interests and national security better than its opponents, has been highlighted in some decisions the Modi government has made over the past five years in both Kashmir and the North East, albeit both instances having divergent approaches on countering insurgencies and terrorism.

As previously mentioned, India's approach to countering terror is vastly different to the American-led global war on terror, which has itself led to significantly less dividends than Western coalitions may have hoped for, with Afghanistan standing tall as an example of a failed war against the Taliban now entering its 18th year without any resolution in sight.

While India has suffered terror attacks regularly through the 1990s, the Mumbai bomb blasts of 1992, the attack on the Indian Parliament in 2001 (a mere month after 9/11) and attacks on Delhi, Hyderabad and other Indian cities at regular intervals, Indian policymakers failed to evolve long-term plans, systems and policies to counter terrorism. Much of the reactions historically have been ad-hoc, and this trend remains to this day, with announcement of new plans, agencies, weapons, technologies and so on commemorating both a lack of ideation on what exactly India, with its available capacities, can do regarding Pakistan's support for terrorism and the fact that its policies only find semblance by the Chinese support it gains both economically and politically, with the latter more than happy to use Pakistan as a counter to keep India engaged on both fronts.

The divisions between the forms of terror that India has to fight do not make the job easier for any all-encompassing policy. The Modi government was expected to fill this void but its performance too has been underwhelming. While Kashmir remains the harbinger of almost every counter-terror policy India has, the rise of global jihadist groups such as the Islamic State of Iraq and the Levant (ISIS/ISIL), known as *Daesh* in Arabic, single-handedly made much of the global counter-terror practices obsolete.[10]

The distinction between global jihadist groups and the ones India fight on a daily basis on its borders with Pakistan are vast, both ideologically and militarily, and pose a new set of daunting challenges despite traditional counter-terror operations still being conducted largely on an ad-hoc basis. Such an approach to these threats has been unsustainable, and have cost India in terms of vast amounts to the exchequer and more importantly, in the number of lives lost. While it can be argued that India's military-heavy approach to counter terrorism has also saved thousands of lives, both civilian and military, the fact remains that the policies currently in place seem comfortable with a status-quo, accepting that the state of Jammu & Kashmir and other Indian cities are susceptible to frequent violence of various magnitudes both from the level of stone pelting in the Valley to 26/11 in Mumbai. It is equally pertinent to observe the fact that no major terror attack on an Indian city outside Jammu and Kashmir has taken place in the last five years.

The rise of the so-called Islamic State, officiated over by its self-declared caliph, Abu Bakr al-Baghdadi at the Al Nuri mosque in the northern Iraqi city of Mosul in 2014, was an event that would change counter-terror practices and narratives world over. The so-called Islamic State captured and plundered territory at a breakneck pace, leaving the international community and its response to it delayed as the world grappled with this new jihadist entity which, by the end of 2015, controlled combined territory in Iraq and Syria roughly the same size as the United Kingdom.[11] However, ISIS was not just another terror organisation such as its peers in al-Qaeda or the Taliban. In fact it had its own share of differences with them, but its global ambitions compared to Osama bin Laden's limited anti-US and anti-Israel fixations.

India's reaction against the threat of ISIS was lax, and largely failed to understand the disruptions this new terror group had created which contested the traditions of geographical boundaries by using the general open source nature of the internet, and the free highways of information. The terror group, while not concentrating heavily on making a presence in the sub-continent, showcased its ability to influence operations, more specifically, individuals, to undertake low-cost terror strike that cost the price of a broadband connection bill. India's response to this international terror threat was driven by two factors: first being national security, and second the fact that it had more than seven million of its citizens working in the larger West Asian region. However, it till date lacks the sense of urgency, with terror groups often out-manoeuvring Indian intelligence agencies on the online front, and the lethargic manner in which this new threat is being addressed.

Nonetheless, India was one of the least affected countries from ISIS's rise and the attacks conducted in the terror group's name in major cities around the world. The fact that there have been less than 190 pro-ISIS cases in the country and less than 30 of those attempted to travel to Iraq or Syria to join ISIS is a tribute to India's ability to manage pluralism more effectively than most other societies of similar diversity.[12] The Indian Muslim population, second largest in the world only next to Indonesia, straightforwardly rejected the ideology ISIS propagated. This allowed Indian intelligence agencies to set up targeted perimeters from 2013 onwards at airports to monitor Indian travellers, specifically single males going to the Middle East. As the years went by, Indian intelligence got stricter with its arrests of suspected ISIS sympathisers, which in turn started to dissuade people from looking to travel to the 'caliphate' as per multiple case accounts accessed by the author. Beyond intelligence, states such as Andhra Pradesh, Telangana and Kerala developed successful de-radicalisation programmes, a rarity in this field of study, which became models for other states to follow as well.

Currently, no white paper or an overview on India's aims, motives and ideas to countering terrorism both on domestic and international realms exists. From its Kashmir policies to its Afghanistan outreach, combating these narratives both politically and militarily is decided and based on other state's actions. While India's cross-border counter-terror operations from a military perspective on the Pakistan border take place primarily as reactions, India has conducted operations against insurgencies in the North East, including crossing over the sovereign boundaries of Myanmar to target insurgents from the National Socialist Council of Nagaland (NSCN-K), a pro-Naga state group dedicated to the Naga tribe in search for an independent state of Greater Nagaland, putting together the Naga inhabited regions in India and Myanmar run by Naga patriarch S.S. Khaplang, a Burmese Naga, who died in 2017.

In 2015, NSCN-K, which had dishonoured a 14-year-old ceasefire agreement with New Delhi, conducted a terror strike against an Indian Army convoy of the 6 Dogra Regiment in the Chandel district of the state of Manipur, killing 18 soldiers. The Indian Army reacted with a 'surgical strike' across the Myanmar border, hitting NSCN-K camps around 15 km inside the Burmese jungle. The operation, which reportedly took 40 minutes, is known to have neutralised nearly 50 members of the NSCN-K and the Kanglei Yawwol Kanna Lup (KYKL),[13] an anti-state revolutionary movement in Manipur. The operation could today be seen as the first instance of Prime Minister Narendra Modi's electoral promises of strengthened national security aims, specifically against terrorism as he blamed the Congress party and government of Prime Minister Manmohan Singh for security failures that led to 26/11. The Myanmar operation was conducted under then General Officer Commanding (GoC) of the Dimapur-based 3rd Corps, General Bipin Rawat, who was later appointed Chief of Army Staff in December 2016. Using these operations on a regular basis, the government has recaliberated the tolerance levels against terror strikes of both the political ecosystem and the average citizen of the country. This not only highlights a greater will to confront terror from the forefront, but also forces the global community to confront the entrenched state-sponsored terrorism that is inflicted on India from across the border. This direct confrontation gives the global community fewer excuses of not acting against Islamabad for the part it plays in the Islamist industrial complex.

Surgical Strikes, Modi and India's Counter-Terror Apparatus

In September 2016, Indian troops stepped across the Line of Control (LoC) in Jammu and Kashmir and orchestrated another 'surgical strike', targeting terrorist launch pads in the aftermath of a terror strike against a military base in Uri, which killed 19 soldiers and left Indian intelligence in an embarrassing situation as militants struck at an opportune time when a change of guard was taking place.

The year 2016 turned out to be a watershed year, with two major attacks on Indian military installations. On 2 January of that year, heavily armed terrorists attacked the Pathankot Air Force Station in the state of Punjab, one of the more significant forward bases of the Indian Air Force's Western Command. The attack saw terrorists successfully challenge the base's defences and enter the facility, and the siege lasting three days before the last of the five attackers (reports suggest there could have been more who escaped or aided them from outside) were killed. However, the attack could be deemed as a success for the attackers, as eight personnel of the Indian armed forces were killed along with leaving the military red-faced by successfully defeating their defences at one of its major bases. This raised many questions on both the military front and counter-terrorism and intelligence front, as to what institutional failures allowed not just the attack to happen in the first place, but so cravenly defeat Indian defences.

While these questions were being raised, another attack of a larger magnitude took place in Uri, Kashmir, on 18 September of the same year, with even more devastating results. This was also a period when a general uptick in militancy was being observed in Jammu and Kashmir, with the killing of terrorist Burhan Wani, a commander of the banned outfit Hizbul Mujahideen, who took a leaf from the operational book of ISIS and used the internet to bolster his popularity. Wani was killed on 8 July, leading to widespread protests in the Valley, adding further complications in Indian contextualising of counter-terror approach. The protests led to thousands being injured and reportedly dozens of civilians killed.

The Modi government's response to the surgical strikes across the LoC can be seen from three perspectives of counter-terrorism, strategic leverage and diplomatic narratives, with the operations themselves dividing both civilian and military discourse on what they aimed to achieve. The debate shifted from Indian counter-terror posture being largely based around management of the fallout of terror strikes to that of prevention.

The Indian military and political establishments have had distinctive interpretations on what these strikes mean, and what they achieved. The effectiveness of these actions purely from a counter-terror front are statistically questionable, as more than 230 terrorists were reportedly killed in Kashmir in 2018.[14] The upward trajectory has been continuous for a while, as in 2017, the year after the surgical strikes, a 166 per cent rise in civilian casualties was observed as a result of terror or counter-terror operations. In 2016, 150 terrorists were reportedly killed in the Valley, while 2017 saw the neutralisation of 213 terrorists.[15] The number of terrorist attacks after the surgical strikes remained constant, with a slight increase. In 2016, a total of 322 incidents of terror were reported while 2017 saw 342 such incidents. While the number of casualties observed in the armed forces decreased during this period, the number of attacks saw no major swing raising questions on the effectiveness of the surgical strikes.

The strikes served a bigger political purpose for the Modi government than a purely strategic one as it was promoted in public discourse as India hitting back at Pakistan after years of allowing Islamabad to get away with its sponsorship of cross-border terrorism. The precedence that the surgical strikes set in 2016 was built upon in 2019. On 14 February, a convoy of the CRPF travelling on the Jammu–Srinagar national highway was attacked by a vehicle-borne suicide bomber which resulted in the death of more than 40 soldiers. The terror attack was claimed by Pakistan-based Jaish-e-Mohammed (JeM), and was conducted by a Kashmiri youth, Adil Ahmad Dar, from the state's Pulwama district. The Pulwama attack became the worst attack against Indian security establishment in Kashmir since 1989, and generated unparalleled public outcry. The Modi government, mere two months away from general elections, found itself in a bind on what sort of reaction it should initiate, whether one that is diplomatic or one that is military. New Delhi chose to go with a mix of both, with the latter taking precedence on the global stage.

On 26 February, 12 days after the Pulwama terror strike, Indian Air Force jets conducted a bombing run at Balakot, in Pakistan's Khyber-Pakhtunwa province. These strikes shattered many glass ceilings in the

India–Pakistan dynamic and built narratives now to be considered a 'new normal' of directly targeting terror infrastructure not just across the Line of Control (LoC) but beyond international borders. The raid reportedly targeted a JeM training camp, and as per some officially unconfirmed reports created fatalities nearing the 300 mark. Technically, this could be classified as a counter-terror strike by India. However, from this particular perspective it also raises the viability and realistic use of air power as a counter-terror tool from here on as part of a 'new normal' thinking.

The fact that the Indian Air Force Mirage 2000 fighter jets were able to break Pakistani air defences without detection until a later stage is first and foremost a (rare) victory on the intelligence front. The fact that India knew the exact potential of Pakistan's defence systems and the ways to avoid it for such a raid was a critical achievement. However, it can be argued that New Delhi's plans of one-upping Islamabad, either diplomatically or militarily was short-changed a day after Balakot, when during a rare air combat between the two countries, India lost a MiG 21 after it was shot down during a dog fight with a Pakistani jet, and its pilot taken into custody. Despite the pilot's release a day later, the narrative around the Balakot strike slipped from the Indian hands significantly, despite efforts to maintain its claims of both imparting damage to terror strongholds in the country and also claiming to shooting down a Pakistani F-16.[16]

However, these strikes will be difficult to develop as a 'new normal' in counter-terror methods. First and foremost, despite taking advantage of the lack of air-defence preparedness of Pakistan, the attacks will now force them to plug these issues on a war footing. Second, unlike other theatres such as those in the Middle East, Afghanistan or the African Sahel where Western forces use air power effectively against terror groups, Pakistani terror groups such as JeM and LeT conduct terror strikes under the safety of Pakistan's nuclear umbrella which ties India's hands significantly on what kind of response it can orchestrate as far as counter-terror strikes go. Balakot was a success in signalling, a departure from any lazy interpretations in Islamabad and Rawalpindi that India would not react in face of attacks such as Pulwama. How much of this can be an institutionalised military response from India for the future remains a much debated issue, and will remain so for the time to come.

Apart from the military front, perhaps one of the largest successes of the Balakot strikes took place on the diplomatic stage, where Delhi has managed to make terrorism and by association the isolation of Pakistan the core mantra of its global outreach. While not as ostentatious as a dog fight in the Himalayas, the international support New Delhi gathered against Pakistan and its harbouring of JeM chief Masood Azhar, whose organisation claimed credit for the Pulwama attack, was a window into the heft that now backs Indian diplomatic outreach. Mere hours after the Balakot strikes, Minister of External Affairs Sushma Swaraj landed in Abu Dhabi to represent India which was for the first time invited as the Guest of Honour to address the inaugural plenary of the Organisation of Islamic Cooperation (OIC). This was a full circle in the making for India, as after 50 years, when Pakistan scuttled India's invitation to the first OIC plenary in September 1969 at Rabat, Morocco[17], this time Islamabad's calls to some of its closest allies in the Gulf to cancel New Delhi's invitation fell on deaf ears. Pakistan's representation at Abu Dhabi was an empty seat.

Beyond the OIC, nations rallied behind India's narrative of sanctioning Masood Azhar. France was one of the first countries to impose sanctions on Azhar, and freeze his assets, followed by Germany with Berlin initiating a move at the EU to designate Azhar a global terrorist. Prior to this, China had stalled a France-UK-Germany sponsored move at the UN for a proposal to put Azhar under the United Nations Security Council (UNSC) 1267 Al Qaeda Sanctions Committee. This was the fourth time Beijing had blocked Azhar's listing, however, this time they were forced to play coy as China's stance stood tall, and in solitude, as the only one protecting a terrorist. The Chinese ambassador in New Delhi, Luo Zhaohui, was forced to sound measured for damage control. 'We are optimistic that this matter will be resolved,' Luo said[18]. The post-Balakot diplomatic offensive gives teeth to counter-terror strikes themselves in making global powers recognise that India's actions are warranted for its own protection, the same global powers that have often showed ignorance to India's plight in the past, are now being forced to take notice after experiencing the likes of al-Qaeda and ISIS on their home turf.

From a strategic point of view, both these strikes themselves can have multiple interpretations. While the aim of these strikes remains a matter of contestation, similar operations had been conducted in the past as well, sans the public relations push the 2016 operations got. Today, multiple articles, books and even television shows give the strikes a depth that goes well beyond purely military and strategic aims. One school of thought, on the strategic front, highlights that the strikes offered the Pakistani establishment a challenge to react, and up the stakes militarily. In case of the 2016 strikes, the reaction of Pakistan was to dismiss the strikes, and deny that they ever took place, or that it faced any casualties due to the same on its side of the Line of Control (LoC). New Delhi maintained its vocal support on the success of the strikes, which claimed it had destroyed terror launch pads.[19]

The Indian counter-terror apparatus has both systemic challenges emitting from lack of cohesive, long-term thinking to systemic rot that successive governments have failed to address. This is visible in both examples from 2016 and 2019. While the world struggles with expansion of global terrorism with coming of groups such as ISIS, other countries have made far better adjustments on how to deal with these threats. The mandate of the Modi government, enjoying a unique absolute majority in Parliament, and its nationalistic character which by its own political design gives utmost importance to national security has only managed to continue the snail-paced bureaucratic procedures to develop a modern, adaptive and robust counter-terror understanding and infrastructure akin to the needs of the twenty-first century threat. Events such as surgical strikes cannot and should not be seen as well-adjusted counter-terror thinking, and such reactionary measures will not dent terror policies of India's adversaries. A deeper, well-thought out process against terrorism needs to find roots in Indian strategic thinking. The avenues where terrorism is committed today are expanding faster than traditional approaches to counter-terrorism can keep up, and governments are yet to address this policy paralysis despite rhetoric around national security and the grave threats that terrorism poses not just nationally, but globally. While the Modi government did offer a comparitively braver posture when it comes to tackling cross-border terror threats, institutional reforms in areas of defence to expedite modernisation and tackle the threats of the twenty-first century is still a significantly underperforming area. While the political intent to take terror head-on is a much needed and a welcome development, the ecosystem to support these actions in a manner which would give India a long-term upper hand against modern-day material and ideological terror infrastructure still eludes the nation.

NOTES

1 The Global Terrorism Index 2018, Institute for Economics and Peace, 2018, https://reliefweb.int/sites/reliefweb.int/files/resources/Global-Terrorism-Index-2018-1.pdf (accessed December 2018).

2 Claudia Hofmann and Ulrich Schenkener, 'Engaging non-state armed actors in state and peace-building options and strategies', International Review of the Red Cross, September 2011: p. 3, https://www.icrc.org/en/doc/assets/files/review/2011/irrc-883-schneckener.pdf (accessed November 2018).

3 Terrorists, Gunmen, Militants: How do we define acts of violence?, *The Quint*, https://www.thequint.com/explainers/terrorists-gunmen-militants-how-do-we-define-acts-of-violence (accessed November 2018).

4 Maya Mirchandani, 26/11 and the Media: Where were the protocols? *The Wire*, 26 November 2018, https://thewire.in/media/26-11-mumbai-attack-media-coverage

5 BBC Editorial Guidelines: Language When Reporting Terrorism, *BBC*, https://www.bbc.co.uk/editorialguidelines/guidance/terrorism-language/guidance-full (accessed November 2018).

6 Harsh V. Pant and Ivan Lidarev, 'Indian counter-terrorism policy and influence of the Global War on Terror,' *India Review*, 27 April 2018, https://www.tandfonline.com/doi/abs/10.1080/14736489.2018.1452416 (accessed September 2018).

7 Boaz Ganor, *The Counter-Terrorism Puzzle: A Guide for Decision Makers*, (USA: International Institute for Counter-Terrorism, Israel, 2008), p. 3

8 TADA document, http://www.satp.org/satporgtp/countries/india/document/actandordinances/tada.htm#21 (accessed October 2018).

9 Jayanth K. Krishnan, 'India's patriot act: POTA and the impact on civil liberties in the world's largest democracy,' *Law & Equality: A Journal of theory and practice*, 2004, https://scholarship.law.umn.edu/cgi/viewcontent.cgi?article=1058&context=lawineq (accessed December 2018).

[10] Kabir Taneja, 'Understanding ISIS: from conception to operations,' ORF, 2017, https://www.orfonline.org/research/understanding-isis-from-conception-to-operations/

[11] Ibid.

[12] ORF ISIS Tracker, 2019 http://trackingisis.orfonline.org/

[13] KYKL, South Asia Terror Portal, http://www.satp.org/satporgtp/countries/india/states/manipur/terrorist_outfits/kykl.htm (accessed November 2018).

[14] 'Over 230 terrorists killed in Jammu & Kashmir in 2018, say officials.' *NDTV*, 8 December 2018, https://www.ndtv.com/india-news/over-230-terrorists-killed-in-jammu-and-kashmir-in-2018-say-officials-1959763

[15] '213 terrorists killed in 2017: J&K govt,' *The Times of India*, 18 January 2018, https://timesofindia.indiatimes.com/india/213-terrorists-killed-in-2017-jk-govt/articleshow/62556052.cms (accessed November 2018).

[16] Arzan Tarapore, 'Balakot, Deterrence and Risk: How this India – Pakistan Crisis Will Shape The News,' *War On The Rocks*, 11 March 2019, https://warontherocks.com/2019/03/balakot-deterrence-and-risk/

[17] Gurbachan Singh, 'How Pakistan Scuttled India's Invitation to the First OIC Plenary,' *The Wire*, 23 February 2019, https://thewire.in/diplomacy/india-pakistan-oic-first-plenary

[18] 'Optimistic this matter will be resolved, says China's Ambassador on blacklisting JeM Chief Masood Azhar at UN,' *Business Today*, 17 March 2019, https://www.businesstoday.in/top-story/optimistic-this-matter-will-be-resolved-says-china-ambassador-on-blacklisting-jem-chief-masood-azhar-at-un/story/328493.html

[19] 'Terror launchpads destroyed across LoC in surgical strikes active again: Army,' *Financial Express*, 12 April 2017, https://www.financialexpress.com/india-news/terror-launch-pads-destroyed-across-loc-in-surgical-strikes-active-again-army/625591/ (accessed November 2018).

6

India's Counter-insurgency Strategy and Maoist Challenge: A Success Story?

Niranjan Sahoo

IN the recent times, one of the most visible success stories of India's counter-insurgency (COIN) strategy is with regard to Maoist insurgency. Not long ago, Maoist insurgency was termed as India's biggest internal security challenge.[1] From an absolute dominance over the Indian state in the mid-2000s spreading across almost one-third of territory in varying degrees, Maoist insurgency is now staring at its sunset. Coordinated and concerted efforts from the Centre and affected states have brought down incidences of Maoist violence to a drastic level, have killed many important leaders of the insurgent organisation, squeezed their dominance to handful of districts in Southern Chhattisgarh, Jharkhand and Odisha and so on. How was such a mighty insurgency brought down to this level? Can this be credited to renewed counter-insurgency (COIN) strategy of Indian state? Can this be termed as the Narendra Modi government's finest achievement as far as national security is considered? This chapter is an attempt to evaluate the successes (and failures) of COIN with regard to Maoist insurgency from a comparative perspective. It endeavours to study the policies and strategies of the successive governments that have invested on COIN and pioneered many of the tactics against Maoist insurgency. However, the main thrust of the chapter is to evaluate the five years of the Modi government in taking forward the fight against Maoists.

History of India's Counter-insurgency (COIN) Strategies: A Snapshot

Over seven decades, India has been subject to insurgencies of all kinds, some foreign but mostly domestic driven ones. India has fought (in many cases successfully) more than a dozen insurgencies so far. However, the country is today principally confronted with three major insurgencies. A long running low-intensity insurgency in its North East, discontentment in Kashmir mainly from the local Muslims contesting India's so-called occupation and the Maoist insurgency (a left-wing extremist movement mostly led by tribal population based on socio-economic grievances based rebellion) in central and eastern regions. Of course, this is not to ignore past insurgencies such as the Khalistani movement that took a massive turn in Punjab. Khalistani extremism was successfully brought down by the Indian state and since the late 1990s has not shown any active sign of reviving, although occasional flare-ups have been noticed, albeit outside India. Today, the Indian state's most pressing engagement is over two major insurgencies viz, Kashmir and Maoist insurgency or left-wing extremism, while North East separatist movements have ebbed and flowed as political approaches to their issues and demands have delivered successes at great length.[2]

For a long time, India's counter-insurgency strategy has wavered between "force and compromise'.[3] India formally espouses population-centric strategy with emphasis on winning "hearts and minds", although on numerous occasions it has followed 'enemy-centric approach" that focusses mainly on combating or targeting the insurgent leadership and key members and their organisations. In this, there is undeniable western influence in the manner in which Indian military and security establishments have conceptualised and operationalised COIN. India had retained most of British legal and police systems and the military ethos including its COIN strategies which the country employed during its campaigns against rebellion by Nagas and Mizos.[4] This apart, there is enough evidence to suggest that the Indian approach to COIN has a heavy leaning to British-Malayan approach to COIN, and largely came through strategies and tactics shared through Commonwealth military exchanges during 1950s and 1960s.[5] The British campaigns in pre-colonial Malaysia to deal with Maoist insurgency, its tactics of "draining the pond to get fish from the water" meaning systematically relocating population into secure areas had a deep impact on Indian military and security apparatus.

The other major influence on population-centric strategy can be traced to well-known French military officer David Galula who advocated that in counter-insurgency, the government must work with the population and best utilise its strengths by making progress on key projects that would win over the population. This is necessary to deprive the insurgents any popular support in their operations. Galula had gained such rare insights from his own experiences in Algeria and his studies of insurgencies in China and Indochina. The same was suggested by British counter-insurgency expert Sir Robert Thompson in dealing with the insurgents of Burma (referred to Myanmar now), Malaya and Vietnam.[6]

With regard to population-centric approach, the major thrust of security agencies is of recovering and maintaining the support of the population. The key focus has been to improve the government's relationship with the local population by protecting them and then carrying out activities, such as building roads, health centres, schools and other basic amenities to win the hearts and minds of the people. This is being done to win citizens' trust and earn their legitimacy. In short, population theory as popularly used by the US military strategists is "first protect and support the population, and all else will follow".[7]

Compared to population-centric strategy, the enemy-centric approach relies on combating the insurgents and eliminating the insurgent organisations. According to this approach, defeat of the enemy is the primary objective, not 'winning hearts and minds'. While the enemy-centric approach has many variants,[8] its key goal is to 'first defeat the enemy and all else will follow.'[9] The end objective of enemy-centric strategy is to suffocate an insurgency through a 'saturation of forces'.[10] This often may involve the co-option of elites to 'buy-out' and contain an insurgency.[11]

Although India's official approach lays emphasis on a population-centric approach, the country's long experience in dealing with large number of insurgencies since 1947 has allowed it to experiment with diverse COIN strategies unlike the West that relies more on population COIN. Sheer diversity of insurgencies from North East, Punjab and Central region to Kashmir has forced India to employ COIN strategies of all kind that have wide variation depending on terrain, force structures, insurgent goals and external involvement.[12] For instance, while Punjab and Kashmir have faced secessionist movements, its COIN strategies have been vastly different from the western approaches[13]. In Punjab, India used enemy-centric strategies[14] to its best use, whereas in Kashmir, all along it has been population-centric COIN. Nothing exemplifies this better than the creation of a separate COIN force—the Rashtriya Rifles—penetrating an army ethos into a paramilitary specifically equipped and trained to drive counter-insurgency operations in Kashmir.[15] In North East involving seven states, India has followed a mixed approach of the buy-out and political accommodation of insurgents with fair degree of success.[16] In short, India's counter-insurgency strategy combines multiple options that are evolving with each campaign.

COIN and Maoist Insurgency

In the recent times, one of the most visible success stories of India's counter-insurgency strategy is with regard to a protracted Maoist insurgency. Maoist insurgency is one of the oldest and most lethal home-grown insurgencies that the Indian state has been grappling with since the country's independence in 1947. While the origin of this left radical movement goes back to the famous Telangana Peasant Rebellion (1946-51), the extremist movement took the young republic by storm in 1967. On 25 May 1967, poor peasants, landless labourers, hapless *adivasis* with their *lathis,* arrows and bows undertook most daring raids of landlords and their granaries at Naxalbari village of West Bengal. The Naxalite movement (named after the village where it originated from) led by the charismatic Charu Majumdar and his close associates Kanu Sanyal and Jangal Santhal created an instant buzz among nearby villages.

The Naxalbari rebellion was put down by strong police action in a matter of days. Yet, its sparks had flown to as far as Srikakulam of Andhra Pradesh and Ganjam district of Odisha.

The surprise arrest of Charu Majumdar and his subsequent death in police custody prompted many analysts to pen obituaries for the Naxalite movement. Their belief was short lived. Within a decade, the new Naxalite movement turned its head in other regions of the country mainly Andhra Pradesh and Bihar. Notably, the early 1980s saw the revival of the movement in its most violent form when Andhra-based Kondapalli Seetharamaiah formed the People's War Group (PWG) in 1980. When Andhra police through strong police action decimated the PWG in the late 1990s, many called curtains down for this armed insurgency.

However, the left-wing insurgency revived again in the late 1990s by spreading into Central India, particularly the mountainous Dandakaranya and adjoining regions. The decisive merger of the Communist Party of India (Maoist-Leninist), PWG, Maoist Communist Centre of India (MCCI) and 40 other armed factions to form the Communist Party of India (Maoist) in 2004 turned the tide in favour of the insurgents. At one point, the CPI (Maoist) dominated over 200 districts of India (in varying measures) prompting Prime Minister Manmohan Singh to call them as 'the greatest internal security threat to India' in 2006. With their rapid rise came consequences: daring attacks on security forces including the famous Tadmetla massacre of 76 jawans in Chhattisgarh and clinical elimination of many of the top leaders of the Congress Party in Chhattisgarh that woke up Indian policymakers to the threats posed by the rebel groups.

The State Response

The state response to Maoist insurgency has evolved in various phases largely governed by the intensity of threats and nature of political dispensations at the Centre and the affected states. While the current National Democratic Alliance (NDA) government has hugely accelerated the pace, the real foundation for COIN was laid down by the previous

United Progressive Alliance (UPA) government.[17] The Centre has provided the resources both security and financial, paramilitary, intelligence and strategic direction, whereas the affected states have been the lead agents of COIN. This is primarily because under the Indian Constitution, 'law and order' is a state subject, therefore states have primary duties to counter insurgency-related activities/threats. A scrutiny of various COIN initiatives indicates that the Indian state has been following a mix of both population-centric and enemy-centric approaches to quell the Maoist menace in India's heartlands. These are in the forms of 'two-pronged approach' that combines both law and order and development instruments/tactics.

The Law and Order Approach

The official 'law and order' approach, which is modelled on enemy-centric strategy of raising special combats, and empowering police and intelligence to mount offensive actions against insurgents and their organisations has been the official strategy ever since the left-wing insurgency took its head in 1967. For instance, as has been well documented, the first cycle of Left-Wing Extremism (LWE), which erupted in West Bengal and spread to Andhra and Odisha in the late 1960s, were dealt with a heavy hand called Operation Spring Thunder.[18] Same strategy was emulated with fair degree of success in the undivided Andhra Pradesh through the creation of Greyhound unit that quelled a violent insurgency threatening a large part of the southern state.[19]

The insurgency in the third cycle (present) spread over a much bigger geography than ever and much more formidable is being dealt largely through the prism of law and order approach, and this is best exemplified by the Centre's deployment of more than 532 companies of paramilitary forces in the affected states.[20] The 2004 merger of some 40 splinter Maoist groups and formation of a new outfit called Communist Party of India—Maoist (CPI-Maoist) proved to be the wake-up call for the Central government and affected states. After rebels launched many audacious attacks against the security forces delivering huge number of casualties and nearly stalled many industrial projects in mining bearing states, around mid-2000, the Union government took a proactive stand in coordinating counter-insurgency measures across India.

The federal government for the first time brought out a security blueprint to tackle the Maoist threat as prominently featured in its 14-point policy[21] and subsequently took a series of security-led countermeasures to address the growing Maoist menace. Beyond the Centre, various affected states have initiated their own state-specific blueprints and security measures to face off the rebels.[22] Following is a summary of major security-related measures initiated by successive Central governments since the mid-2000 to counter LWE.

Modernisation of Police

With the realisation that Maoists are able to run their writ freely in vast swathes of territories largely because of lack of effective policing, the Centre in coordination with the states came out with an innovative Police Modernisation Scheme. Under this scheme, the Centre provided substantial sum of aid to states in modernising and upgrading their police forces including modern weaponry, latest communication equipment, fortification and other infrastructure. The Centre (current NDA government) in recent times furthered this assistance to include Mine Protected Vehicles (MPVs) to affected states. According to recent findings, police modernisation and improvement in intelligence gathering have brought major dividends for Indian states vis-à-vis Maoists.[23]

Strengthening the Intelligence Mechanism

To aid policing and combat operations, the Centre has revamped the intelligence-sharing infrastructure with states. Through Multi Agency Centre (MAC) at the Central level and State Multi Agency Centre (SMAC) at the state level there is intelligence sharing on 24x7 basis. Other noteworthy steps are setting up of Joint Command and Control Centre at Jagdalpur in Chhattisgarh and Gaya in Bihar in recent times.

Security Related Expenditure (SRE) Scheme

A game-changing step in improving anti-Maoist operations was the setting up of a Security Related Expenditure (SRE) scheme. This scheme allowed state governments to reimburse 50 per cent expenses on provisions like insurance scheme for police personnel, community policing, rehabilitation of surrendered Maoists, and other security related items not covered under the Police Modernisation Scheme. In recent times, the NDA government raised the SRE reimbursement up to 100 per cent. In addition, new items like compensation for incapacitation of security forces and property damage have been included for the first time.

Deployment of Central Paramilitary Forces

The most visible counter-insurgency initiative from the Centre has been the deployment of Central Para Military Forces (CPMFs). In order to complement the efforts of affected states and check the further spread of Maoists, the Centre has extended the deployment of CPMFs on a long-term basis in almost a copy of its approach in the cases of North East and Kashmir. So far, more than 70,000 CPMFs have been deployed in LWE affected states. In addition, the Centre has helped in the raising of 14 Specialised Commando Battalions (CoBRA) equipped and trained in guerrilla and jungle warfare techniques to be located in the worst affected districts. Further, the Centre has assisted in creating two dozen Counter Insurgency and Anti-Terrorist Schools (CIATSs) for long-term sustainability of counter-offensives.

Special Infrastructure Scheme

To fill the critical infrastructure gaps (that cannot be covered under existing government schemes), the Centre brought in a Special Infrastructure Scheme. These include requirements of mobility for the police/security forces by upgrading existing roads/tracks in inaccessible areas, providing secure camping grounds and helipads at strategic locations in remote and interior areas and so on. Under this scheme, some 250 fortified police stations were opened in LWE-affected states. The current Central government has increased this to 400.

The Surrender Policy

Another noteworthy step to enhance the effectiveness of COIN was setting up of an attractive surrender policy. While the UPA government initiated it in 2007 with a scheme of Rs 1.5 lakh for surrendered Maoist, the NDA regime has revamped it further. The Centre has increased the stipend of the surrendered from Rs 3,500 per month to Rs 6,000 per month and the one-time grant from Rs 1.5 lakh to Rs 4 lakh.

Ban on the CPI (Maoist) and the Passage of UAPA Act, 2009

To step up the pressure on rebels, the Central government in 2009 imposed a country-wide ban on CPI (Maoist). This apart, the government enacted the Unlawful Activities (Prevention) Act[24] in June 2009 to put a check on their activities apart from providing police and paramilitary autonomy and sweeping powers to go after the banned organisation and their activities.

Strengthening Monitoring and Coordination Mechanisms

It needs to be reiterated that until the mid-2000s, anti-Maoist operations lacked strength and coherence partly because of lack of strong leadership from the Centre and missing urgency from the state governments. A series of steps including a Unified Command—unofficially known as Operation Green Hunt[25]—was put to tackle Maoist.

The Centre and states agreed to have a series of structures and mechanisms to coordinate this mammoth task spread over 12-13 states. To begin with, the Centre set up a high-level Task Force under the Cabinet Secretary, and created a Coordination Centre headed by the Union Home Secretary to review the efforts of state governments concerned. Similarly, a Task Force was set up under a Special Secretary (Internal Security) in the Ministry of Home Affairs with senior officers from Intelligence agencies, Central paramilitary forces and state police forces. Importantly, recognising the seriousness of the issue, a dedicated Naxal Management Division[26] headed by an Additional Secretary was brought in within the Home Ministry to oversee and provide actionable inputs.

Some Notable Recent Initiatives

To step up the anti-Maoist efforts and further enhance their effectiveness, the Narendra Modi government has brought out a fresh dose of initiatives. A noteworthy policy is SAMADHAN which was announced by the Minister of Home Affairs in May 2017. According to this new acronym, S - Smart Leadership, A - Aggressive Strategy, M - Motivation and Training, A - Actionable Intelligence, D -Dashboard Based KPIs (Key Performance Indicators) and KRAs (Key Result Areas), H- Harnessing Technology, A - Action plan for each theatre and N - No access to Financing. While this is more like going back to the basics of COIN, the key thrust behind this new policy is to reenergise the anti-Maoist measures.[27] This apart, the NDA government has brought in systems and processes to enforce usage of unique identification numbers in smart guns, gelatine and other explosive materials. It has also expanded the ambit of existing provisions under the Explosives Act as well as the Prevention of Money Laundering Act to monitor the transportation of explosive substances and means to choke the finances of Maoists.

The Development Approach

The population-centric COIN to help win hearts and minds of locals in Maoist affected states came as an afterthought for successive governments at the Centre. Starting with the suppression of Naxalite movement in 1967 to Maoist movement in mid-1990s, for a long time the Indian state relied on enemy-centric law and order approach to counter Maoist insurgency. However, since this did not end the insurgency which took newer avatars and spread afar, the Centre initiated a series of development measures to win over the affected population. This approach was best illustrated in the Union government appointing an expert committee (headed by D. Bandyopadhyay, the architect of famous 'Operation Barga')[28] to carry out a detailed study of socio-economic developments in the affected regions and suggest measures to address these deficits. Following the suggestions of the Expert Committee and the government's own assessment of the evolving situation, an unprecedented amount of resources has been transferred to areas affected by Maoist insurgency.[29]

One of them is the flagship Integrated Action Plan (IAP) launched by the UPA government to implement a special scheme which addresses the development deficiencies in LWE-affected districts with a financial package over Rs 6,000 crore per annum. While the current government has disbanded the IAP scheme, it has come out with its own scheme called Special Central Assistance (SCA) to cover 35 most LWE-affected districts.

Most significant steps taken by the Centre to address the longstanding grievances of *adivasis* are in terms of bringing out some landmark legislations that clearly recognise the rights of *adivasis* to access forest resources, self-governance and so on. The passage of Forest Dwellers Act in 2006 despite stiff resistance from environmentalists and NGOs is a clear statement of the Centre's resoluteness to address the grievances of tribal populations living in the Naxal-affected areas.

In addition, the NDA government has launched a new scheme, Civic Action Programme (CAP) providing financial grants for the Central Armed Police Forces (CAPFs) to undertake various welfare activities in the LWE-affected areas. This scheme aims to win the goodwill of the affected population. Another notable development scheme, mainly to enhance connectivity in inaccessible Maoist affected regions, by the current government is the Universal Services Obligation Fund (USOF).[30] With a cost of Rs 7,330 crore, this novel scheme provides financial and administrative support to expand mobile services at 4,072 tower locations identified by the Ministry of Home Affairs (MHA) in 96 districts in 10 states.

Further, to address issues of education and employment in Maoist-affected regions, the Ministry of Skill Development & Entrepreneurship (MoSDE) launched two new schemes, namely, 'Skill Development in 47 LWE-affected districts' and 'Pradhan Mantri Kaushal Vikas Yojana (PMKVY)' for creating infrastructure and providing employment-linked skill training to youths in affected areas. Similarly, the NDA government has made major headways in electrifying the un-electrified villages in the LWE-affected districts under the Deen Dayal Upadhyay Gram Jyoti

Yojana (DDUGJY). Out of 7,164 un-electrified villages, electrification has been completed in 7,065 villages so far. Further, penetration of education has received a major boost under the current regime at the Centre. Under the Rashtriya Madhyamik Shiksha Abhiyan (RMSA) 1,590 schools have been upgraded and 350 girls hostels sanctioned in 35 most affected LWE districts. In short, the current NDA government has largely continued with the UPA government's development strategy in Maoist-affected districts and in many cases given new leg up to these schemes to bring better results for COIN.

An Appraisal of COIN

India's COIN strategy against Maoist insurgency which has followed a two-pronged approach of combining security and development has taken positive traction on many fronts. As mentioned earlier, not very long ago, Maoist insurgency was termed as India's 'biggest internal security threat'. From an absolute dominance over state forces in mid-2000s, Maoist insurgency is now staring at its sunset. While there are contrary views on this,[31] the key developments attest to this trend. For instance, as per the recent data of MHA, Maoist insurgency, which at one point had peaked over 200 districts spreading its wings over as many as 20 Indian states, is down to its lowest in decades.[32] While the casualties suffered by Maoists have shot up to highest (231 in 2018), the security forces have taken one of the lowest hit ever (See Table1). This is more strongly vindicated when MHA recently removed a record 44 districts from Naxal-affected list, while the 'worst-affected category' was reduced from 36 to 30.[33] Importantly, security forces have been able to recapture some of the fortresses of Maoists when they penetrated Saranda forest in Jharkhand and are threatening once impregnable Abujhmar in Chhattisgarh.

More importantly, the once mighty movement now looks very weak and dispirited. This five-decade-old armed movement is growing fissures within and its top leadership is getting thinner.[34] In recent years, security forces of various states have achieved the impossible by eliminating many top leaders including Kishenji alias Koteswar Rao, Cherukuri Rajkumar alias Azad and more recently Serisha. The security forces have succeeded in capturing more than 7,000 active cadres in the last three years while an equal number of Maoists have surrendered before authorities in various states.[35]

Table 1: Comparative Statistics of Naxal Violence (2005-2018)

Years	*Civilians*	*Security Force Personnel*	*LWE/ CPI-Maoists*	*Total*
2005	281	150	286	717
2006	266	128	343	737
2007	240	218	192	650
2008	220	214	214	648
2009	391	312	294	997
2010	626	277	277	1180
2011	275	128	199	602
2012	146	104	117	367
2013	159	111	151	421
2014	128	87	99	314
2015	93	57	101	251
2016	123	66	244	430
2017	109	74	150	333
2018	109	73	231	413

Sources: South Asia Terrorism Portal 2018 and Ministry of Home Affairs, GoI, 2017-18

To sum up, the two-pronged COIN strategy has dealt a heavy blow to the once invincible Maoist movement restricting it to a handful of districts of three bordering states. After more than 50 years of its existence and dominance in various stages, the left radical movement appear a spent force. A combination of improved state actions, change in political economy and internal dynamics of Maoist organisation might finally end this recurring insurgency. Loss of strongholds, declining appeal of ideology and leadership crisis along with improved performance from the affected states on socio-economic fronts addressing the key issues of *adivasis* may make it difficult to regain its lost aura or same momentum that it gained decades ago.

Modi Government's Approach to Maoist Insurgency

How much of the credit for bringing down the mighty insurgency to a fringe level can go to COIN (policies and initiatives) of the Modi government? The available statistics of insurgency related incidences including heavy casualty borne by Maoists particularly its top leadership and trends of several districts being declared free from Maoist influence. While there is no denying the critical role of the previous government in mounting a comprehensive COIN which began hitting rebels hard as early as 2012,[36] the real acceleration of such trend began in 2015 and continues to corner the rebels. The Modi government's early recognition of the kind of threats posed by Maoists seems to have helped it put a coherent and aggressive COIN against rebels. This is clearly vindicated from the fact that soon after it took power in May 2014, it came out with a multi-pronged National Policy and Action Plan[37] to fight the Maoist insurgency. Although the real COIN took nearly three years to fructify in the form of SAMADHAN as explained in the earlier section, since its coming to power in 2014 the new government ensured in giving enough teeth to the policies of the previous regime. On developmental front, the Modi government launched an ambitious Aspirational Districts Programme[38] in January 2018. Out of 115 districts selected by the NITI Aayog, as many as 35 districts with strong LWE presence have been selected. Under the scheme, the Centre will infuse funds and technical and capacity building support to address 49 indicators across five core sectors involving education, health, financial inclusion, agriculture among others. If implemented in right earnest, this may act as a strong deterrence to Maoist spread that largely built on the narrative of underdevelopment and state neglect.

While it has built on the population-centric approach of the UPA government by introducing more result-oriented socio-economic/ infrastructure schemes,[39] at the same time the BJP government put its premium on proven 'enemy-centric approach' on the lines of Punjab militancy.[40] This is clearly reflected in a significant hike in Security Related Expenditure (SRE) to further improve the policing (creation of 400 fortified police stations), doubling up the number of combat training schools, making surrender policy more attractive (raised compensation amount from Rs 1.5 lakh to Rs 4 lakh), providing 100 per cent central assistance under SRE and releasing these grants in advance to states, revamping intelligence cooperation with states, etc.

Additionally, to go after the Maoist organisation and leadership, the Modi government adopted several measures which were shunned by the previous government such as using helicopters, drones or unmanned aerial vehicles among others. The Central government also brought more problems for Maoists by speeding up development works under Special Infrastructure Projects schemes, installed more phone towers in remote districts, constructed roads in most difficult terrains, brought electricity and so on. Improved coordination with state police and intelligence agencies meant Maoists are finding it difficult to move arms, funds and their senior leadership from one place to other.[41] Thus, improved coordination between the Centre and affected states and sustained pressure on Maoists due to well-coordinated COIN has put the once mighty insurgency on the back foot.

Of course, some of the affected states, particularly Odisha and West Bengal, have taken commendable steps to check ultras. Mamata Banerjee after assuming power in 2011 went after the Maoist leadership while providing substantial socio-economic packages to the impoverished population.[42] Similarly, Odisha under Naveen Patnaik's leadership followed a strong security and development approach combining judiciously with numerous pioneering socio-economic measures/speedy grievance redressal particularly on land-related issues combined with major revamp in policing infrastructure to make major gains.

Challenges and Way Forward

Over the last decade, Maoist insurgency has ebbed substantially and now is restricted to a few tri-junction districts bordering Chhattisgarh, Jharkhand, Odisha and Maharashtra. Yet, the Centre as well as the affected states should not live on laurels of counter-insurgency. As long as the rebels have strong foothold let alone in tri-junction districts, they are a force to reckon with. Geographically speaking, tri-junctions districts form too large a territory. Besides, development-governance related grievances of locals are still present,[43] providing new recruits as cannon fodder for the Maoists. While it would be impossible for them to dominate the way CPI-Maoist did in the 2000s, one should not forget their ability to commit violent acts and disrupt development and governance. For instance, despite being too weak and on the run, the Maoists were able to kill 25 CRPF jawans on the Dornapal-Jagargunda road in Chhattisgarh in June 2018. In another daring attack, they gunned down 12 CRPF men in Sukma's Bhejji village. The series of attacks in recent times indicate the continued strengths of Naxals to act as an agency of disruption and chaos. More importantly, there are inputs indicating the rebels' determined efforts to penetrate into urban pockets as well. In short, the Naxal insurgency is anything but history yet.

What is the way forward? There are no easy answers. The official two-pronged (security and development) COIN strategy, which has done well to restrict the Maoists spread and substantially weaken them, is still not good enough to address other structural issues, especially weak governance and low spread of service delivery institutions sustaining such a protracted insurgency over decades.[44] Security operations and law and order approach have their limits. Therefore, the Centre needs to think out of box to arrive at a solution that can address the roots of the rebellion. While Aspirational District programme is an excellent initiative to bring up development by improving social and physical infrastructure in those poverty stricken and extremely backward districts, the Central initiative cannot be substitute to state level apathy.

While there is no substitute to law and order approach as one is dealing with violent insurgents, should not efforts be made to persuade the rebels for a dialogue with the Centre? If the Colombian state could persuade its population for a dialogue and clinch a process accord with FARC (Revolutionary Armed Forces of Colombia) to end the world's most violent left-wing insurgency that left more than 200,000 people dead and 5.7 million displaced since early 1960s, why should the Indian state hesitate to hold dialogue with its own rebels? In fact, being very weak and with their back to the wall, Maoist rebels might be more eager for political dialogue than ever. After liquidating the FARC top leadership and weakening their firepower, the Colombian government could push the insurgent group to the negotiation table. In short, time is ripe for dialogue and meaningful negotiations with the rebels. To end, armed means alone cannot crush a revolutionary movement that draws its roots from underdevelopment, injustice, exclusion and lack of governance.

NOTES

[1] Former Prime Minister Manmohan Singh in his 2006 address termed Maoist insurgency as single biggest national security threat. For details, see: *The Times of India*, 13 April 2006, https://timesofindia.indiatimes.com/city/delhi/Naxalism-is-gravest-internal-threat-PM/articleshow/1489633.cms

[2] N.J. Christian, 'The counter-insurgency policies of the Hindu nationalist Bharatiya Janata Party of India and the Naxalite Insurgency,' *Master Thesis*, Naval Post Graduate School, Monterey, USA, 2016, https://apps.dtic.mil/dtic/tr/fulltext/u2/1030821.pdf

[3] Rajesh Rajagopalan, 'Force and Compromise: India's counter-insurgency grand strategy,' *Journal of South Asian Studies*, no. 1 (April 2007).

[4] Kaushik Roy, *The Army in British India: From Colonial Warfare to Total War 1857-1947* (London: Bloomsbury, 2013).

[5] D. Banerjee, 'The Indian Army's Counter-insurgency Doctrine,' in *India and Counter-insurgency: Lessons Learned*, ed. Sumit Ganguly and David P. Fidler (London: Routledge, 2009).

[6] N.J. Christian, Ibid *op.cit.*

[7] U.S. Government Interagency Counter-insurgency Initiative, Counter-insurgency Guide, January 2009. https://www.state.gov/documents/organization/119629.pdf

[8] These include soft versus hard, violent versus non-violent, decapitation versus marginalisation among other.

[9] Thesis p8.

[10] Anit Mukherjee, 'India's experiences with Insurgency and Counter-insurgency,' in *Handbook of Asian Security Studies*, ed. Sumit Ganguly, Andrew Scobell and Joseph Chinyong Liow (London & New York: Routledge, 2018).

[11] Sameer Lalwani, 'India's Approach to Counter-insurgency and the Naxalite Problem,' *CTC Centinel*, Vol. 4, (October 2011).

[12] Lalwani, 2011.

[13] Ibid.

[14] During its Punjab campaign, India militarised the police and reversed their role with the military to capitalise local knowledge and legitimacy and lead kinetic operations. Police officer KPS Gill who led the operation popularised enemy-

centric strategy which was otherwise known as kinetic operations. Sameer Lalwani, 2011.

[15] Rajesh Rajagopalan, 'Innovations in Counter-insurgency: The Indian Army's Rashtriya Rifles,' *Contemporary South Asia*, No. 31 (2004).

[16] Lawrence Cline, 'The Insurgency Environment in Northeast India', *Small Wars and Insurgencies*, No.27 (2009)

[17] Ajay Sahni, a well-known security expert says year 2011-12 can be considered turning point in COIN against Maoist insurgency. He says Maoist movement witnessed a rapid rise from 2004-2009, but a change in government strategy altered the dynamics. We replicated the Andhra Pradesh model to get cracking on ultras. https://www.hindustantimes.com/india-news/red-terror-new-strategy-puts-a-leash-on-maoists/story-a8eaFvV9qGeKdqPPmelFpL.html

[18] See Sumanta Banerjee, *India's Simmering Revolution, the Naxalite Uprising* (London: Zed Book, 1984).

[19] See K. Srinivas Reddy, *Seminar*, http://www.india-seminar.com/2007/569/569_k_srinivas_reddy.htm

[20] See MHA Annual Report, 2017.

[21] See Vinay Kumar, 2006, http://india.eu.org/spip.php?article5013

[22] For a detailed response of states, see this exhaustive report, Jacob N. Shapiro, Oliver V. Eynde, Katherine Ingram and Emefa A. Agawu, 'Indian State Counter-insurgency Policies: Brief historical summaries', *ESOC Empirical Studies of Conflict*, 5 November 2017. https://esoc.princeton.edu/files/indian-state-counter-insurgency-policies-brief-historical-summaries

[23] PTI, 'Big crackdown against Maoists' "overground" supporters planned,' *The Economic Times*, 3 September 2018, //economictimes.indiatimes.com/articleshow/65654346.cms?utm_source=contentofinterest&utm_medium=text&utm_ campaign=cppst https://economictimes.indiatimes.com/news/defence/big-crackdown-against-maoists-overground-supporters-planned/articleshow/65654346.cms

[24] See the detailed Act, https://mha.gov.in/sites/default/files/A1967-37.pdf

[25] See a perceptive analysis on Operation Green Hunt: Nitin Pai, 'Operation Green Hunt and its challenges,' *The Indian Express*, 8 October 2009, https://indianexpress.com/article/opinion/columns/operation-green-hunt-and-its-challenges/

[26] https://mha.gov.in/division_of_mha/left-wing-extremism-division

[27] Shaurya Karanbir Gurung, 'SAMADHAN: Rajnath Singh coins an acronym to wipe out left-wing terror,' *The Economic Times*, 8 May 2017, https://economictimes.indiatimes.com/news/politics-and-nation/rajnath-singh-calls-for-unity-of-purpose-to-tackle-naxals/articleshow/58571588.cms

[28] In 2006, the Planning Commission of India under the leadership of D. Bandyopadhyay set up the committee to look into this political phenomenon. The Expert Committee Report which came out very critical of government's track records and approach (which it thought heavily security centric) traced the growing LWE phenomenon to land alienation, poverty amongst scheduled

tribes and dalits and lack of access to basic forest resources. Detailed report: htttp://planningcommission.nic.in/reports/publications/rep_dce.pdf>

29 According to the Planning Commission (2012) estimates, more than Rs 80,000 crore has been allocated to 100 odd districts affected by Maoist insurgency in the last 10 years. See Approach paper to 12th Five Year Plan, Government of India.

30 For details, See PIB release, http://pib.nic.in/PressReleaseIframePage.aspx?PRID=1533122

31 Some long-time observers of LWE think, the extremist movement is facing one of its low phase, but would likely gain back their supremacy any time soon. For more see, Sudeep Chakarvarti, 'Why Maoists will endure despite Chhattisgarh elections,' *Mint*, 20 November 2018, https://www.livemint.com/Politics/xqdBFQErKMpwvdWpWFw56O/Why-Maoists-will-endure-despite-Chhattisgarh-elections.html

32 Rahul Tripathi, 'Four years of Modi government—Home Affairs: Turning the heat down in Northeast,' *The Indian Express*, 28 April 2019, https://indianexpress.com/article/india/four-years-of-modi-government-home-affairs-turning-the-heat-down-in-northeast-5190158/

33 According to MHA report, an overall 20 per cent reduction in violent incidents (908 compared to 1136) and 33.8 per cent decrease in LWE-related deaths (263 from 397) were reported in 2017 compared to 2013.

34 According to confessions of arrested Naxalites, nearly four dozen Left-wing factions that had opportunistically merged in 2004 to form a hotchpotch coalition to fight Indian state are in now in open war against each other. For instance in Jharkhand alone, there 16 breakaway groups mainly People's Liberation Front of India or PLFI, Tritiya Prastuti Committee or TPC that challenge CPI (Maoist) leadership and compete in terms of resources and influence. There are similar trends in Bihar, Chhattisgarh and Odisha as well.

35 MHA Annual Report 2016-2017 .

36 Ajai Sahni, Ibid *op.cit.*

37 N.J. Christian, 'The counter-insurgency policies of the Hindu nationalist Bharatiya Janata Party…,' n. 2

38 'Aspirational Districts: Unlocking Potentials,' NITI Aayog, Government of India, http://niti.gov.in/writereaddata/files/AspirationalDistricts-Book.pdf

39 Its National Policy declared that 'winning the hearts and minds of the tribal population and other marginalised groups will lie at the core of the counter-insurgency strategy'. See: Aman Sharma, 'Govt can use any element of its national power against Maoists: Rajnath Singh's new anti-Naxal Policy,' *The Economic Times*, 17 October 2014, //economictimes.indiatimes.com/articleshow/44848311.cms?utm_source=contentofinterest&utm_medium=text&utm_ campaign=cppsthttps://economictimes.indiatimes.com/news/politics-and-nation/govt-can-use-any-element-of-its-national-power-against-maoists-rajnath-singhs-new-anti-naxal-policy/articleshow/44848311.cms

[40] Master thesis.

[41] Azaan Javaid, 'Red terror: New strategy puts a leash on Maoists,' *Hindustan Times*, 16 April 2018, https://www.hindustantimes.com/india-news/red-terror-new-strategy-puts-a-leash-on-maoists/story-a8eaFvV9qGeKdqPPmelFpL.html

[42] For West Bengal response, see: Aniruddha Ghosal, 'How Mamata Banerjee tamed Maoists in Bengal,' *The Indian Express*, 2 May 2017, https://indianexpress.com/article/india/how-mamata-banerjee-tamed-maoists-in-bengal/

[43] The underlying causes of its sustenance (as reported by the expert committee of erstwhile Planning Commission) such as underdevelopment, lack of governance, injustice, exploitation of adivasi population remain at large. Although a substantial resources have been channelled through flagship Central Welfare Schemes such as MGNREGA (rural jobs scheme), and NHRM, the Centre has allocated a humongous sum of money to these districts under various specialised schemes including Integrated Action Plan (each affected district getting roughly Rs.30 crore annually), still there are no visible improvement on the ground. Many *adivasis* are still under the spell of Maoist ideology and their utopian idea of People's War or protracted guerrilla war is very much the work in progress.

[44] For a detailed analysis of governance paradox in Maoist affected areas, see Niranjan Sahoo, 'Dealing with Maoist threats: Development and Governance Conundrum,' *ICSSR Astract and Review, Political Science*, 2013, http://citeseerx.ist.psu.edu/viewdoc/download?doi=10.1.1.819.2752&rep=rep1&type=pdf

7

India's Cyber Defence Future: Issues and Challenges

Bedavyasa Mohanty

FOR the last five years, since Prime Minister Narendra Modi assumed office, cyber regulation has proved to be an unpredictable challenge. Amidst numerous threats to data privacy and critical information infrastructure, the ambitious Digital India programme has seen considerable successes but also its fair share of failures.

Three big developments have caused a shift in the technology landscape in the last few years. *First*, the rollout of the ambitious Aadhaar programme has thrown up difficult questions around privacy, autonomy and data integrity. The Aadhaar project with reportedly 99 per cent of Indians having an Aadhaar number has created a one of a kind public data infrastructure to rival the biggest service providers in the world[1]—US's FAANG (Facebook, Amazon, Apple, Netflix and Google) and China's BAT (Baidu, Alibaba and Tencent). It is the only digital platform in the world that has over one billion people on it but isn't privately owned.

Second, on the basis of government initiatives like the Jan Dhan-Aadhaar-Mobile and measures like demonetisation, the rate of adoption of digital payments in the country has increased exponentially. Digital wallets constitute the biggest mode of payment in India outside of plastic cards and have shown 300 per cent growth since demonetisation until 2018.[2] Payments over Unified Payments Interface and Aadhaar Enabled Payments System are said to have also burgeoned with a reported growth of over 1000 per cent.[3]

The Aadhaar database by providing authentication as a service has also spurred the creation of an ecosystem of applications that cater to peoples' everyday needs called the IndiaStack. The IndiaStack, a suite of Application Programme Interface, provides organisations with a toolkit to deliver services in a presence-less, paperless and cashless manner.[4] A person can now sign up for a service using just her mobile with Aadhaar KYC (Know Your Customer), store and verify documents online through DigiLocker and pay for services through the Unified Payments Interface (UPI)—India's public and interoperable digital payments infrastructure. In addition to building layers to deliver these services transparently, IndiaStack has also incorporated individual rights by design through a 'consent' layer. This layer will enable users to control their information and how it is shared. The Aadhaar ecosystem has enabled private corporations to build on this layer. Private banks in India have adopted the Aadhaar framework to verify customer identities and open new bank accounts. The integration of Whatsapp with UPI is also symbolic—where one of Silicon Valley's crown jewels has converged with a locally created architecture.

All of these developments have spurred the growth of the digital economy and also driven home the necessity of securing India's information architecture. The *third* big development, therefore, has been efforts over the past two years to create laws and policies to modernise India's data protection regime. The Narendra Modi government had in August 2017 established a high-level Committee under the chairmanship of retired justice B.N. Srikrishna to draft a modern legislation on data protection that secured individual rights and maintain trust in the digital economy. The Committee, in its report accompanying the draft Personal Data Protection Bill has highlighted the importance of information integrity to protecting India's national security from threats like foreign surveillance and attacks that can debilitate critical information infrastructure.[5]

While these efforts are timely and laudable, many challenges remain. One unique aspect of technology's interplay with national security is the fluid institutional boundary between civilian and military systems.

Protecting national security in cyberspace depends on a combination of factors, from building capacity and articulating a coherent strategy to investing in state of the art technology for both civilian and military institutions. While the government has succeeded in some of its efforts, there are other aspects that have not been given the attention they deserve.

Overarching Cyber Security Policy

One hinderance to the creation of a holistic cyber security architecture is the lack of a modern cyber security policy. India's National Cyber Security Policy,[6] first articulated by the United Progressive Alliance (UPA) government in 2013 remains a statement of first principles only. The policy identifies areas of priority such as building resilience of Critical Information Infrastructure (CII) from external interference and a national agency to coordinate all matters relating to cyber security in the country. The Policy also highlights the necessity of creating a workforce of cyber security professionals to help secure the country's burgeoning digital economy.

While some aspects of the Policy's vision have been acted upon, many other critical components remain unaddressed. The National Critical Information Infrastructure Protection Centre (NCIIPC) for instance was established in 2014. The next year, the Modi government appointed a National Cyber Security Coordinator within the Prime Minister's Office (PMO) to oversee technology reforms to strengthen national security.[7] On the other hand, key recommendations from within the policy such as training five lakh information security professionals by 2013 have not yet been acted upon. Even the National Cyber Coordination Centre (NCCC), despite being greenlit[8] first in 2013 with a sanctioned budget of Rs 800 crore, has not yet become fully operational.

Moreover the policy itself is in need of being both updated and more specific in its next iteration to account for developments over the past five years and to deal with new challenges around disinformation and widespread misuse of data by technology companies.

Supply Chain Integrity

A long-standing threat to India's national security in the cyber realm has been weak oversight of the devices and networks that fuel the nation's digital economy. The proliferation of cheap and unsecured devices combined with a vast number of first-generation internet users creates a vulnerability both on the technical and user front. Four out of the top five most popular smartphones by market share in India are Chinese—accounting for nearly 42 percent of the entire market.[9]

This is cause for serious concern amidst reports from around the world that the Chinese government often leverages network infrastructure provided by Chinese manufacturers to conduct espionage. In early 2018, reports emerged of how the Chinese government after building the African Union headquarters, networks and data servers spied on the organisation for five years by copying data on to servers in Shanghai.[10] Similarly, the Australian[11], British and Japanese[12] governments have also begun investigations against Chinese tech giants Huawei and ZTE over alleged foreign surveillance concerns. The United States too has begun taking action against Chinese manufacturers orchestrating the arrest of a top executive at Huawei in 2018.[13]

India, however, has reversed its earlier stance where it had excluded Huawei from partnering with the government on 5G trials.[14] This decision comes despite the Indian government questioning the privacy and security of Chinese phones in the aftermath of the Doklam crisis.[15] In 2018, the Indian government had begun an investigation into Alibaba Group-owned UC Browser for allegedly sending data of Indian users to servers in China even after being uninstalled from users' phones.[16] The Indian government must, therefore, seriously rethink any potential partnership with organisations that have a part of their supply chain in China.

Cybercrime

India has witnessed a steady rise in cybercrimes with some estimates claiming that over 40 million cyber or cyber-enabled crimes occur in India in a year. While the numbers continue to rise, it has now been established that there are many more crimes that go unreported. These statistics are further complicated by transnational cybercrimes and the ephemeral nature of cyber forensic evidence. To collect this extra-territorial evidence, India relies on an outdated bilateral mechanism called Mutual Legal Assistance Treaties (MLAT) that more often than not does not yield timely results.[17] By one estimate, it can take up to three years and four months for electronic evidence to be made available following an MLAT request.[18]

This insecurity drives home the importance of creating the correct architecture, from up-skilling cybercrime expertise, to developing the best technologies, to ensuring legislation enables successful prosecutions, to adopting Standard Operating Procedures in investigation and prosecution of crimes to preserving of digital evidence. Developments in this area, however, have not been promising. The lack of specific expertise among Indian law enforcement agencies in handling cybercrimes has led to abysmal levels of successful prosecution. Statistics show that cyber criminals in India have a nearly 98 percent chance of escaping conviction.

Cyber Attacks

Equally serious is the threat of cyber-attacks that can cause large scale economic damage to networks and infrastructure. During the infamous WannaCry ransomware attack that affected over 150 countries, India was among the four worst affected countries.[19] In addition to extensive damage to private sector infrastructure, the malware also affected four state government systems including the Andhra Pradesh Police.[20] Similarly, the ATM hack of 2016 affected 3.2 million debit cards issued by six major banks.[21] The potential of damage from cyber-attacks runs into billions of dollars and the Indian market with its proliferation of unsecured smart devices and low levels of digital literacy presents an attractive target for would-be hackers.

A positive step towards tackling this problem that the Narendra Modi government has taken is the establishment of the Cyber Swachhta Kendra[22] or the Botnet Cleaning and Malware Analysis Centre that creates awareness among users around security of their data and devices and partners with Internet Service Providers to automatically detect infected systems and suggest fixes.[23] According to government estimates, the introduction of this tool has resulted in a 51 per cent decrease in malware infections across the country.[24]

Another milestone in this regard has been the establishment of the NCIIPC which has designated five sectors as critical information infrastructure: Power & Energy, Banking, Financial Institutions & Insurance, Information and Communication Technology, Transportation, E-governance and Strategic Public Enterprises. The identification of these sectors as 'protected' automatically makes any malicious attack on these systems an act of cyberterrorism under the Information Technology Act.[25] This carries a higher quantum of punishment and acts as a deterrent.

Encryption

While the creation of institutional frameworks for cyber security is laudable, the Modi administration has continued to create policies that can harm the technical architecture of the internet. In September 2015, the government circulated a Draft National Encryption Policy seeking to establish protocols and algorithms for encryption, key exchange and digital signatures for government agencies, businesses and individual users.[26] The Policy required vendors of encryption products to register their products with the government and submit working copies of software and hardware used for encryption.[27] It also required businesses using encryption to enter into an agreement with the government and upon request by law enforcement hand over the encrypted text, plaintext and hardware and software used for encryption.[28]

The policy had the potential to adversely affect legitimate use of anonymisation technologies used by journalists and whistle-blowers. In the process of making decrypted information readily available for law enforcement it would also have made systems less secure and more vulnerable to malicious cyber-attacks. Many of the policy's provisions were neither enforceable nor technologically feasible. Unsurprisingly, the policy faced a massive backlash from technologists, civil society and the media causing it to be withdrawn within a few days of being released for public comments.[29]

In late 2018, however, the government decided to once again turn its crosshairs on encryption. Currently proposed amendments[30] to Intermediary Liability Rules under the Information Technology Act mandate all communication service providers to introduce traceability into their systems—ensuring that origin of any message or content is readily identifiable. Over end-to-end encrypted platforms, this does not appear to be technologically possible. If compliance with the amendment results in services rolling back or reducing the strength of encryption then India's information ecosystem as well as national security will be significantly jeopardised.

Cyber Defence Infrastructure

Apart from the civilian information infrastructure, India's military institutions tasked with ensuring national security in the information realm remain inadequate. India currently does not have a dedicated cyber command that can lead information warfare and information integrity efforts. Despite a joint recommendation submitted by the Indian Army, Air Force and Navy to create cyber warfare tri-command in 2013, the creation of this central body remains in a preliminary phase. Even when institutionalised, it seems likely that the agency will lack the necessary autonomy to effect any real change. News reports indicate that the government is considering the creation of a Defence Cyber Agency that will report to the National Cyber Security Coordinator.[31] As experts have pointed out a comprehensive cyber defence response requires more than a nodal agency that can coordinate cyber defence activities. For a cyber command to be effective, it needs to be independent, reporting to the PMO and multi-pronged in its structure. It should not only have the ability to recommend polices for cyber defence but also the budget to undertake research into advanced technologies and a dedicated cadre of officials for specialised response.[32]

Another urgent necessity is the establishment of dedicated state-of-the-art cyber ranges. Cyber ranges are sandbox platforms where the resilience of both civilian and military networks can be tested. These can be used to conduct penetration testing of IT infrastructure and devices. Currently, the government has not established any dedicated cyber ranges for this purpose. The only operational cyber range has been established by Cisco in Gurugram, Haryana, to test products before deployment and to train information security professionals.[33] Although the Defence Research and Development Organisation (DRDO) has built ranges for testing electronic warfare capabilities,[34] it is paramount that similar efforts be made to accurately assess the resilience of military networks.

Public Private Partnership

Given the involvement of both state and non-state actors in malicious cyber behaviour and the blurred lines between public and private infrastructure the need for cooperation between the government and private sector is paramount. The Modi administration has made some inroads into this area by actively onboarding private actors in some of its more ambitious endeavours.

The government's Cyber Swachhta Kendra for instance has been developed in collaboration with QuickHeal—an industry leader in malware detection.[35] The government has similarly partnered with Cisco for threat intelligence sharing. Under the partnership, Cisco will establish a Security and Trust Office in India and a Security Operations Centre to monitor and manage cyber threats.[36]

Multilateral Cooperation

The Modi government must be credited for increasing the scope of multilateral cooperation in cyberspace. During its tenure, the Modi government has signed over 41 agreements on cooperation in cyberspace in the form of bilateral treaties, Memorandums of Understanding or as joint framework agreements.[37] The crown jewel among these is the Communications, Compatibility and Security Agreement (COMCASA) signed between India and the United States in September 2018.[38] The COMCASA allows the transfer of secure data and surveillance equipment from the US to India and allows the militaries of both nations to share data on a real-time basis. The agreement also allows the United States to retain advanced communication equipment on the military platforms sold to India, thus significantly bolstering India's surveillance and threat detection capabilities.

Equally noteworthy has been the administration's ability to sign these agreements for cyber cooperation not just with traditional allies like the United Kingdom,[39] France,[40] and Russia,[41] but also its adversaries like China.[42] These agreements not only enable the cross-pollination of expertise and help expedite investigations, they also help establish norms of responsible behaviour in a largely uncharted domain.

In 2017, India and the US signed a Framework to govern their cyber relationship. Through the Framework Agreement both states decided to share information and undertake practical cooperation to mitigate cyber threats. It also provides for the creation of a high-level Cyber Dialogue led by the Special Assistant to the President and Cybersecurity Coordinator of the United States and the Deputy National Security Advisor, Government of India. Similarly, during the visit of Crown Prince Sheikh Mohamed bin Zayed Al Nahyan of the United Arab Emirates in 2016, India and the UAE signed an MoU on Technical Cooperation in Cyber Space and Combating Cybercrime. While the initial focus of the MoU was training and cooperation for cybercrime investigations, a joint statement issued during the Crown Prince's second visit in 2017 indicates that the remit may have been expanded to include online extremism.

With China, however, the Modi administration has begun taking the first steps of what could possibly be a comprehensive bilateral relationship on cyber issues. In 2015, the two countries decided to set up a Home Minister-level mechanism for information sharing on critical issues such as terrorism, drug-trafficking and cybercrime. There has not been any significant headway since this announcement partly because of rising border-tensions between the two nations. In the future, however, given the significant economic interest that the Chinese tech industry has in the Indian market, a formal bilateral mechanism will be necessary to resolve issues around cyber security.

Conclusion

Overall, the Modi government's performance on cyber security has been adequate in certain domains while remaining vastly wanting in others. As the Potomac Institute's Cyber Readiness Index noted in 2016, the only area where India has achieved significant maturity is in cyber diplomacy.[43] This appears to still be the case in 2019.

It is impossible for any country that relies on technology to completely mitigate cyber threats. Increasing numbers of vulnerabilities with each passing year are an idiosyncratic aspect of the medium itself. However, many of these vulnerabilities can be managed by building institutional capacity and investment in technologies. An important precursor to this is acknowledging that the vulnerabilities exist in the first place—something that the current government is yet to do. Multiple breaches of Aadhaar demographic data over the past few years, have all been met by outright denials and ham-fisted responses from the government. As reliance on the internet for commerce and communication increases and the rest of the Indian population comes online, this will need to change.

Equally important is acknowledging that the protection of civilian infrastructure is as important as the protection of the national security apparatus—because today, both are inextricably linked. The government, therefore, needs to stop adopting policies that inadvertently impede cyber security. Policies like the draft amendments to intermediary liability law and mandatory data localisation under the Personal Data Protection Bill will likely hamper India's national security in the long run. For India to become a self-reliant and a secure digital economy, these policies must be abandoned.

NOTES

[1] P.P. Chaudhary, former Minister of State for Electronics And Information Technology, 'Issuance Of Aadhaar', Lok Sabha Un-starred Question No. 4373, 29.03.2017, https://uidai.gov.in/images/loksabha/LS_USQ_4373_answered_on_29032017.pdf; Mahendra Singh, '99% of Indians over 18 now have Aadhaar cards', *The Times of India*, 28 January 2017, https://timesofindia.indiatimes.com/india/99-of-indians-over-18-now-have-aadhaar/articleshow/56820818.cms; see: Ronald Abraham, Elizabeth S. Bennett, Noopur Sen and Neil Buddy Shah, State of Aadhaar Report 2016-17, *IDinsight*, May 2017, http://stateofaadhaar.in/wp-content/uploads/State-of-Aadhaar-Full-Report-2016-17-IDinsight.pdf (accessed 28 January 2019).

[2] Pratik Bhakta, 'Demonetisation effect: Digital payments India's new currency; debit card transactions surge to over 1 billion', *The Economic Times*, 27 May 2017 https://economictimes.indiatimes.com/industry/banking/finance/banking/digital-payments-indias-new-currency-debit-card-transactions-surge-to-over-1-billion/articleshow/58863652.cms (accessed 28 January 2019); Ajay Kumar, Former Additional Secretary, Ministry of Electronics and Information Technology, 'Bits and Bytes: Reaching money to the bottom of the pyramid,' 'India, Raisina Dialogue, 2017,' https://www.facebook.com/firstpostin/videos/1318701534856165/ (accessed 28 January 2019). For more information, watch Arvind Gupta, CEO of MyGov, 'Reimagining the State: Government as Service', AIMA's 4th National Leadership Conclave 2018.

[3] 'Digital Payment Revolution: Facts & Figures - Payments Progress', Press Information Bureau, Government of India, NITI Aayog, 14 April 2017, http://pib.nic.in/newsite/PrintRelease.aspx?relid=161040 (accessed 28 January 2019).

[4] 'What Is India Stack?, *IndiaStack*, http://indiastack.org/about/ (accessed 28 January 2019).

[5] 'A Free and Fair Digital Economy Protecting Privacy, Empowering Indians,' Committee of Experts under the Chairmanship of Justice B.N. Srikrishna, http://meity.gov.in/writereaddata/files/Data_Protection_Committee_Report.pdf (accessed 28 January 2019).

[6] 'National Cyber Security Policy, 2013,' Department of Electronics and Information Technology, 2 July 2013, available at: http://meity.gov.in/sites/upload_files/dit/files/National% 20Cyber%20Security%20Policy%20%281%29.pdf (accessed 28 January 2019).

[7] Varun Aggarwal, 'Gulshan Rai becomes first chief of cyber security; post created to tackle growing e-threats,' *The Economic Times*, 22 April 2015, https://economictimes.indiatimes.com/news/politics-and-nation/gulshan-rai-becomes-first-chief-of-cyber-security-post-created-to-tackle-growing-e-threats/articleshow/46449780.cms (accessed 28 January 2019).

[8] PTI, 'Government clears setting up of National Cyber Coordination Centre,' *The Economic Times*, 10 April 2015, https://economictimes.indiatimes.com/news/

defence/government-clears-setting-up-of-national-cyber-coordination-centre/articleshow/46864939.cms (accessed 28 January 2019).

[9] Shabi Hussain, 'India Smartphone Market sees a healthy growth of 20% in Q2 2018 as Xiaomi retains leadership, According to IDC India,' International Data Corporation, 13 August 2018, https://www.idc.com/getdoc.jsp?containerId=prAP44210918 (accessed 28 January 2019).

[10] Abdi Latif Dahir, 'China "gifted" the African Union a headquarters building and then allegedly bugged it for state secrets,' *Quartz*, 30 January 2018, https://qz.com/africa/1192493/china-spied-on-african-union-headquarters-for-five-years/ (accessed 28 January 2019).

[11] Joe Uchill, 'Report: Australian intelligence knows Huawei was used in espionage,' *Axios*, 4 November 2018, https://www.axios.com/report-australian-intelligence-know-huawei-1541285886-42f1eb64-98de-422f-9686-4174e41ef37e.html (accessed 28 January 2019).

[12] Yoshiyasu Shida and Yoshifumi Takemoto, 'Japan government to halt buying Huawei, ZTE equipment: sources,' *Reuters*, 7 December 2018, https://www.reuters.com/article/us-japan-china-huawei/japan-government-to-halt-buying-huawei-zte-equipment-sources-idUSKBN1O600X (accessed 28 January 2019).

[13] Kate Fazzini, 'US files criminal charges in two Huawei cases, seeks extradition of CFO Meng Wanzhou,' *CNBC*, 28 January 2019, https://www.cnbc.com/2019/01/28/us-seeks-extradition-of-huawei-cfo-meng-wanzhou.html (accessed 28 January 2019).

[14] Anandita Singh Mankotia, 'India unlikely to ban Huawei's 5G equipment,' *The Economic Times*, 21 December 2018, https://economictimes.indiatimes.com/industry/telecom/india-unlikely-to-ban-huaweis-5g-equipment/articleshow/67186519.cms (accessed 28 January 2019).

[15] PTI, 'Amid Doklam Standoff, Government Sends Notice to Chinese, Other Mobile Phone Makers Over Data Privacy,' *India.com*, 17 August 2018, https://www.india.com/news/agencies/govt-puts-mobile-phone-makers-on-notice-over-data-privacy-2406152/ (accessed 28 January 2019).

[16] PTI, 'Alibaba's UC Browser under govt scanner over data leaks,' *The Economic Times*, 23 August 2017, available at: https://economictimes.indiatimes.com/small-biz/startups/alibabas-uc-browser-under-govt-scanner-over-data-leaks/articleshow/60177266.cms (visited on 28 January 2019).

[17] Bedavyasa Mohanty and Madhulika Srikumar, 'Hitting Refresh: Making India-US Data Sharing Work,' Observer Research Foundation Special Report No. 39 (9 August 2017), https://www.orfonline.org/research/hitting-refresh-india-us-data-sharing-mlat/ (accessed 28 January 2019).

[18] Neha Alawadhi, 'CBI & FBI join hands to reduce time required to fulfil requests on information and evidence,' *The Economic Times*, 7 December 2015, https://economictimes.indiatimes.com/news/politics-and-nation/cbi-fbi-join-hands-to-reduce-time-required-to-fulfil-requests-on-information-and-evidence/articleshow/50069794.cms (accessed 28 January 2019).

19 Anirudh Regidi, 'WannaCry ransomware: Despite govt denials, experts say that India is the third largest source of attacks', *Firstpost*, 17 May 2017, http://tech.firstpost.com/news-analysis/wannacry-ransomware-despite-govt-denials-experts-say-that-india-is-the-third-largest-source-of-attacks-376439.html (accessed 28 January 2019).

20 IANS, 'Andhra police computers hit by cyberattack', *The Times of India*, 13 May 2017, http://timesofindia.indiatimes.com/india/andhra-police-computers-hit-by-cyberattack/articleshow/58658853.cms (accessed 28 January 2019).

21 Rimin Dutt, 'Massive ATM Card Hack Hits Indian Banks, 3.2 Million Debit Cards Affected,' *Huffington Post*, 21 October 2016, https://www.huffingtonpost.in/2016/10/20/massive-debit-card-hack-hits-indian-banks-3-2-million-cards-aff_a_21587810/ (accessed 28 January 2019).

22 Cyber Swachhta Kendra, https://www.cyberswachhtakendra.gov.in/about.html (accessed 28 January 2019).

23 Kriitka Sharma and Himani Chandna, 'Modi govt launches big revamp of official computer systems to counter hacking & cybercrime,' *The Print*, 29 November 2018, https://theprint.in/governance/modi-govt-launches-big-revamp-of-official-computer-systems-to-counter-hacking-cybercrime/156082/ (accessed 28 January 2019).

24 Surabhi Agarwal, 'Sarkari bot tool takes global malware to the cleaners,' *The Economic Times*, 31 January 2018, https://economictimes.indiatimes.com/tech/software/sarkari-bot-tool-takes-global-malware-to-the-cleaners/articleshow/62716203.cms (accessed 28 January 2019).

25 Section 66(F), Information Technology Act, 2000.

26 Ministry of Electronics and Information Technology, Draft National Encryption Policy, https://netzpolitik.org/wp-upload/draft-Encryption-Policyv1.pdf (accessed 28 January 2019).

27 Clause V(1), Draft National Encryption Policy, 2015.

28 Clause IV(4), Draft National Encryption Policy, 2015.

29 Betwa Sharma, 'Modi Government Withdraws Draft Encryption Policy: IT Minister,' *Huffington Post*, 22 September 2015, https://www.huffingtonpost.in/2015/09/22/draft-encryption-policy_n_8174870.html (accessed 28 January 2019).

30 Ministry of Electronics and Information Technology, 'he Information Technology [Intermediaries Guidelines (Amendment) Rules] 2018,' http://meity.gov.in/writereaddata/files/Draft_Intermediary_Amendment_24122018.pdf (accessed 28 January 2019).

31 ET Online, 'India is quietly preparing a cyber warfare unit to fight a new kind of enemy,' *The Economic Times*, 14 July 2018, https://economictimes.indiatimes.com/news/defence/india-is-quietly-preparing-a-cyber-warfare-unit-to-fight-a-new-kind-of-enemy/articleshow/61141277.cms

32 Arun Mohan Sukumar and Col R.K. Sharma, 'The Cyber Command: Upgrading India's National Security Architecture,' Observer Research Foundation, Special Report No. 9 (March 2016), https://www.orfonline.org/wp-content/uploads/

2016/03/SR_9_Arun-Mohan-Sukumar-and-RK-sharma.pdf (accessed 28 January 2019).

33 PTI, 'Cisco launches 5th global cyber range lab in Gurugram', *The Economic Times*, 12 April 2017, http://economictimes.indiatimes.com/tech/internet/cisco-launches-5th-global-cyber-range-lab-in-gurugram/articleshow/58142965.cms (accessed 28 January 2019).

34 Press Trust of India, 'India to build two test ranges of electronic warfare systems,' *Business Standard*, 20 January 2013, https://www.business-standard.com/article/economy-policy/india-to-built-two-test-ranges-of-electronic-warfare-systems-110112400166_1.html (accessed 28 January 2019).

35 Quick Heal Technologies, 'Cyber Swachhta Kendra—A Digital India Initiative for a Secure Cyber Ecosystem,' Quick Heal Blogs, 6 March 2017, https://blogs.quickheal.com/cyber-swachhta-kendra-digital-india-initiative-secure-cyber-ecosystem/ (accessed 28 January 2019).

36 Mohd Ujaley, 'Cisco Signs MoU With Modi Govt To Work On Cybersecurity Threat In India,' Express Computer, 25 July 2018, https://www.expresscomputer.in/news/cisco-signs-mou-with-modi-govt-to-work-on-cybersecurity-threat-in-india/20133/ (accessed 28 January 2019).

37 Leilah Elmokadem, 'Mapping of India's Cyber Security-Related Bilateral Agreements,' Centre for Internet and Society, 2017, https://cis-india.org/internet-governance/files/CyberSecurityAgreements_Infographic_04.pdf (last accessed 28 January 2019)

38 'Joint Statement on the Inaugural India-U.S 2+2 Ministerial Dialogue,' Press Information Bureau, Ministry of Defence, Government of India, 6 September 2018, http://pib.nic.in/newsite/PrintRelease.aspx?relid=183300 (accessed 28 January 2019).

39 'Framework for the UK-India Cyber Relationship,' Government of the United Kingdom, available at: https://assets.publishing.service.gov.uk/government/uploads/system/uploads/attachment_data/file/732480/Framework_for_the_UK-India_Cyber_Relationship_FINAL_for_upload__ 002_.pdf (accessed 28 January 2019)

40 'India-France Joint Statement on the occasion of the State Visit of President Francois Hollande of the French Republic to India (25 January 2016),' Ministry of External Affairs, Government of India, 25 January 2016, https://www.mea.gov.in/bilateral-documents.htm?dtl/26297/India France (accessed 28 January 2019).

41 'India, Russia to set up expert group on cyber-security, counter-terrorism,' Embassy of the Russian Federation in the Republic of India, 8 September 2015, http://rusembindia.com/home/actual-topics/104-actualnews/7470-india-russia-to-set-up-expert-group-on-cyber-security-counter-terrorism (accessed 28 January 2019).

42 'India, China to set up framework on terrorism, cyber crime,' *Hindustan Times*, 20 November 2015, https://www.hindustantimes.com/india/india-china-to-set-

up-framework-on-terrorism-cyber-crime-drug-trafficking/story-kuyAypr8wWKABbue9h0i0L.html (last visited on 28 January 2019); 'Joint Statement between the Ministry of Home Affairs and the Ministry of Public Security of the People's Republic of China,' Press Information Bureau, Ministry of Home Affairs, 21 November 2015, http://pib.nic.in/newsite/PrintRelease.aspx?relid=131765 (accessed 28 January 2019).

43 Melissa Hathaway, et al., 'India Cyber Readiness at a Glance,' Potomac Institute for Policy Studies, December 2016, http://www.potomacinstitute.org/images/CRI/CRI_India_Profile.pdf (accessed 28 January 2019).

8

Environmental Security Challenges and India

Aparna Roy

ENVIRONMENTAL security has emerged as a unique feature of national and international politics in the twenty-first century. As indispensable factors in the solution to environment and climate crisis, rising powers such as India are playing an increasingly decisive role today. At the international negotiation stage of global environmental politics (GEP), India has been regarded as a 'game changer' for its environmental negotiation strategies based on equity.[1] India has adopted a series of key environmental policies since 2006 such as the National Environment Policy (NEP) and the National Action Plan on Climate Change (NAPCC) that reflect optimism and commitment to secure the environment and resolve the crisis surrounding it.[2]

In the past five years, Prime Minister Narendra Modi's government has earned accolades for demonstrating leadership towards environment security and climate action. Modi was awarded the 2018 'Champions of the Earth' award—the highest environmental honour by the United Nations Environment Programme (UNEP) under 'Policy Leadership' category for his 'pioneering work in championing the International Solar Alliance (ISA) and promoting new areas of cooperation on environmental action'.[3] In 2017, after the United States withdrew from the Paris Agreement, the world turned to India for climate leadership. India is leading the world in the path of green energy transitions and has embarked on an ambitious goal of achieving renewable power capacity of 227 gigawatts (GW) by the year 2022—with the primary objective of achieving energy security by developing indigenous manufacturing capacity.[4] Indeed, the country has been a shining example for other developing nations of 'how stronger [environment and] climate actions could be successfully aligned with development imperatives'.[5]

While India has made significant achievements in environment and climate action in the past decade, however, the question is: Has India, under the leadership of Modi, been successful in ensuring environment security at the national and regional levels?

During the past five years, the Modi government has worked on a host of environment acts and regulations. These include the third National Wildlife Action Plan (2017-31) of India, *Namami Gange*, Swachh Bharat Abhiyan, draft National Forest Policy (NFP) 2018, draft National Energy Policy (2017), draft CRZ Notification 2018, and the Plastic Waste Management (Amendment) Rules, 2018. Yet, they have not yielded significant reforms on the ground. India stands 177 out of 180 countries on the Environmental Performance Index, 2018.[6] The country also has the dubious distinction of having the maximum number of environmental conflicts in the world, with the Environmental Justice Atlas (an international database) recording 271 cases in India in 2017.[7] Fourteen out of top 20 most polluted cities in the world are in India.[8] Its most important water resource—the 2,525-km-long Ganga that flows through Uttarakhand, Uttar Pradesh, Bihar, Jharkhand and West Bengal, serving water to 40 per cent of India's population—is grappling with extreme pollution. Despite *Namami Gange* project—the cleaning, conservation and revival of the river by March 2019—being Modi's key electoral promise the National Green Tribunal observed in 2017 that 'not a single drop of the Ganga has been cleaned so far'.[9]

Today, India is faced with diverse and multidimensional environmental challenges—air and water pollution, growing scarcity of water and natural resources, groundwater depletion, lack of clean water, energy shortage, climate impacts, loss of biodiversity and poor plastic and solid waste management among others—that have severe ramifications for key national development priorities such as poverty alleviation, health, livelihood and infrastructure. As a threat to the economic and social well-being of people, environmental challenges, therefore, have the potential to spur conflict.[10] The environment is one of the most transnational issues, the security of which is imperative for national as well as regional peace and stability.

The environment—security nexus

The increasing impact of environment degradation and climate change on individual, national as well as global security has created a new agenda in the security studies discourse. The scarcity of natural resources, reducing cropland, forest degradation and depleting fresh water , coupled with demographic pressures and lack of structural ingenuity could potentially lead to clashes between various social groups, thereby impeding the process of development.[11] This security-environment linkage act as a determinant of violence and conflicts, especially in the developing countries as[12] poor governance, existing development challenges, political instability, reduced foreign assistance and mobilised anti-state activities add to the severity of impacts. The lack of institutional capacity and strong governance mechanism for conflict resolution over issues related to natural resources, further exacerbates such vulnerabilities.[13] It needs to be ensured that environmental security issues are 'interconnected with decision-making patterns, anthropogenic threats to ecosystem health, global systems and state institutions, and a normative context within which to achieve sustainable development'.[14] A secure human environment dynamic is imperative, not just for the realisation of sustainable development goals (SDGs), but to attain internal and human security, social equity, justice and social rest.[15]

The emerging domain has led to an understanding of non-conventional security issues such as the role of conservation, restoration, resilience building and mitigation to promote peace, stability and human security.[16]

The new discourse encourages the translation of environmental security concerns into national security practices, thereby broadening the security agenda of a country.[17]

'Environment' in India's security doctrine

The increasing impact of environmental change on the tactics, operations and strategy has led to the emergence of environment as a critical area in India's security paradigm. Following the devastation brought by the 2004 Indian Ocean tsunami on the Car Nicobar Air Force Base, 2014 Cyclone Hudhud on India's Eastern Naval Command Air Base, frequent storms and sea-level rise impacting India's naval assets worth more than US$300 million, 'environment' has been recognised as a security threat in the 2017 Joint Doctrine of the Indian Armed Forces.[18] The doctrine lists a range of non-traditional security threats related to the environment such as climate change impacts, ecosystem disruption, energy population issues and unsustainable modes of production that has the potential to influence conflict and war, and calls for a military response if environmental degradation and related issues increase security risks.[19]

Since the Indian troops are deployed in some of the most ecologically and politically sensitive zones, environmental and climate change impacts have the potential to physically alter their battlefields.[20] For example, changes in Himalayan glaciers could impact water levels in downstream rivers, thereby limiting the military's range and impacting water supplies for military installations.[21]

Environment degradation and climate change are impacting shared resources between India and Pakistan, causing one of the world's highest battleground, the Siachen glacier to recede by nearly 800 metres in the last 20 years. Piles of human waste, plastic sheets, empty artillery shells, ammunition boxes, parachutes and food packets have polluted the world's highest battlefield as well as the Indus River.[22] While the Indian Army launched the 'Green Siachen, Clean Siachen Campaign' to mitigate the impact,[23] the army still needs to address the problem of waste in the glacier and prepare for the long-term impacts of environment threats and climate change.

On India's east, the environmental impacts of climate change such as sea-level rise and depleting natural resources are causing large-scale illegal migration. Increased inundation and saline contamination of the soil are affecting crop production and incomes, and will force nearly 200,000 coastal residents of Bangladesh to migrate in search of alternative livelihoods.[24] Such large-scale illegal migration could stress the resources of the receiving country, thereby pushing India and Bangladesh into potential tensions and conflict. While the challenges are extremely complex and it is difficult to address the threat that the resource constraints of neighbouring nations pose to stability, India has the opportunity to lead the way by deeper integration of resource considerations into its national and regional security policy and planning.

As part of the Indian military's efforts to promote environmental sustainability and efficiency, the army has allowed installations for solar energy generation on defence lands across the country.[25] Following suit, the Indian Navy is committed to achieving zero carbon footprint and is in the process of upgrading its 'blue water' capabilities. At the 2016 International Fleet Review, the Indian Navy launched its first warship running entirely on biofuel. India's largest naval base in the east of the Suez Canal, Karwar in Karnataka has been made 'Smart Green Naval Base' with efficient energy, water and wastewater management systems.[26] Furthermore, since the 2004 Indian Ocean tsunami, encouraging military-to-military cooperation around humanitarian assistance and disaster response has become a priority area for the Indian armed forces. Besides, in collaborating with the United States, Japan and other countries, India is at the forefront of conducting joint regional disaster response strategies.[27] Its relief exercise to Typhoon Haiyan in the Philippines is a case in point.

While the Indian military is taking notable steps to address environmental security risks, yet they remain fragmented and sporadic. To attain environment security at the national and regional level, it is imperative for the military to align its efforts with the country's environmental and climate change objectives, especially under the National Action Plan for Climate Change (NAPCC) and the Sendai Framework for Disaster Risk Reduction (2015-2030). Going forward, to maintain a sustained operational capability, the Indian military should seek to build resilience of its equipment (including tanks, submarines and aircraft) and strategies to the impacts of environmental changes such as temperature rise. It is also important that the military adheres to environmental accountability norms and regulations such as meeting the requirements of Ozone-Depleting Substances regulations and take a more holistic and institutionalised approach to achieve long-term national security objectives threatened by environmental degradation.

Environment security challenges and conflict in India

South Asia is one of the most environmentally insecure regions in the world. The region is host to nearly a quarter of the world's population and faces severe vulnerabilities ranging from rising sea levels, coastal flooding, depleting natural resources and glacial melt.[28]

South Asia contains less than 5 per cent of its annual renewable water resources. A three-fold increase in human population since 1950 has resulted in a sharp decline in South Asia's water availability from over 21,000 cubic metres per capita in the 1960s to about 8,000 in 2005. The availability of arable land for agriculture has fallen from over one hectare per person at the beginning of the twentieth century to less than 0.1 ha today.[29] The region is projected to face severe water scarcity by 2025, impacting food security, health and livelihoods.

The region is also energy scarce and has one of the world's worst electricity grid systems.[30] With the increased demographic pressures on scarce natural resources, the prospect of inter-state and regional conflicts in South Asia is gaining viability.

India, due to its size of population, military, economy and geography, is an overwhelming presence in the subcontinent. However, nearly 40 million people of the country's population are projected to be at heightened risk of dying from impact of sea-level rise by 2050.[31] A study has estimated that rising temperature is most likely to cause a sharp fall in India's agricultural productivity- by 30 to 40 per cent by 2080.[32] While India hosts nearly 20 per cent of the world's population, it has only four per cent of the world's water resources at its disposal. About 63 million of India's population lack access to safe drinking water at home. India's extensive water consumption demand has led users to voraciously raid groundwater supplies.[33] The Central Ground Water Board (CGWB) monitoring data suggests that water levels in 61 per cent of the country's wells have declined by more than 70 per cent between 2007 and 2017 (pre-monsoon).[34] Similarly, in case of energy, India's economic growth has led to an increased demand, projecting it to be world's third-largest energy consumer by 2030. India has made significant achievement in its renewable energy target. However, the nation still cannot guarantee energy access to about 32 million homes and struggles to meet the minimum energy demand in some regions.[35] Consequently, resource scarcity and degrading environment have already begun to spur tensions and conflict in India and vis-a-vis the region.

Domestic Issues

India has the worst history of environment conflicts. Climate vulnerability and resource constraints have sharp ties with stability and national security. The Maoist anti-government insurgency—the country's gravest internal security threat—is a case in point. The insurgency base lies in India's eastern and central reaches that are rich reserves of coal—India's most heavily consumed energy source.

The local communities in these mineral rich areas are not benefited from heavy resource extraction, fuelling grievances among poor villagers that in turn aid the Maoists to spark recruitment. Intensive coal mining often leads to large-scale displacement and hazardous living conditions, strengthening insurgency even further.[36]

The Modi government has launched effective military operations to curb the Maoists.[37] However, it has failed to address environmental insecurity that had spurred insurgencies. The government needs to address the underlying problem associated with environment and resource exploitations in the region and its operations have to be coupled with an effective development agenda for people vulnerable to join the Maoists.

Apart from organised insurgency conflicts, food shortages due to climate change regularly fuel political agitation, social violence and unrest. Devastating crop losses due to severe drought in India has led to series of incidences of farmer suicides and street protests to demand debt relief and better crop prices.[38] In a number of states, there were reports of clashes between protesting farmers and policemen leading to several human injuries and casualties.[39] According to a study by the University of California, suicides among Indian farmers have increased with the rise in temperature. The study suggests that an increase of 1° Celsius above the average temperature is associated with approximately 70 additional suicides.[40]

A country's failure to address such 'climate-driven risks' could lead to increased conflict over water, food, energy and land, particularly in already unstable regions. The Modi government had the opportunity to go beyond addressing the immediate causes of distress through loan waivers and subsidies to develop long-term strategies focused on sustainable management of natural resources such as arable-land management and water conservation, for helping agricultural communities survive bad harvests and recover from distress.

Regional Issues

Environmental security is emerging as a key player in determining India's relationship with its neighbourhood. There is a growing understanding that without addressing the environment security concerns, many of the regional development issues cannot be tackled effectively. This is especially so as substantial amount of environmental issues that India faces are trans-boundary.[41]

Indo-Pakistan relations that have remained hostile since 1947 have now an emerging discourse on the environmental aspects. There is a realisation of the strategic significance of Kashmir for Pakistan to gain complete control over the Indus River.[42] However, this shared resource is impacted by environmental stressors such as pollution, glacial melt and waste.[43]

There is also a rise in bone of contention between India and Pakistan over the former's construction of hydropower projects on the western rivers of Indus basin. Although the Indus Waters Treaty has allocated these waters to Pakistan, India is allowed to develop dams and build hydropower projects.[44] Pakistan's accusation of India 'stealing' Pakistan's water has emerged as a security issue as Lashkar-e-Taiba (LeT), an anti-India militant group, has threatened to attack India in response.[45]

Environmental change is also altering the battlefields between the two armies. Glacier melt and avalanches have cost the lives of Indian and Pakistan soldiers posted in the Siachen glacier.[46] Since the glacier melt is projected to accelerate in pace, it is imperative to realign military strategy or the need for a renewed dispute settlement mechanism.

Similarly, a water-rich Arunachal Pradesh has become an environment battleground between India and China. China, like India, suffers from water scarcity. Its northern region is parched with per capita availability of only 225 cubic metres of water per year. The shared river Brahmaputra that emerges in Tibet and flows through Arunachal Pradesh in India and Bangladesh before falling into the Bay of Bengal, has attained an increased strategic significance.[47] There are reports that China is testing techniques to build a 1,000-km-long tunnel to divert the Brahmaputra river to its arid north, impacting the lower riparian.[48] Furthermore, security analysts predict the Bay of Bengal and its rich, untapped natural resources could be a future source of Sino-India conflict.[49]

India has the capacity to turn the potential conflicts over shared natural resources into opportunities for cooperation. This could be through an integrated, collaborative mechanism for sustainable management of all shared rivers. Joint patrolling of waterways to check illegal activities in the resource bases could be another avenue.

Both India and Bangladesh have been and will continue to be impacted by cyclones and other climate and environmental stressors. Cyclone Aila, that hit the India-Bangladesh border in 2012, affected the lives and livelihood of people of both the countries. Massive flooding and salt water intrusion post the disaster destroyed agricultural crops and contaminated fresh water resources threatening lives and economy.[50]

It is, therefore, imperative for countries in the region to adopt an integrated and effective cooperation for climate change, natural disaster management, and environment protection.

The Modi government had focused on increased cooperation in the region through its policies such as 'Act East,' 'Neighbourhood First' and has been pushing for the revival of the Bay of Bengal Initiative for Multi-Sectoral Technical and Economic Cooperation (BIMSTEC). However, as a country leading the 'environment and disaster management' agenda under BIMSTEC, the government failed to create institutional frameworks under the regional fora to empower a paradigm policy shift from a traditional country-centric, reactive approach to environment security and climate change towards a joint, proactive, holistic one that encompasses mitigation, adaptation and preparedness.[51] The government also did not seek to establish the relevance of military-to-military cooperation between countries in disaster preparedness, management, rehabilitation and relief.

The government certainly has failed to mobilise significant support of a majority of developing countries on environment cooperation. Given that BIMSTEC is being revitalised today, two decades since its establishment, there is an opportunity for India to embark on preparing an ambitious climate action and environment security framework for regional cooperation. This should inculcate a 'multi-hazard and multi-sectoral approach towards common outcomes through the institutionalisation of partnerships across all levels of governance' among the neighbouring countries.[52]

Way forward

The Modi government has tried to address environmental security concerns by framing more stringent laws on conservation of natural resources, limiting the environmental impacts of industrialisation, and offering compensation to sufferers of industrial impacts. However, India still ranks highest in the world on the rate of environmental conflicts. According to the Environmental Justice Atlas, an international database,

India had 271 listed conflicts, while Colombia is second on the list with only 128 cases. India is at the bottom of the heap on environmental health and third-worst in the world on air quality. The lapse in environmental security governance has led the judiciary of India fight for environmental causes. According to an analysis in the State of India's Environment (SoE) 2018, there were 21,145 environmental cases pending for trial in 2016.[53]

Governance mechanisms for environmental security in India are poor not only because of the policies but also of their lack of implementation. The top-down approach does not allow meaningful public participation. There is a need, therefore, for a multi-layered environmental security governance system that goes beyond formulation of centrally designed rules and one size-fits-all solutions. Such system must include the voice and agency of local people and should blend conservation goals with sustainable development. At the regional level, India should push for a transformative approach that entails recognising and overcoming the differences between countries on the issues of environment and shared natural resources such as India and Bangladesh's divergences over water-sharing of trans-boundary Teesta. The countries of the region need to recognise that considering their regional setting and geographical proximity, the security of states is contingent upon each other. Our future government must, therefore, prioritise building 'environment and climate change' as a common security agenda in the region.

NOTES

[1] Mintu Barua, 'India's Environmental Strategy in the Global Climate Negotiations,' International Studies, Vol. 51, no. 1-4 (2014): pp. 195-211.

[2] Ibid.

[3] Urvashi Sarkar, 'UN's Green Award for Modi Comes Despite Criticism of Environmental Record,' *The Wire*, 3 October 2018, https://thewire.in/environment/un-green-award-narendra-modi-controversial-environmental-record

[4] 'India has embarked upon an ambitious plan to install 227 GW of renewable energy by 2022,' *The Financial Express*, 28 June 2018, https://www.financialexpress.com/opinion/india-has-embarked-upon-an-ambitious-plan-to-install-227-gw-of-renewable-energy-by-2022/1223046/

[5] Aparna Roy, 'Only India can save the Paris climate agreement,' *Hindustan Times*,

15 June 2017, https://www.hindustantimes.com/analysis/only-india-can-save-the-paris-climate-agreement/story-okq67Pw4m4Pc8A6hHOyMsI.html

[6] PTI, 'India ranks 177 out of 180 in Environmental Performance Index,' *The Hindu*, 24 January 2018, https://www.thehindu.com/sci-tech/energy-and-environment/india-ranks-177-out-of-180-in-environmental-performance-index/article22513016.ece

[7] Soumya Sarkar, 'India has more environmental conflicts than any other country in the world,' *The Hindu*, 2 June 2018, https://www.thehindu.com/sci-tech/energy-and-environment/india-has-more-environmental-conflicts-than-any-other-country-in-the-world/article24066709.ece

[8] PTI, 'India had 14 out of world's 20 most polluted cities in terms of PM2.5 levels in 2016, says WHO,' *The Hindu*, 2 May 2018, https://www.thehindu.com/sci-tech/energy-and-environment/14-out-of-worlds-20-most-polluted-cities-in-india-who/article23745178.ece

[9] Aparna Roy, 'Ganga won't be cleaned even after 200 years ... unless we learn why generous flows of funds have failed so far,' *The Times of India*, 15 February 2018, https://timesofindia.indiatimes.com/blogs/toi-edit-page/ganga-wont-be-cleaned-even-after-200-years-unless-we-learn-why-generous-flows-of-funds-have-failed-so-far/

[10] Gurneeta Vasudeva, 'Environmental security: A South Asian Perspective,' Tata Energy and Resources Institute, Arlington (2002).

[11] Stefano Bocchi, Stefano Peppino Disperati and Simone Rossi, 'Environmental security: A geographic information system analysis approach—the case of Kenya,' Environmental Management, Vol. 37, no. 2 (2006): pp. 186-199.

[12] Nina Graeger, 'Environmental security?' Journal of Peace Research, Vol. 33, no. 1 (1996): pp. 109-116 .

[13] UNIFTPA , 2012, 'Toolkit and Guidance for Preventing and Managing Land and Natural Resources Conflict,' The United Nations Interagency Framework Team for Preventive Action, New York, USA.

[14] Mabroor Hassan, Manzoor Khan Afridi and Muhammad Irfan Khan, 'Environmental diplomacy in South Asia: Considering the environmental security, conflict and development nexus,' Geoforum, Vol. 82 (2017): pp. 127-130.

[15] S.R. Khan, 2001, 'Environmental Security in Pakistan, Are There Grounds for Optimism? Sustainable Development Policy Institute, Islamabad, Pakistan.

[16] Niloy Ranjan Biswas, 'Is the environment a security threat? Environmental security beyond securitization,' International Affairs Review, Vol. 20, no. 1 (2011): p.1.

[17] Maria Julia Trombetta, 'Environmental security and climate change: analysing the discourse,' Cambridge Review of International Affairs, Vol. 21, no. 4 (2008): pp. 585-602.

[18] '2017 Joint Doctrine of the Indian Armed Forces,' Headquarters Integrated Defence Staff, Ministry of Defence, New Delhi, India, https://bharatshakti.in/wp-content/uploads/2015/09/Joint_Doctrine_Indian_Armed_Forces.pdf

[19] Ibid.

[20] Joseph P. Hupy, 'The Environmental Footprint of War,' Environment and History, Vol. 14, No. 3 (2008): pp. 405-421.

[21] Dhanasree Jayaram, 'Indian Military Recognizes Environment as "Critical" Security Issue, But Response Is Still Fragmented,' Wilson Centre, 29 January 2018.

[22] Agencies, 'Siachen has receded 800 m in 20 years: UN,' *The Indian Express*, 19 August 2009, http://archive.indianexpress.com/news/siachen-has-receded-800-m-in-20-years-un/503886/

[23] Anil Chopra, 'Unforgiving Battleground: Army jawans posted at Siachen serve in the toughest of conditions,' *DNA*, 6 February 2016, https://www.dnaindia.com/analysis/standpoint-unforgiving-battleground-army-jawans-posted-at-siachen-serve-in-the-toughest-of-conditions-2174505

[24] Ananya Bhattacharya, 'Climate change may force 200,000 people in Bangladesh to migrate,' *QUARTZ India*, 23 October 2018, https://qz.com/india/1432375/climate-change-may-force-200000-people-in-bangladesh-to-migrate/

[25] National Solar Mission (NSM) vision document, The Ministry of New and Renewable Energy (MNRE).

[26] Manu Pubby, 'International Fleet Review 2016: Navy to showcase warship running on biofuel at Vizag,' *The Economic Times*, 14 July 2018, https://economictimes.indiatimes.com/news/defence/international-fleet-review-2016-navy-to-showcase-warship-running-on-biofuel-at-vizag/articleshow/50858844.cms

[27] India-Japan Vision Statement, Ministry of External Affairs, https://www.mea.gov.in/bilateral-documents.htm?dtl/30543/IndiaJapan_ Vision_Statement

[28] Sangit Sarita Dwivedi, 'Understanding South Asian Vulnerability: Perspectives of Regional Security, Crimson Publishers, 18 December 2017, https://crimsonpublishers.com/aaoa/pdf/AAOA.000515.pdf

[29] Tushaar Shah and Uma Lele (Ed.), 'Climate Change, Food and Water Security in South Asia: Critical Issues and Cooperative Strategies in an Age of Increased Risk and Uncertainty,' GWP and IWMI Workshop, Colombo (23-25 February 2011), Global Water Partnership (GWP), Stockholm, Sweden.

[30] 'South Asia has the most unreliable power supply in the world,' *The Economic Times*, 17 December 2018 https://energy.economictimes.indiatimes.com/news/power/infographics-south-asia-has-the-most-unreliable-power-supply-in-the-world/67129573

[31] PTI, '40 million Indians at risk from rising sea levels: UN report,' *The Economic Times*, 20 May 2016, https://economictimes.indiatimes.com/news/politics-and-nation/40-million-indians-at-risk-from-rising-sea-levels-un-report/articleshow/52358231.cms?utm_source=contentofinterest&utm_medium=text&utm_campaign=cppst

[32] B. Bapuji Rao, P. Santhibhushan Chowdary, V. M. Sandeep, V. U. M. Rao, and B. Venkateswarlu, 'Rising minimum temperature trends over India in recent decades: Implications for agricultural production,' Global and Planetary Change 117 (2014): pp. 1-8.

[33] Prachi Salve, '63 million Indians do not have access to clean drinking water,' *Hindustan Times*, 21 March 2017, https://www.hindustantimes.com/india-

news/6-3-crore-indians-do-not-have-access-to-clean-drinking-water/story-dWIEyP962FnM8Mturbc52N.html

[34] Badri Chatterjee, 'Water levels fell in 61% of India's wells in last decade, says report by Union ministry,' *Hindustan Times*, 9 April 2018, https://www.hindustantimes.com/mumbai-news/water-levels-fell-in-61-of-india-s-wells-in-last-decade-says-report-by-union-ministry/story-A7Y0uiwMv9TvL4 KAR8pzAI.html

[35] Rajesh Kumar Singh and Saket Sundria, 'India Nears Power Success, But Millions Still in the Dark,' *Bloomberg*, 27 April 2018, https://www.bloomberg.com/news/articles/2018-04-26/india-nears-power-success-but-millions-are-still-in-the-dark

[36] Michael Kugelman, 'India's nexus between resources, climate change - and stability,' NATO review, https://www.nato.int/docu/review/2012/food-water-energy/India_Nexus_Climate_resources_stability/EN/index.htm

[37] Kamaljit Kaur Sandhu, '12 takeaways from Centre's new strategy to deal with Naxals,' *India Today*, 8 May 2017, https://www.indiatoday.in/india/story/naxals-mha-rajnath-singh-narendra-modi-government-strategy-975991-2017-05-08

[38] Joyjeet Das, 'State election results grim reminder to how deep India's rural crisis is,' *Down to Earth*, 17 December 2018, https://www.downtoearth.org.in/news/agriculture/state-election-results-grim-reminder-to-how-deep-india-s-rural-crisis-is-62481

[39] Peeyush Khandelwal, 'Police-farmers clash near Delhi, Opposition alleges 'brutal crackdown',' *Hindustan Times*, 2 October 2018, https://www.hindustantimes.com/india-news/kisan-rally-cops-use-tear-gas-water-cannons-as-protesting-farmers-try-to-enter-delhi/story-6RgpgNtHSK0fHaDirev0mI.html

[40] Tamma A. Carleton, 'Crop-damaging temperatures increase suicide rates in India.' Proceedings of the National Academy of Sciences, Vol. 114, no. 33 (2017): pp. 8746-8751.

[41] Mintu Barua, 'India's Environmental Strategy in the Global Climate Negotiations,' International Studies, Vol. 51, no. 1-4 (2014): pp. 195-211.

[42] Gregory Pappas, 'Pakistan and Water: New Pressures on Global Security and Human Health.' American Journal of Public Health, Vol. 101, no. 5 (2011): pp. 786-788.

[43] Walter W. Immerzeel, Ludovicus P.H. van Beek and Marc F.P. Bierkens, 'Climate change will affect the Asian water towers,' Science, Vol. 328, no. 5984 (2010): pp. 1382-1385.

[44] Gregory Pappas, 'Pakistan and Water: New Pressures on Global Security and Human Health,' American Journal of Public Health, Vol. 101, no. 5 (2011): pp. 786-788.

[45] Myra MacDonald, 'Lashkar-e-Taiba threatens more violence in Kashmir,' *Reuters*, 25 March 2009, http://blogs.reuters.com/pakistan/2009/03/25/lashkar-e-taiba-threatens-more-violence-in-kashmir/

[46] Ritu Sharma, 'Changing climate new adversary of India's armed forces,' India Strategic, September 2009, http://www.indiastrategic.in/topstories376.htm

[47] S.K. Mahapatra and K. C. Ratha, 'Brahmaputra River: A bone of contention between India and China.' Water Utility Journal, Vol. 13 (2016): pp. 91-99.

[48] Stephen Chen, 'Chinese engineers plan 1,000km tunnel to make Xinjiang desert bloom,' *South China Monitoring Post*, 29 October 2017, https://www.scmp.com/news/china/society/article/2116750/chinese-engineers-plan-1000km-tunnel-make-xinjiang-desert-bloom

[49] David M. Malone and Rohan Mukherjee, 'India and China: Conflict and Cooperation,' *Survival*, Vol. 52, no. 1 (2010): pp. 137-158.

[50] Sebak Kumar Saha, 'Cyclone Aila, livelihood stress, and migration: empirical evidence from coastal Bangladesh,' *Disasters*, Vol. 41, no. 3 (2017): pp. 505-526.

[51] Aparna Roy, 'BIMSTEC and climate change: Setting a common agenda,' *ORF Issue Brief*, 18 October 2017, https://www.orfonline.org/research/bimstec-climate-change-setting-common-agenda/

[52] Ibid.

[53] 'State of India's Environment (SoE) in Figures, 2018 is out,' Down to Earth, 6 June 2018, https://www.downtoearth.org.in/news/latest-state-of-india-s-environment-soe-in-figures-2018-is-out-60767

9

Towards a Gender Responsive National Security Policy

Vidisha Mishra

NATIONAL security discourse has a gender blind spot.[1] The decades-long academic siloing of national security and gender studies—with infrequent methodical intersections—has translated into real world policy outcomes.[2] As women have steadily gained more representation in crucial decision-making roles in international politics as well as in peace and security processes, it may be argued that gender dimensions are now integrated into national security policy considerations. The unprecedented advocacy for gender equality as a fundamental right,[3] and its recognition as a pre-condition for development and has led policymakers to commit, at least in theory, to mainstreaming gender considerations across sectors.

In reality, however, stereotypes have proven to be rigid,[4] and institutional architectures have been slow in catching up with normative progress—reinforcing the historical neglect of the conceptual and political intersections of gender and security constructs.[5] Further, discourse on the broader topic of gender and national security is often restricted to the topic of women in combat roles. While representational parity is significant, the causal inter-relationship between gender equality and national security needs a more nuanced consideration.

With regards to representation, India has witnessed dramatic changes in the last few years. In 2019, the country's 70th Republic Day parade involved many firsts: for the first time, a woman army officer, Lieutenant Bhavana Kasturi led an all-male contingent of the Indian Army Service Corps (ASC).[6] In addition, Captain Bhavna Syal, a third-generation officer in the armed forces, led the transportable satellite terminal's contingent.[7]

In another first, Major Khushboo Kanwar created history by leading the all-women Assam Rifles contingent, which participated in the parade for the first time.[8] Assam Rifles—India's oldest paramilitary force, started the recruitment of women personnel in 2015, with the first batch of 124 women passing out in April 2016.[9] Demonstrating another shift in tradition, Lieutenant Ambika Sudhakaran led a marching naval contingent of 144 sailors.

While the demonstration of women's strength at the 2019 Republic Day parade is more symbolic of a gradual shift in attitudes than a radical disassociation of power, security and war with masculinity, it is certain that under Prime Minister Modi's administration, gender has been more central in core national security and foreign policy discussions than before. The fact that since 2017, Modi's Cabinet Committee on Security (CCS) included two women members—Sushma Swaraj, Minister of External Affairs, and Nirmala Sitharaman, Minister of Defence—is made more significant by the fact that they were the first two women to hold these portfolios which are traditionally considered as male bastions, in over three decades.[10]

At the same time, it is important to recognise that the link between women office holders and gender in national security is complex. Previous studies establish that the ability of female officeholders to represent women's interests is 'context dependent—varying with the level of party control over legislators and the gender stereotypes that officeholders confront'.[11] Both ministers have been notable in their leadership—Swaraj in pioneering what is now known as 'Twitter diplomacy',[12] and Sitharaman in being the face of military reforms at a crucial time in India. The two ministers have also been vociferous advocates for gender equality in society—Swaraj recently urged men to share household responsibilities for breaking stereotypes,[13] and Sitharaman criticised the baseless association of sexual violence with women's choice of clothing—both unprecedented statements by holders of these portfolios.[14] However, neither minister has taken a stand for the Women's Reservation Bill or the Constitution (108th Amendment) Bill, 2008 advocating 33 per cent reservation for women in Parliament.[15] Even so, a day after Sitharaman took charge as Defence Minister, it was declared that 800 women would be inducted in the military police.[16] In addition, Sitharaman has reiterated the government's commitment to 'seriously' work towards having women in combat roles.[17] While it is clear that the presence of women in previously male-dominated leadership roles in the national security arena is a step in the right direction, it is also true that women's political gains do not automatically translate into substantive differences in national security outcomes which, in practice, intersect with gender in a more intrinsic manner and, therefore, require broader measures in addition to representational parity.

In this context, the rest of this chapter aims to unpack the complex commensurabilities between gender and national security constructs and attempts to analyse the Modi government's reforms to security with regard to gender. It ends with identifying key challenges that remain and how the existing gaps can be bridged.

Linking gender and national security

A growing body of research has established the inter-linkages between gender equality and national security. A 2016 study on perceptions of gender diversity in national security by New America argues that gender inclusivity improves peacebuilding and peacekeeping operations.[18] There is compelling evidence that the global advancement of gender equality around the world helps in the growth of global gross domestic product, decrease in hunger and can aid the prevention and countering of violent extremism.[19]

The gender and security link has further been cemented by on-going research involving gender-differentiated data and creation of global databases that provide empirical proof of women's societal status being inextricably linked to state power, stability, corruption and prosperity, amongst other indicators.[20] Previous research has established a strong correlation between gender inequality and levels of conflict—societies that are more gender-unequal and have higher rates of violence against women are more prone to violence and instability.[21] The reverse, that violent and unstable societies witness more adverse gender gaps and a lower societal status of women, is true as well.[22] However, while policy discourse and policymakers generally accept that promoting political stability and economic growth can improve the status of women; the reversed causal arrow is yet to gain wider acceptance. [23]

Gender refers to the particular roles and relationships, personality traits, attitudes, behaviours and values that society ascribes to men and women. 'Gender' therefore refers to learned differences between men and women, while 'sex' refers to the biological differences between males and females. Gender roles vary widely within and across cultures and can change over time. Gender refers not simply to women or men but to the relationship between them.

Gender mainstreaming is the process of assessing the implications for women and men of any planned action, including legislation, policies or programmes, in all areas and at all levels.

Source: Peter Albrecht and Karen Barnes, 'National Security Policy-Making and Gender,' *Gender and Security Sector Reform Toolkit*, Eds. Megan Bastick and Kristin Valasek. Geneva: DCAF, OSCE/ODIHR, UN-INSTRAW, (2008)

There are other significant examples of how gender dimensions matter in security outcomes as well. For instance, young, unmarried men who lack economic prospects are more at risk for recruitment by extremists groups.[24] The only surviving attacker involved in the 26/11 Mumbai attacks had told interrogators that one of his motivations to join the terror organisation was to earn bride prices for himself and his brother. [25] Further, terrorist organisations are more likely to recruit women in societies with significant inequalities. For instance, research suggests that the existence of female suicide bombers is most evident in societies where women do not have the same rights and freedoms as men.[26] Similarly, the Islamic State of Iraq and Syria (ISIS) has been able to exploit existing gender inequalities to recruit women with its 'quasi female empowerment' propaganda in societies.[27] In fact, it can be argued that terrorist organisations have been quicker to recognise the links between gender and security than national security establishments, and have actively used the 'gender blind spot' in their favour. ISIS women have been involved in reproduction, consolidation of territory and aiding in the building of statehood. Further, as security officials and policymakers still maintain the overwhelming stereotype of women as passive victims of violent conflicts, recruited women are able to avoid suspicion and pass through security more easily than male counterparts in many cases.[28]

Despite glaring evidence of the links, those in-charge of taking national security and foreign policy decisions—even in countries that perform relatively better than India in terms of gender equality indicators—have not fully embraced the integration of the gender as an important lens through which to design policies to address internal and external security threats. For instance, a US-based 2017 survey of 500 foreign policy leaders working in and with the government showed that only 13 per cent of the respondents believed international gender inequality to be a vital threat to US interests. Further, less than a third of those surveyed believed women and girls' full political and economic participation to be a foreign policy goal.[29] It is clear that a lot more needs to be done in changing the perceptions of policymakers regarding the meaningful integration of gender considerations into national security policy debates.[30] In common perception, power, national security, and international relations are still associated with hegemonic masculine constructs, leading to an in-built self-selection mechanism causing the exclusion of women's voices and experiences from academic discourses as well as policymaking.[31]

In recent years, the need to have more women at the table and in the armed forces has gained momentum. This is a much-needed step in the right direction. At the same time, it is clear that symbolic representation is not enough and the cross-cutting nature of gender in national security needs to gain further recognition. Thus, in addition to the appointment of women in key decision-making ministerial bodies and critical branches of security forces, the equal and meaningful participation of women and men in security policymaking processes should include broader consultations with rural and urban community-based organisations as well as national and regional ministries of women's affairs—links that are conspicuously missing at the moment.

This is not to say that progress has not been made at all. Increasingly, there is recognition of the fact that gender-neutral policies do not lead to gender-neutral outcomes. A comprehensive security policy must consider the differential impact of risks to men and women as well as their different security needs, importantly including internal security threats of gender-based violence (GBV).[32] Existing obligations under international laws, instruments and norms already necessitate the integration of gender into national security policymaking. These include: *The Convention on the Elimination of All Forms of Discrimination against Women* (1979), The *Beijing Declaration and Platform for Action* (1995), and most expansively, the *United Nations Security Council Resolution 1325 on Women, Peace and Security (WPS)* (2000) which seeks to lead a 'radical reconfiguration of the gendered power dynamics that characterise our world and a proper global commitment to sustainable and positive peace' through system-wide action plans based on the pillars of participation; protection; relief and recovery; and an occasional normative pillar. [33] Some of the indicators adopted by the UN Security Council that cover each of the four pillars are[34]:

- Women's political participation (national level, but also women as voters and candidates) and/or representation of women among mediators, negotiators and technical experts in formal peace negotiations (participation).
- Percentage of referred cases of sexual and gender-based violence that are reported, investigated and sentenced (protection).
- Number and percentage of women in executive positions of relevant regional and sub-regional organisations involved in preventing conflict (prevention).
- Percentage of benefits from Disarmament, Demobilisation and Reintegration programmes (DDR) received by women and girls (relief and recovery).

The ambitious and comprehensive nature of indicators proves that most countries have committed to a strong framework for the Women, Peace, and Security agenda, at least on paper. However, it is equally clear that normative advances have not been followed by on the ground implementation.[35] Keeping this framework in mind, the next section attempts to highlight the key hits and misses during the Modi administration in India.

Women in the National Peace and Security Agenda

Women in the Indian Armed Forces

The Modi administration has reiterated its commitment to shift 'women's development to women-led development'. In his Independence Day speech in 2018, Prime Minister Narendra Modi declared his government's decision to allow women officers in the armed forces to have the option to take up Permanent Commission just like their male counterparts.[36] Since their first induction as Short Service Commission (SSC) in 1992—where women officers' terms of engagement gradually changed from the initial 5 years to 10 years with the option to extend the period for another 4 years (10+4)—this is a momentous achievement for women officers attempting to dent the 'brass ceiling' in the form of Permanent Commission over the last few years.[37]

In 2008, women officers were granted Permanent Commission in a limited number of non-combat roles, including Army Education Corps (AEC) and the Judge Advocate General (JAG) branch, as well as in the corresponding branches in the navy and the air force, in addition to branches such as accounts in the air force and air traffic controller roles in the navy. However, this resulted in a very marginal increase in vacancies, leading to women officers moving the Delhi High Court in 2010 which ruled in their favour. In a landmark judgment, the Delhi HC granted them the right to Permanent Commission which could be translated into full service tenure of 20 years—a precondition to greater opportunities of leadership and eligibility for pension and other benefits.[38] The current government's 2018 declaration to grant Permanent Commission to all women officers recruited through Short Service

Commission is a positive development. At the same time, there is a lack of clarity on the exact extent to which women will be allowed in the Army, Navy and the Air Force.[39]

In 2016, women comprised of just over 2.5 per cent of India's million-plus armed personnel.[40] According to recent figures, there are 1,561 women officers in the army, 1,594 women officers in the air force, and 644 women officers in the navy.[41] According to the Ministry of Defence, the Indian armed forces were short of over 52,000 personnel and 11,000 officers in 2015.[42] The measures taken to rectify this include improvements in the pay scale. The shortage has also initiated debates on why the Indian armed forces continue to recruit women only in the officer rank, when more women can be inducted as Personnel Below Officer Rank (PBOR).[43]

The debate on gender parity in combat roles often eclipses the broader topic of gender and national security; consequently, more action has taken place on this front. In 2018, Defence Minister Nirmala Sitharaman said the government was seriously considering the inclusion of women in combat roles in the Indian armed forces. If made possible, this would enable women to be eligible to be deployed on-board tanks of the army and submarines of the navy—formerly impenetrable al-male bastions. The Indian Air Force (IAF) has already inducted women fighter pilots. Three women—Bhawana Kanth, Avani Chaturvedi and Mohana Singh—were inducted into the IAF in 2016.[44] Subsequently, two more women fighter pilots, Shivangi Singh and Pratibha, were inducted in 2017—taking the total number of women in the combat wing to five.

These developments under the current administration signify that India is well on its way to shattering its formerly-rigid combat exclusion policy.[45]

In 2022, India will move towards the 75th year of its Independence; the aspirations and under-utilised potential of half of the country's population should not be neglected. Some arguments against the inclusion of women combatants in the army may be valid. However, a significant number of arguments are based on outdated mindsets and stereotypes. For instance, Chief of Army Staff General Bipin Rawat recently commented that women should be excluded from combat roles in the Indian Army because the male soldiers largely hail from small villages in the country, and would not be willing to accept orders from a female commander.[46] While debates pertaining to the armed forces must always prioritise their efficiency and readiness, arguments based on what may be uncomfortable are simply not good enough to restrict the entry of women.

Moreover, as battles become more technologically-driven and increasingly include non-contact standoff operations, the debate on capabilities must undergo reviews.[47] Further, Indian Army women are already involved in UN Peacekeeping missions in post-conflict zone where they contribute towards ceasefire negotiations and post-conflict resolution. In 2018, Lt Gen Sarath Chand, the then Vice-Chief of Army Staff (VCOAS), said the Indian Army aims to double its share of women in peacekeeping missions.[48] These factors indicate the inevitable increase in women's roles and greater integration in the armed forces. Importantly, while debates around women in the armed forces focus on the complexities of women in combat roles, it is essential to acknowledge that female officers also face the same barriers rooted in gender stereotypes that other working women face— such as the lack of gender-sensitive infrastructure, and policies need to be actively gender-responsive in nature to be able to truly integrate women.

Women in the Central Reserve Police Force (CRPF)

The Central Reserve Police Force (CRPF), India's largest paramilitary force consisting of more than three lakh personnel,[49] is also the only paramilitary force in the country that has six Mahila Battalions (all-women battalions). At present, CRPF women personnel are deployed in active duty in Jammu and Kashmir, Ayodhya, Manipur, Assam and other parts of the country. In July 2018, a special contingent of 500 women CRPF personnel was inducted in Kashmir.[50] In addition, each Rapid Action Force (RAF) battalion has a women's component consisting of 96 personnel.

This year, reiterating the Central government's commitment to enhance women's representation in the constabulary of paramilitary forces, Union Minister of State for Home Affairs Kiren Rijiju announced in the Lok Sabha that the Centre aims to increase women strength to 15 per cent in CRPF and CISF (Central Industrial Security Force), and 5 per cent in BSF (Border Security Force), ITBP (Indo-Tibetan Border Police) and SSB (Sashastra Seema Bal).[51]

The first ever women's battalion of CRPF, the 88 Mahila Battalion, became operational in 1987. At present, six such battalions have been approved by the government—88 Bn, 135 Bn, 213 Bn, 232 Bn, 233 Bn and 240 Bn. Women personnel in these battalions are effectively assisting their male counterparts in policing duties as well as other clerical and administrative functions.

The total number of women employees working in CRPF as on 31 October 2018 was:[52]

Category	*Number*
Group A	303
Group B	882
Group C	7025
Total	8210

To facilitate the smooth discharge of duties by the women workforce, CRPF has invested in creating infrastructure facilities like restrooms, recreation rooms, mobile toilets etc. Even during field deployments, separate toilets in the unit vehicles are made available for the convenience of women employees. Other gender-sensitive provisions include relaxations in uniform rules (such as wearing trousers, shirts and belt) during pregnancy. In addition, gender sensitisation is carried out at regular intervals within the force. In order to increase awareness about women's rights, regular interactions and *Sainik Sammelans* are also being held.[53]

The force also makes efforts to focus on the welfare of the families of the force personnel. For instance, CRPF has constructed family welfare centres exclusively for women family members of personnel to encourage them to learn new skills and to supplement their family income through activities like stitching, handicrafts, production of food items etc. Further, special provisions are made for the benefit of the women employees and the family members of the force personnel which include women's hostels, provisions for physical activities, provision of music systems and TV etc. for recreation, gymnasium, day care centres/ crèche including provision of caretaker to look after the children of working women.[54]

The women personnel of CRPF, and the institutional framework of the force make for an interesting case study. CRPF women battalions are conducting extensive operations, such as road building, in sensitive areas such as Maoist-hit Bastar in Chhattisgarh and have played an important role in situations such as the Gorkhaland agitation alongside their male counterparts.[55] Further, an all-women contingent of 125 women peacekeepers made up of CRPF personnel was deployed with the UN mission from 2007 until 2016.[56] According to numbers from United Nations Mission in Liberia (UNMIL), the presence of this all-women contingent resulted in a fourfold increase in the number of Liberian women applying to join police services.[57]

To an extent, they pave the way for a more nuanced, evidence-based conversation on women in combat roles in the armed forces.

Secondly, CRPF makes for an interesting case study for the efficacy of gender budgeting. The Government of India's Gender Budgeting Handbook describes Gender Budgeting as: 'a tool for gender mainstreaming. It uses the Budget as an entry point to apply a gender lens to the entire policy process. Gender Budgeting is concerned with gender sensitive formulation of legislation, policies, plans, programmes and schemes, allocation and collection of resources; implementation and execution; monitoring, review, audit and impact assessment of programmes and schemes, and follow up corrective action to address gender disparities. It is a continuous process that must be applied to all levels and stages of the policy process'.[58]

According to figures provided by CRPF, the government has provided Rs 52 lakh for running crèche facilities for the financial year 2018-19 and Rs 57.20 lakh has also been projected in Budget Estimates for 2019-

20. When arguing the need for greater representation of women in national security, it must be acknowledged that the pervasive social norms—such as lack of childcare facilities and unequal burden of household responsibilities—that cause the severe under-participation of women in the Indian workforce in general,[59] apply to all sectors, including the armed and paramilitary forces, and must be addressed as such. As opposed to using these arguments to restrict women's entry into the forces, it is important to address them in a way that allow for their greater participation as equal members of the Indian society.

National Security Guard (NSG)

At present, the National Security Guard (NSG) is an all-male force. A woman commando was inducted in the NSG in 2011-12 and a squad of women 'Black Cat' commandos was trained for deployment in specialist operations like hostage situations and VIP security.[60] However, in 2017, the last remaining woman NSG commando left the force on maternity leave.

Notably, the first pushback faced by the commandos came from their own gender when former Uttar Pradesh Chief Minister Mayawati and late Tamil Nadu Chief Minister J. Jayalalithaa—both of whom had been accorded Z+ security of NSG Black Cats in 2012—refused to have women combatants as their 'shadows'. The remaining three women officers in NSG are medical officers. Group B Women staff in NSG is mainly ministerial and paramedical staff. Similarly, Group C staffs are either MTS (Multi-Tasking Staff) or office staff.

The total number of women employees working in NSG as on 31 October 2018 was[61]:

Category	*Number*
Group A	3
Group B	25
Group C	5
Total	33

Conclusion

As newer and more complex threats emerge, national security discourse and policymaking will have to evolve to mitigate their impact. Evidence suggests that there is a causal inter-relationship between gender and security outcomes. Therefore, the meaningful adoption of a gender lens can lead to improved policy outcomes. At the same time, it is also clear that discussion on gender in national security have, albeit with best intentions, remained disproportionately focused on increasing women's representation in the high tables of global governance. While this should remain a crucial policy priority, it is equally important to recognise the overlaps between gender and security on other fronts—such as the role of local women's organisations in peacebuilding and peacekeeping.

It is clear that India is undergoing dramatic social, economic and political changes—this is reflected in the changing attitudes towards integrating gender in security frameworks, both symbolically and in practice. It can be argued, however, that institutions are yet to fully catch up with the ongoing normative progress.

The Modi government included the most gender-representative Cabinet Committee on Security (CCS) in India's history. Simultaneous developments in the armed forces—the granting of Permanent Commission to women and the arrival of India's first women fighter pilots—indicate that strides have been made in penetrating the rigid 'brass ceiling' and combat exclusion policy. While the government under Prime Minister Narendra Modi was able to elevate discussions on the topic of women in national security, for gender concerns to be truly integrated within policymaking, there must be a broader representation of voices beyond a few key office holders. In the future, ensuring that women have a seat at all levels of national security policymaking remains critical. For instance, women's representation in the Indian Parliament still remains abysmally low. In the run-up to the 2019 General elections, it will be interesting to note how political parties address this. Notably, women bureaucrats have served, and continue to serve, as senior officers in all relevant ministries. To further ensure that policymaking includes the differentiated security needs of women, efforts to make the drafting of security policies more inclusive, on the ground, of voices, such as women-led organisations in conflict areas, could yield better security outcomes.

Secondly, it is important for the next government to recognise, and formally articulate, the links between gender and national security in a methodical manner. This has not been done so far. For instance, despite the evidence on the role women can play in preventing and countering violent extremism, India's counter-terrorism plans have tended to ignore this dimension. Again, the approach to gender and national security must go beyond representation without compromising the significance of it. Lastly, it is evident that the siloing of gender and security policy discussions has negative outcomes for both. Moving forward, the links and commensurabilities must be explicitly articulated by administrations.

NOTES

[1] Anne-Marie Slaughter and Elizabeth Weingarten, 'National security: A gender blind spot,' World Economic Forum, 21 October 2019, https://www.weforum.org/agenda/2016/10/national-security-a-gender-blind-spot (accessed 1 February 2019).

[2] Elizabeth Weingarten, Heather Hurlburt and Elena Souris, 'From the Classroom to the Capitol: A Missing National Security Gender Link?' *New America*, 23 March 2019, https://www.newamerica.org/political-reform/policy-papers/classroom-capitol-missing-national-security-gender-link/ (accessed 4 February 2019).

[3] Helen Clark, 'Gender Equality: A Human Right Critical for Development Progress,' UNDP, (2019) http://www.undp.org/content/undp/en/home/blog/2015/3/6/Gender-equality-a-human-right-critical-for-development-progress.html (Accessed 1 February 2019).

[4] Michele L. Swers, 'Building a Reputation on National Security: The Impact of Stereotypes Related to Gender and Military Experience,' *Legislative Studies Quarterly*, Vol. 32, no. 4 (2007): pp. 559-595, doi:10.3162/036298007782398512.

[5] Heidi Hudson, '"Doing" Security As Though Humans Matter: A Feminist Perspective on Gender and the Politics of Human Security,' *Security Dialogue*, Vol. 36, no. 2 (2005): pp. 155-174, doi:10.1177/0967010605054642.

[6] PTI, 'Women prowess mesmerises crowd at 70th Republic Day parade on Rajpath,' *The Times of India*, 26 January 2019, https://timesofindia.indiatimes.com/india/women-prowess-mesmerises-crowd-at-70th-republic-day-parade-on-rajpath/articleshow/67700758.cms (accessed 1 February 2019)

[7] Ibid.

[8] Ibid.

[9] Surendra Singh, 'Women Power on full display at Republic Day Parade,' *The Times of India*, 26 January 2019, https://timesofindia.indiatimes.com/india/nari-shakti-on-full-display-during-republic-day-parade/articleshow/67702636.cms (accessed 1 February 2019).

[10] Tarun Shukla and Elizabeth Roche, 'Nirmala Sitharaman 2nd woman defence minister after Indira Gandhi,' *Mint*, 4 September 2017, https://www.livemint.com/Politics/FVQvbbivrpvEuyMkiz3eCM/Nirmala-Sitharaman-becomes-Indias-2nd-woman-defence-ministe.html (accessed 1 February 2019).

[11] Michael T. Koch and Sarah A. Fulton, 'In the Defense of Women: Gender, Office Holding, and National Security Policy in Established Democracies,' *The Journal of Politics*, Vol. 73, no. 1(January 2011), pp. 1–16, doi:10.1017/s00223816 10000824

[12] 'Sushma Swaraj among 15 Global Thinkers for Novel Twitter Diplomacy,' *Hindustan Times*, 14 December 2016, https://www.hindustantimes.com/india-news/sushma-swaraj-among-15-global-thinkers-for-novel-twitter-diplomacy/story-Xo5HrwCC6i1LJViSiTZRiP.html (Accessed 1 February 2019).

[13] Moushumi Das Gupta, 'Men Should Learn To Do Household Work, Women Martial Arts, Says Sushma Swaraj,' *Hindustan Times*, 29 April 2017, https://www.hindustantimes.com/india-news/men-should-learn-to-do-household-work-women-martial-arts-says-sushma-swaraj/story-VeNihxNceSwMwnZq3ofghL.html (accessed 1 February 2019).

[14] 'Dress Not Reason Behind Rape, Says Defence Minister Nirmala Sitharaman,' *NDTV.com*, 8 May 2018, https://www.ndtv.com/india-news/dress-not-reason-behind-rape-says-defence-minister-nirmala-sitharaman-1848806 (accessed 1 February 2019).

[15] 'Women's Reservation Bill [The Constitution (108th Amendment Bill, 2008),'PRS Legislative, (2019) http://www.prsindia.org/billtrack/womens-reservation-bill-the-constitution-108th-amendment-bill-2008-45 (accessed 1 February 2019).

[16] Manjeet Singh Negi, 'Army to induct 800 women in military police, day after Nirmala Sitharaman takes charge as Defence Minister,' *India Today*, 8 September 2017, https://www.indiatoday.in/india/story/indian-army-to-induct-800-women-in-military-police-nirmala-sitharaman-1040604-2017-09-08 (accessed 1 February 2019).

[17] IANS, 'Working "seriously" to have women in combat roles: Nirmala Sitharaman,' *The New Indian Express*, 7 May 2018, http://www.newindianexpress.com/nation/2018/may/07/working-seriously-to-have-women-in-combat-roles-nirmala-sitharaman-1811410.html (accessed 1 February 2019).

[18] Heather Hurlburt and Elizabeth Weingarten, 'Not Secondary, But Central Perceptions of Gender Diversity in National Security,' New America, Policy Paper, 11 October 2016, https://www.newamerica.org/better-life-lab/policy-papers/not-secondary-central/(accessed 1 February 2019).

[19] Tom Donilon and Cathy Russell, 'Lessons from the Obama Administration: Why Gender Equality Should Continue to Be Part of U.S. Foreign Policy,' 4 January 2017.

[20] Slaughter and Weingarten, 'National security: A gender blind spot,' n.1.

[21] Valerie Hudson, 'What Sex Means for World Peace', Foreign Policy, 24 April 2012. https://foreignpolicy.com/2012/04/24/what-sex-means-for-world-peace/ (accessed 1 February 2019).

[22] Ibid

[23] Slaughter and Weingarten, 'National security: A gender blind spot,' n.1

[24] S.V. Raghavan and V. Balasubramaniyan, 'Evolving Role of Women in Terror Groups: Progression or Regression?', *Journal of International Women's Studies*, Vol. 15, no.2(2014): pp. 197-211.

[25] Hurlburt and Weingarten, 'Not Secondary, But Central Perceptions of Gender Diversity in National Security,' n.18

[26] Ibid.

[27] Slaughter and Weingarten, 'National security: A gender blind spot,' n.1

[27] Ibid.

[28] Joshua Busby and Heather Hurlburt, 'Do women matter to national security? The men who lead U.S. foreign policy don't think so,' *The Washington Post*, 2 February 2017, https://www.washingtonpost.com/news/monkey-cage/wp/2017/02/02/do-women-matter-to-national-security-the-men-who-lead-u-s-foreign-policy-dont-think-so/?utm_term=.04d737dcbad2

[29] Ibid.

[31] Vidisha Mishra, 'Women in the Indian Armed Forces' in Defence Primer: India at 75, Ed. Sushant Singh and Pushan Das (2016), https://www.orfonline.org/wp-content/uploads/2016/03/Military_Layout-.pdf (accessed 1 February 2019).

[32] Peter Albrecht and Karen Barnes, 'National Security Policy-Making and Gender,' Gender and Security Sector Reform Toolkit, Eds. Megan Bastick and Kristin Valasek, DCAF, OSCE/ODIHR, UN-INSTRAW, Geneva (2008), https://www.international-alert.org/sites/default/files/publications/Cover_National_ security Policy_Gender.pdf (accessed 1 February 2019).

[33] Paul Kirby and Laura J. Shepherd, 'The futures past of the Women, Peace and Security agenda,' International Affairs, Vol. 92, no. 2 (2016), pp. 373–392.

[34] 'Women, Peace and Security', Gender Tool Box Brief, SIDA, (March 2015). https://www.sida.se/contentassets/3a820dbd152f4fca98bacde8a8101e15/women-peace-and-security.pdf (accessed 1 February 2019).

[35] Ibid.

[36] 'PM Modi Independence Day speech: Women officers to get permanent commissions in defence forces,' *India Today*, 15 April 2018, https://www.indiatoday.in/india/story/pm-modi-independence-day-speech-women-officers-to-get-permanent-commissions-in-defence-forces-1314932-2018-08-15(accessed 1 February 2019).

[37] Vidisha Mishra, 'Women in the Indian Armed Forces' in Defence Primer: India at

75, Ed. Sushant Singh and Pushan Das (2016), https://www.orfonline.org/research/defence-primer-india-at-75/ (accessed 1 February 2019).

[38] Ibid.

[39] IANS, 'Armed Forces To Have Permanent Commission For Women Officers: PM Modi,' *NDTV*, 15 August 2018, https://www.ndtv.com/india-news/armed-forces-to-have-permanent-commission-for-women-officers-pm-modi-1900913(accessed 1 February 2019).

[40] Nita Bhalla, 'Indian armed forces to recruit women for all combat roles – President,' *Reuters*, 24 February 2016, http://in.reuters.com/article/india-women-military-idINKCN0VX1PQ (accessed 1 February 2019).

[41] Armed Forces To Have Permanent Commission For Women Officers: PM Modi,' *NDTV*, 15 August 2018, https://www.ndtv.com/india-news/armed-forces-to-have-permanent-commission-for-women-officers-pm-modi-1900913 (accessed 1 February 2019).

[42] 'Armed forces face shortage of over 52,000 personnel,' *The Indian Express*, 20 March 2015, http://indianexpress.com/article/india/armed-forces-face-shortage-of-over-52000-personnel/(accessed 1 February 2019).

[43] Ibid.

[44] Rajat Pandit, 'Meet India's first three women fighter pilot trainees who will shatter the combat-exclusion policy,' *The Economic Times*, 11 July 2018,https://economictimes.indiatimes.com/news/defence/meet-indias-first-three-women-fighter-pilot-trainees-who-will-shatter-the-combat-exclusion-policy/articleshow/51322570.cms (accessed 1 February 2019).

[45] Srinivasa Rao Apparasu, 'Two more female pilots inducted into IAF, total at 5 now,' *Hindustan Times*, 16 December 2017, https://www.hindustantimes.com/india-news/two-more-female-pilots-inducted-into-iaf-at-dundigal-graduation-parade/story-fWaQzgRjkFHzRN81sHNYXJ.html (accessed 1 February 2019).

[46] Shraddha Chowdhury, 'Armed forces globally reek of misogyny; General Bipin Rawat's remarks on women in combat roles cements theory,' *Firstpost*, 17 December 2018, https://www.firstpost.com/india/armed-forces-globally-reek-of-misogyny-general-bipin-rawats-remarks-on-women-in-combat-roles-cements-theory-5744731.html (accessed 1 February 2019).

[47] Vidisha Mishra, 'Women in the Indian Armed Forces,' n. 37.

[48] Uday Singh Rana, 'Indian Army to Double its Share of Women in UN Peacekeeping Missions,' *News18*, 5 February 2018, https://www.news18.com/news/india/indian-army-to-double-its-share-of-women-in-un-peacekeeping-missions-1651473.html

[49] PTI, 'CRPF inducts 500 women personnel to counter protestors in Kashmir,' *Hindustan Times*, 1 July 2018, https://www.hindustantimes.com/india-news/crpf-inducts-500-women-personnel-to-counter-protestors-in-kashmir/story-WFzbTMGH33NURf1PMkLDQN.html (accessed 1 February 2019).

[50] Ibid.

[51] PTI, 'Women quota in CRPF, CISF to be made 15 per cent,' The Telegraph, 8

January 2019, https://www.telegraphindia.com/india/women-quota-in-crpf-cisf-to-be-made-15-per-cent/cid/1681181 (accessed 1 February 2019).

[52] Accessed by author on 24 January 2019 at the Ministry of Home Affairs, Government of India.

[53] Ibid.

[54] Accessed by author on 24 January 2019 at the Ministry of Home Affairs, Government of India.

[55] Ritesh Mishra, 'Chhattisgarh deploys women commandos to secure road in Maoist hotbed,' *Hindustan Times*, 16 January 2018, https://www.hindustantimes.com/india-news/chhattisgarh-deploys-women-police-commandos-to-secure-road-in-maoist-hotbed/story-5qnG22dOU8t8ROYv6HmS1N.html (accessed 1 February 2019).

[56] PTI, 'Role of all-women Indian contingent in UN peacekeeping mission in Liberia lauded,' *Hindustan Times*, 24 March 2018, https://www.hindustantimes.com/india-news/role-of-all-women-indian-contingent-in-un-peacekeeping-mission-in-liberia-lauded/story-JJeMxhsmGA3NdcgM1NpQbJ.html (accessed 1 February 2019).

[57] Ibid.

[58] Gender Budgeting Handbook: HANDBOOK for Government of India Ministries / Departments State Governments /District Officials Researchers / Practitioners, http://wcd.nic.in/sites/default/files/GB%20-%20Handbook%20October%202015.pdf

[59] Terri Chapman and Vidisha Mishra, 'Rewriting the Rules: Women and Work in India', ORF Special Report No. 80, January 2019, https://www.orfonline.org/research/rewriting-the-rules-women-and-work-in-india-47584/

[60] Kamaljit Kaur Sandhu, 'Battle of sexes: NSG loses its last woman commando after she goes on maternity leave,' *India Today*, 29 October 2017, https://www.indiatoday.in/india/story/nsg-commandos-women-black-cats-crpf-capf-central-forces-1071272-2017-10-29 (accessed 1 February 2019).

[61] Accessed by author on 24 January 2019 at the Ministry of Home Affairs, Government of India.

List of Contributors

Abhijnan Rej is a New Delhi-based analyst. His current research focuses on Indian foreign and defence policies, and international security. Rej's research and analyses have appeared in *The Washington Quarterly*, *War on the Rocks*, The Interpreter, The National Interest (online), Global Policy (online), *Wired* (online), Journal of Physics: A, and Contemporary Mathematics. Along with this, he has published more than a dozen occasional papers, briefs, reports, and book chapters, and over 50 articles in virtually all major Indian English-language media outlets. Rej has been quoted by the *Economist*, *Reuters*, *Voice of America*, *The Australian*, *China Global Television Network*, and *The Nation*, among others.

Aparna Roy is an Associate Fellow working with Observer Research Foundation's Climate Change and Development Initiative. Her current research explores the impact of and vulnerability to climate change with potential for adaptation. As a development practitioner, she has done in-depth research and policy analysis on issues of social development, governance reforms, gender, rights-based social protection/welfare policies, and human rights. Roy holds a Bachelor's degree in Political Science (Honours) and Master's degrees in Sociology and International Development. She was a Commonwealth scholar at the University of Bristol. She writes for various publications including *The Times of India*, *Hindustan Times* and *The Hindu*.

Bedavyasa Mohanty is an Associate Fellow with Observer Research Foundation's Cyber Initiative. His work focuses on encryption and the regulation of lethal autonomous weapons systems. He coordinates ORF's cyber security capacity building for Indian law enforcement officials and is the curator of CyFy, ORF's flagship conference on technology, security and society. Mohanty is a lawyer by training and completed his BA LLB (Hons) from the National University of Juridical Sciences, Kolkata. His latest paper, 'Hitting Refresh', analyses elements in the data sharing process between law enforcement agencies in India and the US and has been cited by prominent stakeholders including the expert committee that drafted India's new data protection law.

Harsh V. Pant is Director, Studies and Head of Strategic Studies Programme at Observer Research Foundation, New Delhi. He holds a joint appointment as Professor of International Relations in Defence Studies Department and the India Institute at King's College London. He is also a Non-Resident Fellow with the Wadhwani Chair in US-India Policy Studies at the Center for Strategic and International Studies, Washington, DC. His current research is focused on Asian security issues. His most recent books include *New Directions in India's Foreign Policy* (Cambridge University Press), *India's Nuclear Policy* (Oxford University Press), *The US Pivot and Indian Foreign Policy* (Palgrave Macmillan), and *Handbook of Indian Defence Policy* (Routledge). Pant writes regularly for various media outlets including *The Japan Times*, the *Wall Street Journal*, the National (UAE), and *Hindustan Times*.

Kabir Taneja is an Associate Fellow with Strategic Studies programme. His research focuses on India's relations with West Asia, specifically looking at the domestic political dynamics, terrorism, non-state militant actors and the general security paradigm of the region. Taneja also recently authored the monograph *The ISIS Phenomenon: South Asia and Beyond*. He has written extensively in *The New York Times, The Hindu, Suddeutsche Zeitung, The Huffington Post, Politico, Quartz, The Wire*, and *The Cairo Review*, among others. Currently, he is working on a book on the terror group ISIS.

Kapil Patil is an Associate Fellow at the Vivekananda International Foundation (VIF), New Delhi and his research focuses on India's nuclear and defence-related policies. Prior to joining VIF, he worked with the Indian Pugwash Society, New Delhi and co-authored a book titled *India's Nuclear Energy Programme: Challenges, Prospects, and Public Concerns*. Patil is a recipient of the 2018 Emerging Leaders Fellowship awarded by the Korean Ministry of Unification, and an alumnus of the Nuclear History Boot Camp (2011) organised by the Woodrow Wilson Center, Washington

DC. His research has featured in peer-reviewed journals as well as in current affairs magazines such as *Global Energy Monitor, Nautilus, The Diplomat, Swarajya,* and the *CBW Magazine.*

Niranjan Sahoo is a Senior Fellow at Observer Research Foundation, New Delhi, with years of expertise on issues of governance, democracy, electoral reforms, insurgency and conflict studies. He serves as a member of the Carnegie Rising Democracies Network (RDN), Washington, D.C.

Rajeswari Pillai Rajagopalan is a Distinguished Fellow and Head of the Nuclear and Space Policy Initiative at Observer Research Foundation. She joined ORF after a five-year stint at the National Security Council Secretariat (2003-2007), where she was an Assistant Director. Prior to joining the NSCS, she was Research Officer at the Institute of Defence Studies and Analyses, New Delhi. She was also a Visiting Professor at the Graduate Institute of International Politics, National Chung Hsing University, Taichung, Taiwan in 2012. Her books include *Nuclear Security in India* (2015), *Clashing Titans: Military Strategy and Insecurity among Asian Great Powers* (2012), *The Dragon's Fire: Chinese Military Strategy and Its Implications for Asia* (2009), and *Uncertain Eagle: US Military Strategy in Asia* (2009).

Tuneer Mukherjee is a researcher of Asian Security Studies. He is currently working on naval modernisation in South Asia. His recent work has focused on artificial intelligence in the naval domain as well as the strategic relationship between India, China and the US in the maritime domain. Mukherjee was previously a Junior Fellow with Observer Research Foundation's Maritime Policy Initiative, and a Research Intern with the Asia Maritime Transparency Initiative at the Center for Strategic and International Studies, Washington D.C. He is a graduate of the double-master's program offered by the University of Warwick and the School of International Service (American University).

Vidisha Mishra is an Associate Fellow at Observer Research Foundation (ORF), New Delhi. She currently leads ORF's work on gender. She was a Managing Global Governance (MGG) Fellow with the Deutsches Institut für Entwicklungspolitik (DIE), Germany during August-December 2018 and continues her association with DIE as a consultant. Mishra is a member of the Women20 (W20) Network and the Think20 (T20) Digital Economy Task Force of the G20. She completed her Masters in Gender, Development, and Globalisation from the London School of Economics and Political Science, and holds a Bachelor's degree in Politics and International Relations from the University of Warwick.

Vidya Sagar Reddy is a Research Analyst at Jane's by IHS Markit. Previously, he was an Associate Fellow in the Nuclear and Space Policy Initiative of Observer Research Foundation, New Delhi. His analyses appeared in Astropolitics and New Space journals as well as in The Space Review, E-International Relations, Georgetown Journal of International Affairs etc. He holds Master's degrees in Space Systems Engineering from the University of Michigan, Ann Arbor and in Geopolitics and International Relations from Manipal University.

Index

Act East policy 51, 150
Ad-hocism 26, 40
Adivasis 109, 116, 118
Advanced Projects Agency 31
Advanced Radar for Topside Ionosphere 76
Aerospace 16, 32
Afghanistan x, xii, 53, 95, 97, 101
  extremist violence in xii
Aircraft 7–8, 16–17, 31, 34, 49, 57–58, 146
Al-Baghdadi, Abu Bakr 96
Al-Qaeda xi, 96, 103
Andaman & Nicobar Command (A&NC) 6, 10-11, 28
Andaman Sea 51
Andhra Pradesh 97, 110–11, 130
Anti-piracy 50, 52, 56
  missions 52
  patrolling 50
Anti-satellite (ASAT) missile test 7, 16
Arianespace 81
Armed forces ix, xii, xv, 4–5, 14, 27, 29, 31, 36, 54, 99–100, 145, 156, 160, 162–64, 166, 168
  defence expenditure of xv
  Indian xv, 5, 99, 145, 163
  modernisation and expansion of xiv, 33
  salaries of 14
  structures/structuring xvi, 36, 109
Armed Forces Tribunals (AFT) 32
Arms and ammunitions x, xii–xiii, xvii, xxi, 15, 30, 32, 39–40, 120, 144
Army Education Corps (AEC) 162
Artificial intelligence xxi, 18, 59
Arunachal Pradesh 149
Asia x–xii, xviii, 2, 51, 52–53, 55–56, 73–74, 118, 146
Aspirational District programme 121
Assam 92, 157, 164
Association of Southeast Asian Nations (ASEAN) 51
Astrosat 82–83, 86
Australia 3–4, 51, 54–55
Azhar, Masood 102

Bab-el-Mandeb 52
Balakot strike 4, 100–102
Ballistic missile defence (BMD) 7
Bangladesh x–xi, 10, 50, 145, 149, 151
BAT (Baidu, Alibaba and Tencent) 126
Bay of Bengal 50–51, 55, 149–50
BIMSTEC 51, 150
Beijing Declaration and Platform for Action 161
Belt and Road Initiative (BRI) 55
Bhabha Atomic Research Centre (BARC) 58
Bharatiya Janata Party (BJP) xix, 1, 15, 27, 31–32, 93–94, 119
Bihar 110, 112, 142
Bin Laden, Osama 96
'Black Cat' commandos 167
Border ix, 94–95, 101
  disputed ix
  India-Bangladesh 149
  international 101
  management 28, 32
  militarised ix
  skirmishes 45
Botnet Cleaning and Malware Analysis Centre 130
BSF (Border Security Force) 165
Budget/Budgetary
  allocation xv, 13, 57–58, 76
  constraints ix, 12
  defence xvii, 5, 14–15, 18, 38
Bureaucracy xii, xvii, 1, 4–5, 8, 18, 38–39
  archaic xii
  civilian 38–39
  military xvii, 18
  national-security 1, 4–5, 8
  reforms 5
Bureaucratic
  architecture 2
  politics 12
  red tape 31
Buy and Make 34
Buy Indian-Indigenously Designed, Developed and Manufactured (IDDM) 34

Cabin Environment Simulation Chamber 84
Cabinet Committee on Security (CCS) xx, 8, 11, 13, 157, 168
Cabin Pressure Control System (CPCS) 84
Capability(ies) ix–x, xii–xiii, xiv–xv, xvii, xxi, 1–3, 5, 7, 10, 13, 16–19, 29, 31, 33–34, 36–37, 48–49, 56–57, 60, 72, 78–80, 94, 133–34, 145, 164
  acquisitions xvii, 13
  asymmetric xvii, 18
  ballistic missile defence (BMD) 7
  combat/combating xv, 31, 33
  development xiii, xiv, 37
  gap ix–x
  generation 5
  hard-power 1
  industrial 29
  material 48
  naval 17, 56
  nuclear 94
  second-strike 57
  surveillance and reconnaissance (ISR) 49
  war fighting ix, 10
Carrier Battle Groups (CBGs) 49, 58
Carrier task forces (CTFs) 49, 58
Ceasefire 98, 164
Ceasefire agreement 98
Central Armed Police Forces (CAPFs) 116
Central Para Military Forces (CPMFs) 113
Central Reserve Police Force (CRPF) 3, 100, 121, 164–66
  women's battalion of 165
Chabahar port 53
Chandrayaan 74, 75, 78
Chhattisgarh 91, 106, 110, 112, 117, 120–21, 166

Index

- Chief of Defence Staff (CDS) 8–10, 12, 29–30, 37–38
- Chiefs of Staff Committee (COSC) xiii, 9, 30, 37
- China ix–x, xiv, 1–2, 4, 8, 10, 13, 15, 19, 26, 30–31, 45, 48–50, 54–56, 60, 78, 81, 94, 102, 108, 126, 129, 134, 149
  - defence modernisation x
  - Indian security policy on xiv
  - rise of x, 26
  - 'salami-slicing' tactics 4
- China and India x, 1, 81, 149
  - capability gap x
  - military standoff 4
- China-Pakistan Economic Corridor (CPEC) 54
- Chinese
  - armed forces 54
  - encroachment 54
  - naval assets 47
  - submarines 47
  - tech industry 135
- Choke points 49, 52
- CISF 165
- Civic Action Programme (CAP) 116
- Civil-military relations 12, 29, 37–39
- Civil war 89
- Clean Siachen Campaign 144
- Climate change 143–45, 148, 150–51
  - environmental impacts of 144
- Close air support (CAS) 10
- CO_2 and Odor Removal System (CORS) 84
- Coastal economic zones (CEZs) 60
- Coastal Security Scheme 46
- Coastal Surveillance Network (CSN) 47
- Cold Start 6, 7
- Colombia 121, 151
- Combined Commanders Conference xiv, 32, 36
- COMCASA 55, 133–34
- Commercial Space Launch Agreement 80
- Communal riots 31
- Communist Party of India—Maoist (CPI-Maoist) 110–11, 114
  - ban on the 114
- Communist Party of India (Maoist Leninist) 110
- Conflicts xx, 9, 28, 53, 142–51, 158, 160–61, 164, 169
  - environmental xx, 142, 150
- Convention on the Elimination of All Forms of Discrimination against Women 161
- Cooperation xviii, 51–53, 55–56, 60, 92, 120, 133–34, 141, 145, 149–50
  - defence 51
  - environmental action 141
  - international 92
  - maritime xviii, 52, 60
  - multilateral 133
  - strategic 52
- Counter Insurgency & Anti-Terrorist Schools 113
- Counter-terror/terrorism xiv, xviii–xix, 91–97, 99–103, 169
  - global practices xix, 95
  - India's approach to xiv
  - operations 96–97
  - policy(ies) xviii–xix, 93, 95
  - strikes 102
  - understanding and infrastructure xix, 103
- Counter-terror/terrorism strikes 101
- Crew Escape System 84
- Crew module Atmospheric Re-entry Experiment (CARE) 84
- Crew Module System 84
- Critical Information Infrastructure (CII) 128
- Cross-LoC special operations 4
- Cross-LoC strikes 6, 15
- Cryogenic engine 74, 76–79, 85
- Cryogenics 77
- Cryosat 82
- CRZ Notification 142
- Cyber x, xiii, xix, 126, 128–35
  - attacks 130–31
  - crime 129–30, 134
  - defence xix, 126, 132
  - diplomacy xix
  - forensic evidence 130
  - regulation 126
  - security xix, 128, 131, 135
  - space 92
  - terrorism 131
- Cyber Swachhta Kendra 130, 133

- Daesh xi, xix, 95
- Dassault Aviation 17
- Deen Dayal Upadhyay Gram Jyoti Yojana 116–17
- Defence
  - acquisitions 12, 16, 29, 32, 34
  - attaché 53
  - budget xvii, 5, 14–15, 18, 38
  - cooperation 51
  - deals xiii
  - diplomacy xiv, 3
  - engagement xiii, 37
  - expenditure xv, 33
  - foreign direct investment in 15
  - intelligence 12
  - manufacturing xiii–xiv, xvii, 15–17, 37, 39
    - domestic 15
    - indigenous 15
    - issue of 16
  - modernisation and production x, xvi–xvii, xx, 26–27, 31, 37–38, 40
  - objectives 5
  - organisation 27, 36
  - planning xiii, xv–xvi, 26, 29, 36–37, 39–41
  - planning and management 26, 37, 40
  - policy xii–xiii, xvi–xvii, 1–3, 5, 8, 12–13, 17, 36, 40
  - policymaking xvi, 40
  - procurement xvii, xx, 27, 31, 33, 35, 39
  - production xvii, xx, 33, 35, 39
  - reforms xvii, 27–28, 31, 37–38
  - spending 15
  - technologies 27, 31
- Defence Acquisition Council (DAC) 12–13, 28, 32
- Defence Advanced Research Projects Agency (DARPA) 31
- Defence Cyber Agency 11, 132
- Defence Innovation Fund (DIF) 35
- Defence Intelligence Agency (DIA) 28
- Defence Planning Committee (DPC) xiii, xiv, 12–13, 36–39
- Defence Planning Guidelines (DPG) 28
- Defence Procurement Organisation 35

Defence Procurement Procedure (DPP) 29, 34–35
Defence Research and Development Organisation (DRDO) 16, 35, 59, 133
Defence Space Agency 11
Deterrent/Deterrence xiv, 3, 6, 57, 94, 119
  by-punishment 6
  credibility xiv
  nuclear 8, 45
Dhirendra Singh Committee 34
Digital India 126
Diplomacy xiv, xviii–xix, 3, 59, 135, 157
  cyber xix
  defence xiv, 3
  maritime 3
  seas xviii, 59
  Twitter 157
Disarmament, Demobilisation and Reintegration programmes (DDR) 161
Doklam crisis x, 4, 54, 129
  Chinese road construction in 4
Draft National Encryption Policy 131
Drones xxi, 18, 59, 120

East Asian Summit 54
Eastern Indian Ocean 10, 51
Eastern Theatre Command 10
Election manifesto 7, 15, 27, 31
Encryption 131–32
Environment x, xiii, xvii, xxi, 1–2, 13, 18, 26, 28, 39, 41, 58, 141–45, 147–51
Environmental Performance Index 142
Environment–security nexus 143
Errorist and Disruptive Activities (Prevention) Act (TADA) 93
European Organization for Nuclear Research 82
Exclusive Economic Zone (EEZ) 51
Expenditure xiii, xv, 8, 13–14, 33–34, 38
  army's 13
  defence xv, 33
  military 14
  modernisation 58
  revenue xv, 8, 13–14, 33, 38
Extremism x, xi, 26, 45, 107, 134, 158, 169
  Islamist xi
  left-wing xi, 45, 107
  radical 26
Extremist xi–xii, 107, 109
Extremist movement 107, 109

Female xx, 157, 159, 164
Foreign direct investment 15
Foreign investments 16
Forest Dwellers Act 116
France 3, 32, 48, 55, 77, 82, 102, 134
Free and Open Indo-Pacific 54–55
Fundamentalism xi

Gaganyaan 83
Galula, David 108
Gandhi, Indira, former Prime Minister 93
  assassination of 93
Ganor, Boaz 92-93
GDP, share of defence budget in 14
Gender x, xiii, xx–xxi, 156–61, 163–69
  cross-cutting nature of 160
  equality 156–58, 160
  gaps 159
  inequality 158, 160
  mainstreaming 159
  national security and 156, 158, 163, 169
  security and 156, 158–59, 168–69
General elections 27, 53, 60, 94, 100
Geostationary Satellite Launch Vehicle (GSLV) 72, 74, 76, 78–79, 80–81, 84–86
Germany 102
Gilgit-Baltistan 54
Global environmental politics (GEP) 141
Global Terrorism Index 89
Goldwater-Nichols-type legislation 18
Government
  Central 111, 113–14, 120, 165
  defence policy xvii, 2, 8
  expenditure 14
Government-to-Government contracts 34
Green Siachen 144
Group-of-Ministers (GoM) on National Security 5
GSAT 49, 72, 78, 85
GSLV Programme 76
Gujarat 94
Gulf Cooperation Council (GCC) 52
Gulf of Aden 50, 52
Gulf of Persia 50, 52

Hacking/Hackers 130
Haryana 133
Headquarters Integrated Defence Staff (HQ IDS) 28–29
Helicopters 32, 34, 120
Hizbul Mujahideen 99
Hubble 82
Humanitarian assistance 45, 48, 53, 56, 145
Humanitarian assistance and disaster relief (HADR) 53
Human space mission 74, 83

Ideation xvii, 1–2, 13, 95
India
  approach to counter-terror xiv
  armed forces xii
  budgetary allocation 57
  challenges to ix–x
  coalition government 93
  conventional military strength xvii, 17
  counter-terror apparatus 98
  counter-terror policy xix, 95
  credible military option against Pakistan xii
  defence
    budget 58
    modernisation x, 26–27, 37
    planning in xiii, 29, 39
    reform campaign xvi
  economic profile xi
  external security challenges 4
  global ambitions 2
  hegemonic status x
  impact of ISIS on xi
  maritime engagement 52
  maritime security
    approach to 47
    issues in 53

Index

military modernisation xiii
military modernisation programme xvi
military power xii
military strength xvii, 17
Narendra Modi government ix, xii, xiii, xvii, xix–xx, 3, 8, 15, 27, 45, 99, 106, 115, 119, 127, 130, 135, 158
national security x, xiii, xviii, xx, 4, 12, 27–28, 31, 40, 127, 129, 135
nuclear triad 57
UPA government xviii, 1, 26–27, 84, 111, 114, 116–17, 119, 128
UPA II government 30–31
Indian aerospace 32
Indian Air Force (IAF) 3, 6, 9–10, 14, 16–17, 31–32, 83, 99–101, 162–63
acquisition 17
Indian Army xv, 4, 6, 10, 13, 15, 18, 33, 98, 132, 144, 156, 164
mountain divisions 13
operational objectives 6
reforms of the 8
restructuring xv
role of the 6
surgical strike across the Myanmar border 98
Indian Army Service Corps (ASC) 156
Counter-insurgency (COIN) xix, 18, 106–09, 112–13, 120
strategy 106–7
Surrender Policy 114
Indian counter-terror narratives 91
Indian cyber defence xix, 126
Indian defence xii, xv–xvii, 2–3, 5, 8, 12, 15, 18, 26, 29, 39
planning xv, 37
Indian defence policy xii, xvi, xviii, xx, 1–3, 5, 8, 12, 36, 53
Modi government on xvii, 2
production 39
stickiness of 3
weaknesses of xii
Indian Integrated Defence Staff Headquarters 5
Indian intelligence 97–98
Indian maritime
connections 48, 53
resolution 48
security agenda 46, 56–57
security apparatus 53, 57
security strategy 60
space 54
Indian National Congress (INC) 93–94, 98, 110
Indian national security x, xiii, xviii, xx–xxi, 4, 12, 18, 27–28, 31, 40, 127, 129, 135
gender-related issues into xx
policy xxi
Indian naval assets 49
Indian Naval Indigenisation Plan (INIP) 57
Indian naval influence 51
Indian Navy 17, 46–50, 52–53, 56–57, 59, 145
modernising the 56
nuclearisation of the 58
Permanent Mission Base Deployments 50
seaborne nuclear force 57
strategy in Indian Ocean 17
Indian nuclear deterrent 8
Indian Ocean ix, xii, xviii, 3, 10, 17–18, 46–48, 50–56, 60, 144–45
Indian Navy's strategy in 17
patrolling xii
Indian Ocean Region (IOR) 48–51
Indian Regional Navigation Satellite System (IRNSS) 73
Indian Remote Sensing (IRS) satellites 72–73
Indian rockets 72
Indian security ix–x, xiv, xxi, 18, 100
challenges to x
policies 12
policy ix, xviii, xiv
predicament 47
Indian space programme xviii, 72–74, 79, 82, 85
Indian Space Research Organisation (ISRO) 72–79, 81–86
Indian Special Forces, cross-Line of Control (LoC) operation 3
India–Pacific Islands Cooperation 52
India-Pakistan War 9
India-US political relations 79
Indonesia 48, 51, 55, 97
Indo-Pacific region xviii, 3, 18, 54–56, 85
Indo-Pakistan relations 148
Indo-US strategic relations 55
Industrial
development 35
innovation 36
policy 34–35
Industrialisation, impacts of xx, 150
Information Management and Analysis Centre (IMAC) 47, 52
Information Technology Act 131–32
Innovation 3, 5, 29, 34–36
INS Arihant 57, 59
INSAT 72, 76
INS Chakra 57, 59
Insurgency(ies) x–xi, xix, 18, 91–93, 95, 97, 106–13, 115, 117–21, 147
anti-government 147
domestic 93
Maoist xi, xix, 106–10, 115, 117, 119–20
organised 147
Integrated Action Plan (IAP) 116
Intellectual property rights (IPRs) 34
Intelligence xii, xvi, xxi, 4, 12, 17–18, 28–29, 47, 49, 59, 91–92, 97–99, 101, 111–12, 114–15, 120, 133
agencies 97, 120
defence, 12
gathering xii, 112
reforms xxi
services 4
sharing 29, 112, 133
International Fleet Review 145
International Solar Alliance (ISA) 141
International Thermonuclear Experimental Reactor (ITER) 82
Intransigence 2, 3
Iran 53
Iraq xi, xix, 89, 95–97, 159
ISIL (Islamic State of Iraq and Levant) xi, xix, 95
Islamic State in Iraq and Syria (ISIS) xi, xix,

95–97, 99, 103, 159–60
impact on South Asia xi
Islamist extremism xi
Islamist extremist groups xi
Islamist terrorism 90, 93
Islamist urban terror cell xi
Israel 16, 17, 35, 96
ITBP (Indo-Tibetan Border Police) 165

Jaish-e-Mohammed (JeM) 100–102
training camp 101
Jammu and Kashmir xix, 3–4, 18, 91–100, 107, 109, 113, 148, 164
counter-insurgency functions in 18
terror attacks in 91
Japan 3–4, 48, 51, 54–55, 145
Jharkhand 106, 117, 120, 142
Jihadist groups xi, xix, 95
global xix, 95
Joint Doctrine of the Indian Armed Forces (JDIAF) 6, 11
Joint Working Group on Aircraft Carrier Technology Cooperation (JWGACTC) 58

Kamov helicopters 32
Kanglei Yawwol Kanna Lup (KYKL) 98
Kargil Review Committee (KRC) 28–30
Kargil War 1, 9, 26, 28, 36, 40
Karnataka 145
Khalistani movement 107
Khalistani terror movement 93
Kissinger, Henry 94
Krivak-III 17

LAC (Line of Actual Control) 31
Land Warfare Doctrine 6
Lashkar-e-Taiba (LeT) 91, 101, 149
Launch vehicle 72, 74–77, 80–82, 84–85
Left-Wing Extremism (LWE) 111–13, 116–19
LEMOA (Logistics Exchange Memorandum of Agreement) 55
Levant xi, xix, 95
Limited air assets 10
Line of Control (LoC) 3–4, 6, 15, 91, 98–99, 101, 103
Long Range Identification and Tracking 47
Long-Term Integrated Perspective Plan (LTIPP) 5, 12–13, 28, 30
'Look East' policy 51

Madagascar 50, 52
Maharashtra 120
Majumdar, Charu 109–10
Make in India xvii, 15–17, 33–35, 39, 57
Malabar naval exercise 4, 49, 55
Malaya 108
Maldives 50, 52
Manifesto
BJP 15, 31
Manipur 98, 164
Man-Portable Anti-Tank Guided Missiles 16
Maoist xi, xix, 106, 112–13, 115, 117–21, 147
Maoist attacks 31
Maoist Communist Centre of India (MCCI) 110
Maoist insurgency xi, xix, 106–10, 115, 117, 119–20
law and order approach 111, 115, 121
Modi Government's approach to 119
state response to 110
tactics against xix, 106
Maritime ix, xviii, 3, 17, 45–61
affairs 45
connections 48, 53
contacts 52
cooperation xviii, 52, 60
diplomacy 3
engagement 52, 56
linkages 50
outreach 50
policy engagement 52
relationships 60
security xviii, 45–49, 51–53, 55–60
space 54–55
Maritime and Coastal Security (NCSMCS) 46–47
Maritime domain awareness (MDA) 47, 49, 53
Maritime security xviii, 45–49, 51, 52–53, 55–60
regional xviii, 45
Maritime Silk Road 51
Mars Mission 72, 74–76, 84, 86
Mars Orbiter Mission (MOM) 75
Martin, Lockheed 16
Mauritius 50, 52
MAVEN 75
MBDs 57
Middle East 97, 101
Migration 144–45
illegal 144–45
Milan exercise 49
Militarisation 48, 55, 85
Military
acquisition xii
affairs xii
assertiveness xii
base 3–4, 98
bureaucracy xvii, 18
change xviii, 27
characteristics xviii, 85
doctrines 3–6
effectiveness 11, 39
exercises 29
expenditure 14
manpower 33, 38
modernisation xiii, xvi, xviii, 26–27, 29, 38–39
objective 13
operations 29, 59, 91, 147
options xii, 11
personnel xviii, 27
power xii, 26
preparedness 15, 31–32
reforms 9, 157
restructuring 27, 39–40
standoff 4
strength xvii, 17
Mine Protected Vehicles (MPVs) 112
Ministry of Defence (MoD) x, xvii, 4, 9, 12, 14, 29–30, 32–36, 38, 163
Ministry of External Affairs (MEA) xiv
Ministry of Home Affairs (MHA) 114, 116–17
Ministry of Skill Development & Entrepreneurship (MoSDE) 116
Missiles xii, 7, 16, 77

Index

Barak 17
indigenous 16
Spike 16
surface-to-air 17
Missile Technology Control Regime (MTCR) 77, 79
Mission-based deployments (MBD) 50
Mizos 107
Modernisation x, xiii, xv–xviii, xx, 26–29, 31–32, 37–40, 46, 57, 104, 112
defence x, xvi–xvii, 26–27, 31, 37–38
effort 38
expenditure 58
funds for xv
military xiii, xvi, xviii, 26–27, 29, 38–39
police 112
Modi government ix, xii–xiii, xiv–xx, 2–3, 5, 7–9, 11–13, 15–16, 27, 32–33, 36–40, 45–46, 50, 54, 57–58, 60, 73, 95, 99–100, 103–04, 106, 115, 119–20, 127–28, 130, 133, 135, 141–42, 147–48, 150, 158, 168
airstrikes xii, xiv
approach to defence reforms 27
approach to Maoist insurgency 119
defence policy xvii
Indian defence policy xvii, 2
performance on cyber security xix, 35
plan to enforce jointness among the three services 8
space programme and policy xviii, 74
success in countering the Maoist xix
surgical strikes across the LoC xii, 99
Modi, Narendra, Indian Prime Minister
addressing the Combined Commanders Conference xiv, 32
counter-terrorism policy of the xviii
election manifesto 7
leadership of 142
maritime diplomacy 3
maritime security framework 53
policy
defence 1–2, 13
foreign 52
military 6
towards Pakistan 6
terror–counter-terror divide 94
Morocco 102
Mumbai, terrorist strikes in xii, 18, 46, 91, 94–96, 159
Musk, Elon 80
Mutual Legal Assistance Treaties (MLAT) 130
Mutually-assured destruction (MAD) 8
Myanmar x, 10, 50, 97–98, 108

Nagrota 4
Namami Gange 142
Nano-biology xxi
Narasimha Rao, P.V. 51, 93
Naresh Chandra Committee 4, 9, 30–31, 38
recommendations of the 9, 31
Nasr tactical nuclear missiles 7
National Action Plan on Climate Change (NAPCC) 141, 145
National Aeronautics and Space Administration (NASA) 75
National Command Control Communications & Intelligence Network (NC3I Network) 47
National Critical Information Infrastructure Protection Centre (NCIIPC) 128, 131
National Cyber Coordination Centre (NCCC) 128
National defence 4–5, 40
strategy 4, 5
National Energy Policy 142
National Environment Policy (NEP) 141
National Forest Policy (NFP) 142
National security ix–x, xiii, xvii–xviii, xx–xxi, 1–5, 8, 12–13, 18, 27–32, 37–38, 40, 45, 72–73, 92, 94–96, 98, 103–04, 106, 127–29, 132, 135, 143, 146–47, 156–61, 163, 167–69
bureaucracy 1, 4–5, 8
gender and 156, 158, 163, 169
Group-of-Ministers (GoM) on 5, 8–9, 28–30
issues ix, 32
objectives 5, 146
outcomes xx, 158
policy xiii, xxi, 156, 160
priorities xxi, 19
strategy ix, xiii, 2, 5, 29–31, 37, 45
China-centric 30
the Modi government's performance in ix
National Security Advisor (NSA) xiii, xiv, 6, 11–12, 36–37, 134
National Security Advisory Board (NSAB) 12
National Security Council (NSC) 8, 11–12
National Security Guard (NSG) 167
National Security Strategy document xiv
National Security Strategy (NSS) xiv, xx, 4–6, 26, 37, 40
Indian 4, 5
National Socialist Council of Nagaland (NSCN) 92, 97–98
NSCN-K 97–98
National War Memorial, New Delhi 32
Nationwide intelligence integration network (NATGRID) 18
Naval
assets 47–49, 57, 59, 144
base 3, 145
logistics agreements 3
Naxalbari 91, 109–10
Naxalite movement 109–10, 115
Naxals/Naxalites xi, 91, 114, 116–18, 121
as 'greatest internal security threat xi
Nehru, Jawaharlal, India's first Prime Minister 74
Neighbourhood First 50, 150
Neighbourhood relations 50
Nepal x, 60
North Andamans 50
North Arabian Sea 50
North Bay of Bengal 50
North East 92, 95, 97, 107, 109, 113
separatist movements 107
Northern Theatre Command 10
Nuclear
arsenal 7
assets 7
blackmail xiv
bluff xiv
capabilities 94
command-and-control 7

deterrent 8, 45
doctrine 3, 7
force xx, 57
missiles 7
'no first use' 7
options 7
triad 8, 57, 58
vulnerability 7
war-fighting posture 7
weapons 1

Odisha 106, 110–11, 120
One Rank, One Pension (OROP) 32
Operation Barga 115
Operation Green Hunt 114
Operation Spring Thunder 111
Organisation of Islamic Cooperation (OIC) 102

Pakistan ix–xii, xiv, 1–4, 6–10, 19, 31, 45–46, 49–50, 54, 89, 91, 94–95, 97, 100–103, 144, 148–49
adventurism xiv
extremist violence in xii
intransigence 2–3
nuclear blackmail xiv
support for terrorism 95
tactical nuclear-weapon (TNW) 8
Pakistani nuclear bluff xiv
Pakistani provocations xiv
Paris Agreement 141
Parliamentary Standing Committee on Defence (PSCOD) xv, 15
Parrikar, Manohar, Defence Minister 9, 33
Pathankot Air Force Station 11, 99
Patnaik, Naveen 120
Pension xv, xvii, 14, 32, 38, 162
People's Liberation Army Navy (PLAN) 47–48
People's Liberation Army (PLA) 4, 10, 47
People's War Group (PWG) 110
Permanent Chairman of the Chiefs of Service Staff Committee (PCCOSC) 9–10
establishment of 9
Personal Data Protection Bill 127, 135
Personnel Below Officer Rank (PBOR) 163
Piracy xii, 45, 50, 52, 56
Polar Satellite Launch Vehicle (PSLV) 72, 75–76, 80–81, 86
Policy(ies)
containment 55
counter-terror/counter-terrorism xviii–xix, 93, 95
cyber security xix, 128
defence xii–xiii, xvi–xvii, 1–3, 5, 8, 12–13, 17, 36, 40
'multi-vector' xiii
encryption 131
engagement 52
foreign xii, xx, 52–53, 60, 73, 80, 157, 160
implementation of, lack of xx
industrial 34–35
institutionalised 89
issues ix, 29
Kashmir 97
Neighbourhood First 50
paralysis 1, 31, 104
procurement 27, 31, 34–35, 39
security ix, xiii–xiv, xviii–xxi, 12–13, 59, 128, 145, 156–57, 160–61, 169
space 72, 73, 86
'splendid isolation' x
Port 50, 53, 60
development 50, 60
Port of Colombo 47
Potomac Institute's Cyber Readiness Index 135
Prevention of Terror Act (POTA) 93
Prime Minister's Office (PMO) 5, 8, 12, 128, 132
Production and procurement xii–xiii, xvii, xx, 27, 29, 31, 33–35, 39–40, 57, 59
arms xiii
cost escalation xiii
defence xvii, xx, 35, 39
emergency xvi
foreign 57
naval assets 57
policy 27, 31, 34–35, 39
procedures xii
process xvii, 33, 40
programmes xiii
reforms 33
scandals xiii
Project Mausam 50
Provocations xiv
PSLV XL 75
Pulwama xii, xiv, 100, 102
terror attack in 4
terrorist attack on a CRPF convoy in 3
Punjab 93, 99, 107, 109, 119

Qatar 52
Quadrilateral Security Dialogue (Quad) 3–4, 54–55

Radar 47, 76
Rafale Medium Multi-Role Combat Aircraft (MMRCA) xiii, 8, 16–17, 32
acquisitions 16
Medium Multi-Role Combat 32
Raksha Mantri's Operational Directive 5
Rapid Action Force (RAF) 164
Rawat, Bipin, General, Indian Army Chief 6, 13, 98, 164
R&D (Research and Development) 16, 27, 31, 34–35, 59, 84–85, 133
procurement and commercialisation 35
spending 35
Red Sea 52
Reforms
agenda 9, 27
army 8
bureaucratic xvii, 5, 8
defence xvii, 27–28, 31, 38
implementation of 39
institutional 36, 104
issue of 10, 27, 31
management 2
managerial 8
military 9, 157
organisational 31
procurement 33
Regional security xi, 41, 145

Index

- Resources xvi–xvii, xx, 2, 4–5, 29–30, 37–38, 41, 111, 115–16, 142–51, 166
  - allocation 5
  - financial 30
  - fresh water 149
  - integration and coordination xvi
  - mobilisation of xvi
  - national 4
  - natural xx, 142–44, 146, 148–51
  - shared 148
  - state xvi
  - technological 30
- Reusable launch vehicle (RLV) 74, 80–81
- Revolution in Military Affairs (RMA) 39
- RLV technology demonstrator (RLVTD) 81
- Rockets 72, 74, 77, 79–82, 84, 86
- Rocket-satellite gap 79
- Rukmini GSAT 49
- Russia 15, 17, 59, 76–77, 79, 82, 134

- Sagarmala Project 60
- SAGAR (Security and Growth for All in the Region) 52
- SAMADHAN 115, 119
- Santhal, Jangal 109
- Sanyal, Kanu 109
- Sarabhai, Dr Vikram 73–74
- Satellite xviii, 7, 49, 72–73, 76–77, 79–82, 86, 156
  - broadcasting 77
  - geostationary 72
- Satellite Instructional Television Experiment 76
- Satellite launch vehicle 80
- S-Band Synthetic Aperture Radar (SAR) 76
- Seaborne nuclear force 57
- Sea Guardian drones 59
- Sea lines of communication (SLOCs) xii, 51–52, 56
- Secretariat of the NSC (NSCS) 11
- Security
  - ambitions 54
  - architecture 46, 53, 128
  - arrangement 46
  - challenges ix–x, xix, 4, 17, 26, 54, 146
  - coastal 46–47
  - continental 45, 60
  - doctrines and strategy xvii, 2
  - energy 141
  - environmental x, xvii, xix–xx, 26, 41, 141, 143, 145, 148, 150–51
    - regional approach to xx
  - external 4, 160
  - gender and 156, 158–59, 168–69
  - global 89, 143
  - information 128, 133
  - internal xi, xix, 28, 46, 106, 110, 117, 147, 161
  - issues ix, xiii, 32, 53, 143
  - maritime xviii, 45–49, 51–53, 55–60
  - non-traditional xiii, 17, 144
  - off-shore 49
  - policy ix, xiii, xiv, xviii–xix, xxi, 12–13, 59, 128, 145, 156, 160–61, 169
  - posture 1
  - processes 156
  - regional xi, 41, 145
  - strategy ix, xiii, 2, 5, 29–31, 37, 45, 49, 60
  - threat ix, xi, 47, 110, 117, 144, 147, 160–61
    - internal xi, 110, 117, 147
    - nature of ix
  - traditional ix, xiii, 17, 144
- Security forces, attacks on 110–11
- Security principles 53
- Security Related Expenditure (SRE) Scheme 113, 119–20
- Sendai Framework for Disaster Risk Reduction 145
- Seychelles 3, 50, 52
- Sharma, Rakesh 83
- Shekatkar Committee 9, 33, 38
- Singapore 51, 55
- Singh, Manmohan, former Prime Minister xi, 47–48, 52, 54, 59, 93–94, 98, 110
- Sino-centric Asian order 55
- Sitharaman 157–58, 163
- Sitharaman, Nirmala, Minister of Defence 157
- Sivan, Dr K. 83
- Smart Green Naval Base 145
- Socio-economic inequities x
- South Asia xi–xii, xviii, 73, 118, 146
  - impact of ISIS on xi
- South Asian Association for Regional Cooperation (SAARC) 50
- South Asian neighbourhood 73
- South Asia satellite xviii, 73
- South China Sea 48, 55
- Southeast Asia 51
- Southern Indian Ocean 50
- Southern Pacific 52
- South Nicobar 50
- South Pacific xviii, 60
- Space Activities Bill 73
- Space Commission xviii, 73
- Space
  - mission 74, 83
  - policy 72–73, 86
  - programme xviii, 72–74, 79, 82, 85
  - telescope 82
- SpaceX 80, 81
- Special Central Assistance (SCA) 116
- Special Infrastructure Projects schemes 120
- Special Infrastructure Scheme 113
- Specialised Commando Battalions 113
- Special Operations, Aerospace and Cyber Command 30
- Special Operations Division 11
- Sri Lanka x, 47, 50, 52
- SSB (Sashastra Seema Bal) 165
- State of India's Environment (SoE) 151
- Strategic Forces Command 10, 28
- Strategic Partnership (SP) 35
- Strategic Policy Group (SPG) 12–13
- S-Triumf anti-aircraft weapon system 7
- Submarines 32, 47–49, 56–58, 145, 163
  - Chinese 47
- Successes (and failures) of counter-insurgency (COIN) xix, 106–07, 109–11, 114–15, 117–21
  - strategy xix, 106
- Surgical strikes xii, xiv, 3–4, 98–100, 103
- Surveillance and reconnaissance (ISR) 49
- Swaraj, Sushma, External Affairs Minister 51, 102, 157

Syria xi, 89, 96–97, 159

Tactical nuclear-weapon (TNW) 8
Tadmetla massacre 110
Taliban 95, 96
Technological
  obsolescence xiii
  resources 30
  solutions ix
Technology(ies) xi, xiv–xvi, xxi, 16, 18–19, 26–28, 31–35, 39–40, 48, 58–60, 72–77, 80–86, 95, 115, 126–28, 130–32, 135
  AI-based 59
  anonymisation 131
  cryogenic engine 77, 85
  defence 27, 31
  dual-use xxi
  foreign 39
  launch vehicle 82
  naval 59
  next-generation 18
  quantum xxi, 18
  Reusable Launch Vehicle (RLV) 74, 81
  warfare xvi
Telangana Peasant Rebellion 109
Territorial seas 51
Terror/Terrorism xi, xiv, xviii–xix, 4, 11, 26, 31–32, 45, 89–104, 118, 134, 159, 169
  acts of 90
  contemporary 90
  cross-border 32, 45, 93, 100
  forms of 95
  infrastructure 101, 104
  Islamist 90, 93
  movement 93
  organisations 96, 159
  Pakistan's support for 26, 95
  systems to tackle 92
  threat of 93
Terror/Terrorism attacks/strikes 3–4, 11, 47, 96, 100
  attack on the Indian Parliament 93, 95
  cross-border 91
  CRPF convoy in Pulwama 3
  military base in Uri 4, 98
  Mumbai attacks 91, 94–95, 159
  Pathankot Air Force Station 99
  Pulwama attack xii, xiv, 3–4, 100, 102
Terror/Terrorism groups, Pakistan-backed 31
Theatre commands, integrated 10–11
Theatre Level Readiness and Operational Exercise (TROPEX) 49
Thermal and Humidity Control System 84
Threats ix–x, xix, 4, 6, 40, 89, 94, 96, 103–04, 110–11, 119, 126–27, 133–35, 143–44, 160–61, 168
  environment 28
  non-state-based x
  perception xv, 89
  security ix, xi, 47, 110, 117, 144, 147
Thumba Equatorial Rocket Launching Station 82
Trilateral Cooperation on Maritime Security 52
Twitter diplomacy 157

UAE 52, 134
UAPA Act 114
Ultra Violet Imaging Spectroscopy Telescope 76
United Kingdom 96, 134
United Liberation Front of Assam (ULFA) 92
United Nations Environment Programme 141
United Nations Mission in Liberia (UNMIL) 166
United Nations Security Council Resolution on Women, Peace and Security (WPS) 161
United Nations Security Council (UNSC) 161
United Nations Security Council (UNSC) Al Qaeda Sanctions Committee 102
United Nations (UN) 82, 89–90, 102, 141, 159, 161, 164, 166
  France-UK-Germany sponsored move at the 102
United States Naval Forces Central Command (NAVCENT) 53
United States of America (USA) 2–5, 48, 53–56, 58–59, 76–80, 82, 90, 96, 108, 126, 129, 134, 141, 145, 160
Urban terror cell xi
Uri attacks 4, 11, 98–99
US Central Command (CENTCOM) 53
US-India-Japan Malabar naval exercise 4
US Quadrennial Defence Review 5

Uttarakhand 142
Uttar Pradesh 142, 167
Vajyapee, Atal Bihari, former Prime Minister 12, 26, 28, 74, 78, 93
Vikram Sarabhai Space Centre (VSSC) 83
Violence xii, 91–92, 96, 106, 118, 143, 148, 157–58, 161
  extremist xii

Wani, Burhan 99
WannaCry ransomware attack 130
Warfare xv, xvi, 9, 15, 18, 30, 49, 59, 113, 132–33
  electronic 18, 133
  nature of xv
  technology xvi
War on terror 90, 95
Warships 32, 34, 56
Weapons xvi, xxi, 1, 7–8, 15–16, 18, 26, 30–31, 34, 39–40, 95
  acquisition of, inferior xxi
  advanced xxi
  anti-aircraft 7
  critical 15
  deficiencies of 15
  gen-next xxi
  hypersonic 18
  nuclear 1
West Asia 52–53
West Bengal 92, 109, 111, 120, 142
Western Indian Ocean xviii, 52–53, 60
Western Theatre Command 10
Women xx, 156–69
  exclusion of 160
  in Central Reserve Police Force (CRPF) 164
  in the Indian Armed Forces 162
  political gains xx, 158
  reservation for 157
  rights 165
  violence against 158
Women's Reservation Bill 157